**lonely planet**

# Maldives

## James Lyon

D1166919

LONELY PLANET PUBLICATIONS
Melbourne • Oakland • London • Paris

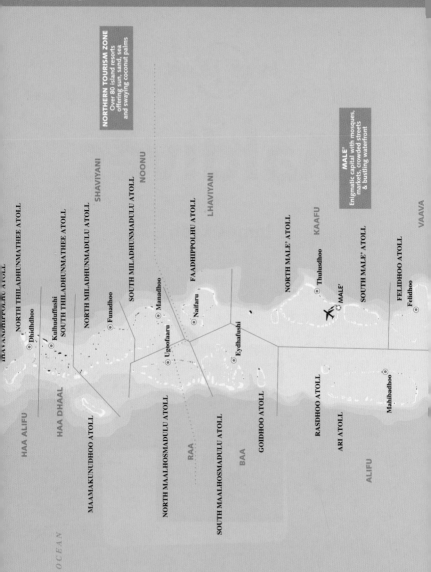

NORTHERN TOURISM ZONE
Over 80 island resorts
offering sun, sand, sea
and swaying coconut palms

MALE'
Enigmatic capital with mosques,
markets, crowded streets
& bustling waterfront

IHAVANDIPPOLHU ATOLL

NORTH THILADHUNMATHEE ATOLL

Dhidhdhoo

Kulhuduffushi

SOUTH THILADHUNMATHEE ATOLL

NORTH MILADHUNMADULU ATOLL

SHAVIYANI

Funadhoo

SOUTH MILADHUNMADULU ATOLL

NOONU

Manadhoo

FAADHIPPOLHU ATOLL

Naifaru

LHAVIYANI

Ungoofaaru

Eydhafushi

NORTH MALE' ATOLL

Thulusdhoo

KAAFU

MALE'

SOUTH MALE' ATOLL

FELIDHOO ATOLL

Felidhoo

VAAVA

HAA ALIFU

HAA DHAAL

MAAMAKUNUDHOO ATOLL

RAA

NORTH MAALHOSMADULU ATOLL

BAA

SOUTH MAALHOSMADULU ATOLL

GOIDHOO ATOLL

RASDHOO ATOLL

ARI ATOLL

ALIFU

Mahibadhoo

INDIAN OCEAN

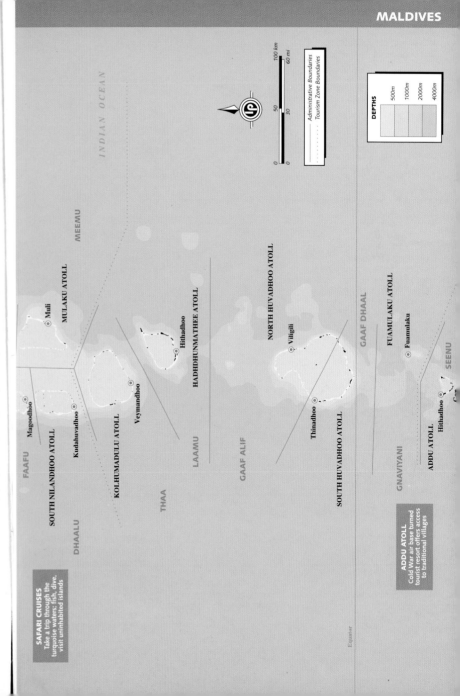

MALDIVES

DEPTHS

500m
1000m
2000m
4000m

Administrative Boundaries
Tourism Zone Boundaries

INDIAN OCEAN

**SAFARI CRUISES**
Take a trip through the turquoise waters; fish, dive, visit uninhabited islands

**ADDU ATOLL**
Cold War air base turned tourist resort offers access to traditional villages

Equator

Maldives
**4th edition** – September 2000
**First published** – November 1985

**Published by**
**Lonely Planet Publications Pty Ltd**, ABN 36 005 607 983
90 Maribyrnong St, Footscray, Victoria 3011, Australia

**Lonely Planet offices**
**Australia** Locked Bag 1, Footscray, Victoria 3011
**USA** 150 Linden St, Oakland, CA 94607
**UK** 10a Spring Place, London NW5 3BH
**France** 1 rue du Dahomey, 75011 Paris

**Photographs**
Many of the images in this guide are available for licensing from
Lonely Planet Images.
w www.lonelyplanetimages.com

**Front cover photograph**
Head over heels in the Maldives
(Stuart McClymont, Tony Stone Images)

Quotes in the Southern Atolls chapter are from *The Maldive Mystery*
by Thor Heyerdahl (Allen & Unwin, 1986)

ISBN 0 86442 700 X

text & maps © Lonely Planet Publications Pty Ltd 2000
photos © photographers as indicated 2000

Printed through Colorcraft Ltd, Hong Kong
Printed in China

# Contents – Text

# Contents – Maps

# The Author

## James Lyon

James worked for five years as an editor at Lonely Planet's Melbourne office, then 'jumped the fence' to become a researcher and writer, and has since worked on guides to Bali, California, Mexico, Maldives, South America and the USA, sometimes travelling with his wife and their two young sons. A social scientist by training and a sceptic by nature, he finds the Maldives especially intriguing for its devotion to Islam, its unique geography, and the astounding richness of its underwater environment.

## FROM JAMES

The Maldives is a difficult destination to research. You can't just walk up to a hotel and ask to see a room, not unless you can walk on water. Many people helped me to get around the country, supplied me with information and provided new perspectives. I am especially grateful (in no particular order) to Ibrahim Abdulla, Andrew Webber, Esther Sassenburg, Anthu at MTPB, Mohamed Arif and Maggie at Paradise Holidays, Firaq at Inner Maldives, Majdy and Asim at AAA, Aishath Suhar and Ahmmed Rasheed, Tim Godfrey, Tony and Zulfa Hussein, Ian Lyon, and Pauline (as ever).

# This Book

Robert Wilcox researched and wrote the first edition of *Maldives & Islands of the East Indian Ocean*, Mark Balla updated the second edition and James Lyon updated the third edition which concentrated solely on the Maldives. James returned to the Maldives to update this fourth edition.

## FROM THE PUBLISHER

This fourth edition of Maldives was edited and proofed in Lonely Planet's Melbourne office by John Hinman, with expert assistance from Bethune Carmichael, Julia Taylor and Adam Ford. Maree Styles was the coordinating designer responsible for maps and layout. The fish section was illustrated by Adriana Mammarella and Trudi Canavan. Shahara Ahmed searched exhaustively in pursuit of reliable climate chart data and edited the health section. Quentin Frayne put together the Language chapter. Leonie Mugavin researched the Getting There & Away chapter. Thanks to seniors Sharan Kaur on the editing side and Adriana Mammarella on the design side for their assistance, insistence, advice and good humour.

Quotes in the Southern Atolls chapter are from *The Maldive Mystery* by Thor Heyerdahl (Allen & Unwin, 1986).

**THANKS**
Many thanks to the travellers who used the last edition and wrote to us with helpful hints, advice and interesting anecdotes. Your names appear in the back of this book.

# Foreword

## ABOUT LONELY PLANET GUIDEBOOKS

The story begins with a classic travel adventure: Tony and Maureen Wheeler's 1972 journey across Europe and Asia to Australia. Useful information about the overland trail did not exist at that time, so Tony and Maureen published the first Lonely Planet guidebook to meet a growing need.

From a kitchen table, then from a tiny office in Melbourne (Australia), Lonely Planet has become the largest independent travel publisher in the world, an international company with offices in Melbourne, Oakland (USA), London (UK) and Paris (France).

Today Lonely Planet guidebooks cover the globe. There is an ever-growing list of books and there's information in a variety of forms and media. Some things haven't changed. The main aim is still to help make it possible for adventurous travellers to get out there – to explore and better understand the world.

At Lonely Planet we believe travellers can make a positive contribution to the countries they visit – if they respect their host communities and spend their money wisely. Since 1986 a percentage of the income from each book has been donated to aid projects and human rights campaigns.

**Updates** Lonely Planet thoroughly updates each guidebook as often as possible. This usually means there are around two years between editions, although for more unusual or more stable destinations the gap can be longer. Check the imprint page (following the colour map at the beginning of the book) for publication dates.

Between editions up-to-date information is available in two free newsletters – the paper *Planet Talk* and email *Comet* (to subscribe, contact any Lonely Planet office) – and on our Web site at www.lonelyplanet.com. The *Upgrades* section of the Web site covers a number of important and volatile destinations and is regularly updated by Lonely Planet authors. *Scoop* covers news and current affairs relevant to travellers. And, lastly, the *Thorn Tree* bulletin board and *Postcards* section of the site carry unverified, but fascinating, reports from travellers.

**Correspondence** The process of creating new editions begins with the letters, postcards and emails received from travellers. This correspondence often includes suggestions, criticisms and comments about the current editions. Interesting excerpts are immediately passed on via newsletters and the Web site, and everything goes to our authors to be verified when they're researching on the road. We're keen to get more feedback from organisations or individuals who represent communities visited by travellers.

> Lonely Planet gathers information for everyone who's curious about the planet – and especially for those who explore it first-hand. Through guidebooks, phrasebooks, activity guides, maps, literature, newsletters, image library, TV series and Web site we act as an information exchange for a worldwide community of travellers.

**Research** Authors aim to gather sufficient practical information to enable travellers to make informed choices and to make the mechanics of a journey run smoothly. They also research historical and cultural background to help enrich the travel experience and allow travellers to understand and respond appropriately to cultural and environmental issues.

Authors don't stay in every hotel because that would mean spending a couple of months in each medium-sized city and, no, they don't eat at every restaurant because that would mean stretching belts beyond capacity. They do visit hotels and restaurants to check standards and prices, but feedback based on readers' direct experiences can be very helpful.

Many of our authors work undercover, others aren't so secretive. None of them accept freebies in exchange for positive write-ups. And none of our guidebooks contain any advertising.

**Production** Authors submit their raw manuscripts and maps to offices in Australia, USA, UK or France. Editors and cartographers – all experienced travellers themselves – then begin the process of assembling the pieces. When the book finally hits the shops, some things are already out of date, we start getting feedback from readers and the process begins again …

## WARNING & REQUEST

Things change – prices go up, schedules change, good places go bad and bad places go bankrupt – nothing stays the same. So, if you find things better or worse, recently opened or long since closed, please tell us and help make the next edition even more accurate and useful. We genuinely value all the feedback we receive. A well travelled team reads and acknowledges every letter, postcard and email and ensures that every morsel of information finds its way to the appropriate authors, editors and cartographers for verification.

Everyone who writes to us will find their name in the next edition of the appropriate guidebook. They will also receive the latest issue of *Planet Talk*, our quarterly printed newsletter, or *Comet*, our monthly email newsletter. Subscriptions to both newsletters are free. The very best contributions will be rewarded with a free guidebook.

Excerpts from your correspondence may appear in new editions of Lonely Planet guidebooks, the Lonely Planet Web site, *Planet Talk* or *Comet*, so please let us know if you *don't* want your letter published or your name acknowledged.

Send all correspondence to the Lonely Planet office closest to you:

**Australia:** Locked Bag 1, Footscray, Victoria 3011
**USA:** 150 Linden St, Oakland, CA 94607
**UK:** 10A Spring Place, London NW5 3BH
**France:** 1 rue du Dahomey, 75011 Paris

Or email us at: talk2us@lonelyplanet.com.au

**For news, views and updates see our Web site: www.lonelyplanet.com**

## HOW TO USE A LONELY PLANET GUIDEBOOK

The best way to use a Lonely Planet guidebook is any way you choose. At Lonely Planet we believe the most memorable travel experiences are often those that are unexpected, and the finest discoveries are those you make yourself. Guidebooks are not intended to be used as if they provide a detailed set of infallible instructions!

**Contents** All Lonely Planet guidebooks follow roughly the same format. The Facts about the Destination chapters or sections give background information ranging from history to weather. Facts for the Visitor gives practical information on issues like visas and health. Getting There & Away gives a brief starting point for researching travel to and from the destination. Getting Around gives an overview of the transport options when you arrive.

The peculiar demands of each destination determine how subsequent chapters are broken up, but some things remain constant. We always start with background, then proceed to sights, places to stay, places to eat, entertainment, getting there and away, and getting around information – in that order.

**Heading Hierarchy** Lonely Planet headings are used in a strict hierarchical structure that can be visualised as a set of Russian dolls. Each heading (and its following text) is encompassed by any preceding heading that is higher on the hierarchical ladder.

**Entry Points** We do not assume guidebooks will be read from beginning to end, but that people will dip into them. The traditional entry points are the list of contents and the index. In addition, however, some books have a complete list of maps and an index map illustrating map coverage.

There may also be a colour map that shows highlights. These highlights are dealt with in greater detail in the Facts for the Visitor chapter, along with planning questions and suggested itineraries. Each chapter covering a geographical region usually begins with a locator map and another list of highlights. Once you find something of interest in a list of highlights, turn to the index.

**Maps** Maps play a crucial role in Lonely Planet guidebooks and include a huge amount of information. A legend is printed on the back page. We seek to have complete consistency between maps and text, and to have every important place in the text captured on a map. Map key numbers usually start in the top left corner.

Although inclusion in a guidebook usually implies a recommendation we cannot list every good place. Exclusion does not necessarily imply criticism. In fact there are a number of reasons why we might exclude a place – sometimes it is simply inappropriate to encourage an influx of travellers.

# Introduction

About 20 years ago, a tourism master plan for the Maldives identified 'the Robinson Crusoe factor' as a key feature of the Maldives' appeal. It said there was a market for unspoilt, palm-fringed tropical islands with squeaky-white beaches and brilliant turquoise lagoons. If you don't need a consultant to tell you that, then you could be a candidate for the Maldives' brand of paradise.

Planning and professionalism are the hallmarks of the Maldives' tourism industry. The same plan recognised that contemporary Crusoes want their creature comforts, and that mass tourism would destroy the appeal of the place. The industry followed the plan, building a limited number of quality resorts, each on its own uninhabited island, free from traffic, crime and crass commercialism. The industry has been enormously successful and

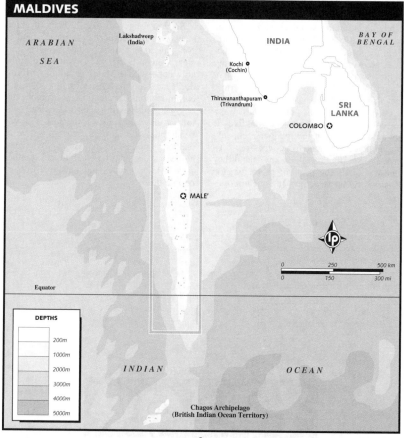

is now recognised as a model for sustainable, environment-friendly tourism development.

The enormously rich underwater world is a huge attraction, and Maldivians have taken great care to preserve it. The damage done by coral bleaching in 1998 is therefore doubly unfortunate, caused by climate change and an El Niño event over which this small country had no control. It is still one of the most beautiful and best-preserved marine ecosystems in the world, and if it has suffered as a result of global warming, that should be a warning to us all. However, the coral is growing back and the marine life is as prolific as ever, with fish of every shape, size and colour. Over three-quarters of the world's reef-fish species can be found in the Maldives, and many can be seen just by snorkelling a short distance from the beach. For scuba divers the Maldives are world famous. As well as the beauty of the fish and soft corals, there is the thrill of diving with turtles, moray eels, manta rays, reef sharks and dolphins.

Of course the quality of this tourism experience comes at a cost. The Maldives is not a destination for low-budget backpackers, and independent travellers aren't allowed to simply drop in on any island they please – that's the price of protecting the sensitive social structure. It's not impossible to visit the outer islands, but it's difficult enough to deter all but the most dedicated and determined.

On the other hand, the capital city is completely open to visitors – Male' is an intriguing place, with mosques, markets and a maze of small streets. Also accessible, at least for short visits, are the island communities close to tourist resorts. These two possibilities are enough to gain an appreciation of local life and culture, both modern and traditional. After seeing these places, most thoughtful people agree that the more isolated Maldivian villages would not benefit from extended visits by an uncontrolled number of tourists.

So you'll have to like the idea of being stuck on a picture-perfect tropical island or condemned to a safari boat cruising crystal-clear waters. If that's OK, you could probably cope with a Maldives holiday. If you don't need any hassles in finding food, accommodation or recreation, you might even enjoy it. But if you're an underwater eco-tourist or water-sports enthusiast, a closet beach bum or a chronic escapist, you're in danger of atoll addiction. You might have to come back year after year to get another fix of Maldivian sea and sunshine. Lots of people do.

# Facts about the Maldives

The Republic of Maldives is a small Islamic nation of about 300,000 people with a history, culture and language all of its own. The country comprises some 1192 tiny islands, none of them more than a couple of km across or more than a few metres above sea level. Traditionally a fishing and trading people, the Maldivians have been able to maintain their independence for centuries.

## HISTORY
The history of the Maldives can be divided into two stages – before and after the conversion to Islam in 1153 AD.

The latter, well-documented stage has passed through a series of sultanic dynasties to the recent birth and rebirth of the republic. The pre-Muslim period, however, is full of hazy, heroic myth mixed with conjecture based on archaeological discoveries.

The Muslim authorities are not interested in what went on before Islam and tend to use the myths of legendary queens and princes as religious stories to support the ensuing conversion.

Foreigners such as archaeologist HCP Bell early in the 20th century and, more recently, Kon-Tiki explorer Thor Heyerdahl have attempted to explain the tangible, although insubstantial, remains of early civilisations.

## Early Days
The first settlers probably arrived in the uninhabited archipelago from Sri Lanka and southern India, not later than 500 BC.

Heyerdahl, however, explores the theory that the existence of the Maldives was well known long before that. Rather than being isolated or ignored, from around 2000 BC onwards they were at the trading crossroads of several ancient maritime nations.

He believes the ancient Egyptians, Romans, Mesopotamians and Indus Valley traders all called by at one time or another. Which ones settled to become the legendary sun-worshipping people called the Redin remains a mystery. The Redin left a pagan heritage of beliefs and customs involving evil spirits, or *jinnis*, which still exists today.

Around 500 BC the Redin either left or were absorbed by Buddhists, probably from Sri Lanka, and by Hindus from north-west India. HCP Bell, a British commissioner of the Ceylon Civil Service, led archaeological expeditions to the Maldives in 1920 and 1922. Among other things, he investigated the ruined, dome-shaped structures called *hawittas*, mostly in the southern atolls, which he believed were Buddhist stupas similar to the *dagobas* found in Sri Lanka. Because the islands were so small and building materials limited, each group built its important structures on the foundations of those left by previous inhabitants, which explains why many mosques in the Maldives face the sun and not Mecca.

## Conversion to Islam
Arab traders en route to the Far East had been calling on the Maldives for many years – the first record of the Maldive islands is from the 2nd century AD. Known as the 'Money Isles', the Maldives provided enormous quantities of cowry shells, an international currency of the early ages. (The cowry is now the symbol of the Maldives Monetary Authority.)

Abu Al Barakat, a North African Arab, is credited with converting the Maldivians to Islam in 1153. According to the legend, young virgin girls in Male' were chosen from the community and left alone in a temple as a sacrifice to Rannamaari, a sea jinni. One night Barakat took the place of a prospective sacrificial virgin and drove the demon away by reading from the Islamic holy book, the Quran. That may seem far-fetched and best treated as a parable, but in fact certain Hindu sects did practise human sacrifice and the skulls of young women have been unearthed where the temple supposedly stood.

Whatever happened, the Maldivian king at the time was sold on Islam, and Barakat went on to become the first sultan. A series of six sultanic dynasties followed – 84 sultans and sultanas in all, although some did not belong to the line of succession. At one stage, when the Portuguese first arrived on the scene, there were actually two ruling dynasties, the Malei (or Theemuge) dynasty and the Hilali.

## The Portuguese

Early in the 16th century the Portuguese, who were already well established in Goa in western India, decided they wanted a greater share of the profitable trade routes of the Indian Ocean. They were given permission to build a fort and a factory in Male', but it wasn't long before they wanted more from the Maldives.

In 1558, after a few unsuccessful attempts, Captain Andreas Andre led an invasion army and killed Sultan Ali VI. The Maldivians called the Portuguese captain 'Andiri Andirin' and he ruled Male' and much of the country for the next 15 years. According to some Maldivian beliefs, Andre was born in the Maldives and went to Goa as a young man, where he came to serve the Portuguese. (Apart from a few months of Malabar domination in Male' during the 18th century, this was the only time that another country has occupied the Maldives.)

The occupation was cruel, and ultimately the Portuguese decreed that Maldivians must convert to Christianity or be killed. There was ongoing resistance, especially from Mohammed Thakurufaanu, son of an influential family on Utheemu Island in the northern atoll of Haa Alifu. Thakurufaanu, with the help of his two brothers and some friends, started a series of guerrilla raids, culminating in an attack on Male' in which all the Portuguese were slaughtered (see the boxed text 'The Legend of Thakurufaanu').

This victory is commemorated annually as National Day on the first day of the third month of the lunar year. There is a memorial centre on the island of Utheemu to Thakurufaanu, the Maldives' greatest hero, who went on to found the next sultanic dynasty, the Utheemu, which ruled for 120 years. Many reforms were introduced, including a new judicial system, a defence force and a coinage to replace the cowry currency.

## Protected Independence

The Portuguese attacked several more times, and the Rajahs of Cannanore (who had helped Thakurufaanu) also attempted to gain control. In the 17th century, the Maldives accepted the protection of the Dutch, who ruled Ceylon at the time. They also had a short-lived defence treaty with the French, and maintained good relations with the British, especially after the British took possession of Ceylon in 1796. These relations enabled the Maldives to be free of external threats while maintaining internal autonomy. Nevertheless, it was the remoteness of the islands, the prevalence of malaria and the lack of good ports, naval stores, or productive land that were probably the main reasons neither the Dutch nor the British established a colonial administration.

In the 1860s Borah merchants from Bombay were invited to Male' to establish warehouses and shops, but it wasn't long before they acquired an almost exclusive monopoly on foreign trade. The Maldivians feared the Borahs would soon gain complete control of the islands, so Sultan Mohammed Mueenuddin II signed an agreement with the British in 1887 recognising the Maldives' statehood and formalising its protected status.

## Early 20th Century

In 1932 the Maldives' first constitution was imposed upon Sultan Shamsuddin. The sultanate became a position elected by a 'council of advisers' made up of Maldivian elite, rather than a hereditary one. As a result, in 1934 Sultan Shamsuddin was deposed and Hasan Nurudin became the next sultan.

WWII brought great hardship to the Maldives. Maritime trade with Sri Lanka was severely reduced, leading to shortages of rice and other necessities – many died of illness or malnutrition. A new constitution was introduced in 1942, and Nurudin was persuaded to abdicate the following year. His replacement, the elderly Abdul Majeed Didi, retired to Ceylon (Sri Lanka) leaving the control of the government in the hands of his prime minister, Mohammed Amin Didi. Amin Didi nationalised the fish export industry, instituted a broad modernisation pro-

## The Legend of Thakurufaanu

As the man who led a successful revolution against foreign domination, and then as the leader of the newly liberated nation, Mohammed Thakurufaanu (sultan from 1573 to 1585) is the Maldives' national hero. Respectfully referred to as Bodu Thakurufaanu (*bodu* meaning big, or great), he is to the Maldives what George Washington is to the USA. The story of his raid on the Portuguese headquarters in Male' is part of Maldivian folklore and incorporates many compelling details.

In his home atoll, Thakurufaanu's family were known and respected as sailors, traders and *kateebs* (island chiefs). The family gained the trust of Viyazoaru, the Portuguese ruler of the four northern atolls, and was given the responsibility of disseminating orders, collecting taxes and carrying tribute to the Portuguese base in Ceylon. Unbeknown to Viyazoaru, Thakurufaanu and his brothers used their position to foster anti-Portuguese sentiment, recruit sympathisers and gain intelligence on the Portuguese. It also afforded the opportunity to visit southern India, where Thakurufaanu obtained a pledge from the Rajah of Cannanore to assist in an overthrow of the Portuguese rulers in the Maldives.

Back in Haa Alifu, Thakurufaanu and his brothers built a boat in which to conduct an attack on Male'. This sailing vessel, named Kalhuoffummi, has a legendary status in its own right – it was said to be not only fast and beautiful, but to have almost magical qualities that enabled it to elude the Portuguese on guerrilla raids and reconnaissance missions.

For the final assault, they sailed south through the atolls by night, stopping by day to gather provisions and supporters. Approaching Male', they concealed themselves on a nearby island. They stole into the capital at night to make contact with supporters there and to assess the Portuguese defences. They were assisted in this by the local *imam*, who subtly changed the times of the morning prayer calls, tricking the Portuguese into sleeping late and giving Thakurufaanu extra time to escape after his night-time reconnaissance visits.

The attack on Male' was carefully planned and timed, and backed by supernatural forces – one story relates how a coconut tree mysteriously appeared in the Portuguese compound, which provided cover for Thakurufaanu as he crept close and personally killed 'Andiri Andirin' Andre with a spear. In the ensuing battle the Maldivians, with help from a detachment of Cannanore soldiers, defeated and killed some 300 Portuguese. Another nice touch is that most versions of the story have the Portuguese drinking heavily on their last night, making it a cautionary tale about the evils of alcohol.

The Thakurufaanu brothers then set about re-establishing a Maldivian administration under Islamic principles. Soon after, Bodu Thakurufaanu became the new sultan, with the title of Al Sultanul Ghazi Mohammed Thakurufaanu Al Auzam Siree Savahitha Maharadhun, 1st Sultan of the 3rd Dynasty of the Kingdom of the Maldives.

gram and introduced a total ban on tobacco smoking.

When Ceylon gained independence in 1948, the Maldivians signed a defence pact with the British, which gave the latter control of the foreign affairs of the islands but not the right to interfere internally. In return, the Maldivians agreed to provide facilities for the British forces for the defence of both islands and the Commonwealth.

In 1953 the sultanate was abolished and a republic was proclaimed with Amin Didi as its first president. Didi was too tough too

soon, however, and the new government was short-lived. Less than a year after he came to power Didi was overthrown and, during a riot over food shortages, was beaten by a mob and died on Kurumba Island. The sultanate was returned, with Mohammed Farid Didi elected as the 94th sultan of the Maldives.

### British Bases & Southern Secession

While Britain did not overtly interfere in the running of the country, it did secure permission to re-establish its wartime airfield on

Gan Island in the southernmost Addu Atoll. In 1956 the Royal Air Force began developing the base as a staging post, employing hundreds of Maldivians, and undertook the resettlement of the Gan islanders. The British were informally granted a 100-year lease of Gan which required them to pay £2000 a year.

When Ibrahim Nasir was elected prime minister in 1957, he immediately called for a review of the agreement with the British on Gan, demanding that the lease be shortened and the annual payment increased.

This was followed by an insurrection against the Maldivian government by the inhabitants of the southern atolls of Addu and Suvadiva (Huvadhoo), who objected to Nasir's demand that the British cease employing local labour. Undoubtedly influenced by the British military presence, they decided to cut ties altogether and form an independent state, electing Abdulla Afif Didi president.

In 1960, however, the Maldivian government officially granted the British the use of Gan and other facilities in Addu Atoll for 30 years (effective from December 1956) in return for the payment of £100,000 a year and a grant of £750,000 to finance specific development projects over a period of years. Later, Nasir sent gunboats from Male' to quash the rebellion in the southern atolls. Afif fled to the Seychelles, then a British colony, while other leaders were banished to various islands in the Maldives.

In 1965 Britain recognised the islands as a completely sovereign and independent state, and ceased to be responsible for their defence (although it retained the use of Gan and continued to pay rent until 1976). The Maldives were granted independence on 26 July 1965 and later became a member of the United Nations.

## The Republic

Following a referendum in 1968 the sultanate was again abolished, Sultan Majeed Didi retired to Ceylon and a new republic was inaugurated. Nasir was elected president. He ruled for 10 years, seemingly becoming more autocratic each year.

The Sri Lankan market for the Maldives' biggest export, dried fish, collapsed in 1972. Fortunately that was the year the tourism industry was born with the opening of Kurumba and Bandos resorts. Unfortunately, the money generated by tourism didn't directly benefit the populace. Prices kept going up and there were revolts, plots and banishments as Nasir clung to power. In response to one protest in 1974, Nasir ordered the police to open fire on a large crowd, which had gathered to air its grievances.

In 1978, fearing for his life, Nasir stepped down and skipped across to Singapore reputedly with US$4 million from the Maldivian national coffers.

A former university lecturer and Maldivian ambassador to the United Nations, Maumoon Abdul Gayoom, was elected president in Nasir's place. Gayoom's style of governing was much more open, and he immediately denounced Nasir's regime and banished several of the former president's associates.

In 1980 a coup plot against Gayoom, involving mercenaries, was discovered and more banishments occurred; the list included more of Nasir's cohorts. Extradition proceedings began, for the second time, to have Nasir brought back from Singapore to stand trial for murder and theft. They were unsuccessful.

Gayoom was re-elected in 1983 and continued to promote education, health and industry, particularly tourism. He also gave the tiny country a higher international profile with full membership in the Commonwealth and the South Asian Association for Regional Co-operation (SAARC).

In January 1986, unable to extradite Nasir, the Maldivian High Court sentenced the ex-president *in absentia* to 25 years banishment. He was pardoned in 1988 as a goodwill gesture recognising the role he played in changing the Maldives' status from that of British protectorate to full independence.

## The 1988 Coup

In September 1988, the 51-year-old Gayoom was re-elected for a third term as president, but his sense of security was shattered only a month later. A group of disaffected Maldivian businessmen attempted a coup, employing about 90 Sri Lankan Tamil mercenaries. Half of these soldiers infiltrated Male' as visitors, while the rest landed by boat. The mercenaries took several key installations on Male', including the power station and the president's office, but failed to capture the National Security Service headquarters.

More than 1600 Indian paratroopers, immediately dispatched by the Indian prime minister, Rajiv Gandhi, ended further gains by the invaders who then fled by boat towards Sri Lanka. They took 27 hostages and left 14 people dead and 40 wounded. No tourists were affected – many didn't even know that a coup had happened.

The mercenaries were later caught by an Indian frigate 100km from the Sri Lankan coast. According to authorities, four hostages were found dead and three were missing.

Sixty of the mercenaries were returned to the Maldives for trial in July 1989. Several were sentenced to death, but reprieved and returned to Sri Lanka. Ibrahim Nasir denied any involvement in the coup attempt. The assault was headed by Abdulla Luthufi, a former Maldivian exporter of tropical fish, who had lived in Sri Lanka since 1985.

## Growth & Development

In 1993 Gayoom was nominated for a fourth five-year term, and his presidency confirmed with an overwhelming referendum vote. Recent years have been characterised by modernisation, a very high rate of economic growth, and improvement in most social indicators. The main contributors to this growth have been the fishing industry, tourism and foreign aid.

At the same time, the Maldives is experiencing many of the problems of developing countries, notably rapid growth in the main city, the environmental effects of growth, regional disparities, youth unemployment and income inequality. Political stability and social harmony have been maintained, but there are growing expectations of open government, a pluralistic society and personal freedoms, as well as the emergence of religious fundamentalism in the region.

A generally high economic growth rate has been maintained, but there is also concern that the economy is too vulnerable to external factors, such as variations in the price of tuna and events which impact on international tourism. The 1991 Gulf War, for example, stalled the growth in tourist numbers. The 1998 El Niño event, which caused coral bleaching throughout the atolls, was not just bad for tourism – it was a warning that global warming is the greatest threat to the Maldives' future. Gayoom began a fifth term as president in 1998, and one of his main concerns is the environment. If sea levels rise he has said, the country could 'sometime in the next century disappear from the earth'.

## GEOGRAPHY

The Maldives is a chain of about 1192 small, low-lying coral islands grouped in clusters, or atolls, about 600km south-west of Sri Lanka. The word 'atoll' actually derives from the Maldivian word *atolu*.

With a total land area of 298 sq km, the 26 atolls stretch out across the equator in a vertical strip 754km long and 118km wide. On these figures, less than 0.4% of the country is dry land. There are no hills or rivers,

### An Alternative Geography

The Maldives has appeared in the Guinness Book of Records as the world's flattest country, with no natural land higher than 2.4 metres above sea level – but you can look at it from another angle.

The Maldives is one of the most mountainous countries in the world. Its people live on the crest of an ancient volcanic mountain range which extends 2000km from the Lakshadweep Islands near India to the Chagos Islands, well south of the equator. The range is over 5000m high and rises steeply between the Arabian Basin in the north-west and the Cocos-Keeling Basin in the south-east. Its upper valleys and plateaus are incredibly fertile and rich with plant and animal life. The entire mountain range is submerged beneath the Indian Ocean and its peaks are capped not with snow, but with coral stone.

and none of the islands rises more than 3m above sea level or is longer than 8km. On the whole they are infertile and support only a limited range of flora and fauna.

The number of islands has been estimated variously from 1300 to 13,000, but the government determines that there are 1192, of which only 202 are inhabited. Counting the islands may seem a simple matter, but when flying over an atoll it's almost impossible to distinguish between a reef that is just below the surface, and a sand bank that is just above it. The situation may change with the next high tide, and an obvious sand bank can be swept away in the next big storm, or be divided into two separate islands.

Officially, it's a matter of vegetation – an island means a vegetated land area, but even this is not definitive. It's easy to spot a tiny sandbank with a patch of scrub and wonder if it would qualify. There are round sandy spots with a single coconut palm, like the desert island of the comic-strip castaway, but the bigger islands have bamboo, banyan, mangroves and towering trees.

To locals, the more important distinction is between inhabited and uninhabited islands. Inhabited means inhabited by Maldivians. The 87-odd resort islands are officially 'uninhabited', as are those used for factories, airfields, or agriculture, but which don't have a village or a mosque.

## GEOLOGY

The Maldive islands are made of coral stone, sand and rubble which have built up over millennia to form a bedrock of limestone many metres thick on the top of a submerged volcanic ridge (see the boxed text 'Coral Atolls' in this chapter).

## CLIMATE

Generally, the year is divided into two monsoon periods – the north-east monsoon or *iruvai*, from December to March, which are the drier months; and the south-west monsoon or *hulhangu*, from May to November, which are wetter months with more storms and strong winds. Transitional periods, in mid-April and late November, are supposed to be calm with exceptionally clear water.

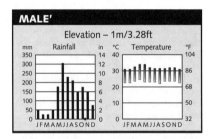

Maldivians further divide the year into 27 *nakaiy*, each about two weeks long, with a characteristic weather pattern. Each nakaiy has its place in the cycle of fishing, planting and harvesting, and its significance for personal and family fortunes.

However, the average maximum temperature is remarkably consistent throughout the year, ranging from 30° to 31.8°C, while nights are between 25.1° and 26.3°C. Sea temperatures remain pretty constant at around 27°C. Almost continual sea breezes keep the air moving and make life quite bearable, but you can't always count on the weather patterns. Heavy rain can fall at any time in the dry season, and you can have clear sunny days in the middle of the wet.

## ECOLOGY & ENVIRONMENT

As a small island nation in a big ocean, the Maldives had a way of life which was ecologically sustainable for centuries, but certainly not self-sufficient. The comparatively small population survived by harvesting the vast resources of the sea and by obtaining the other necessities of life through trade. The impact on the limited resources of their islands was probably minimal. Of course this was achieved under low growth conditions, with low material standards of living, short life expectancy and high infant mortality.

Now, the Maldives' interrelationship with the rest of the world is greater than ever, and it has a high rate of growth supported by two main industries, fishing and tourism. It is well recognised by government, business and the population that both industries depend on preservation of the environment, and there are strict regulations to ensure sustainability.

## Coral Atolls

A coral reef or garden is not, as many people believe, formed of multicoloured marine plants. It is rather, a living colony of coral polyps, which are tiny, tentacled creatures that feed on plankton.

These polyps, related to jellyfish and the sea anemone, are invertebrates with sack-like bodies and calcareous or horny skeletons. After extracting calcium deposits from the water around them, these polyps excrete tiny, cup-shaped, limestone skeletons.

A coral reef is the rock-like aggregation of millions of these animals or their skeletons. Only the outer layer of coral is alive. As polyps reproduce and die, the new polyps attach themselves in successive layers to the skeletons already in place. Coral grows best in clear shallow water, but it grows fastest where waves and currents from the open sea bring extra oxygen and nutrients.

Charles Darwin was the first to put forward the theory that atolls develop from coral growth that has built up around the edges of a submerged volcanic mountain peak.

In a scenario played out over hundreds of thousands of years, coral first builds up around the shores of a volcanic land mass producing a fringing reef. Then, when the island (often simply the exposed peak of a submarine mountain) begins slowly to sink, the coral continues to grow upwards at about the same rate.

This forms a barrier reef separated from the shore of the sinking island by a lagoon. By the time the island is completely submerged, the coral growth has become the base for an atoll, circling the place where the volcanic land mass or mountain used to be. The enclosed lagoon accumulates sand and rubble formed by broken coral, and the level of this lagoon floor also builds up over the subsiding land mass.

As the centuries pass, sand and debris accumulate on the higher parts of the reef, creating islands on which vegetation can eventually take root. The classic atoll shape is oval, with most of the islands around the outer edges where the coral growth is most vigorous. Coral growth can also create reefs and islands within the lagoon, but these are smaller and less numerous. The sea usually forms breaks in the reef rim and these gaps are enlarged by the erosion of water flowing in and out.

Most of the scientific evidence for these theories comes from elsewhere in the world. In the Pacific, for example, where volcanic islands still protrude above the ocean, features of terrestrial erosion, such as river valleys, can be seen well below the sea surface. This shows that the volcanoes are in fact sinking back into the sea.

The most extensive geological research was undertaken at a number of Pacific sites, with drilling penetrating to volcanic rock as deep as 1400m beneath coral atolls. The core samples revealed a sequential build-up of coral-based limestone which was deeper at the edges of the atoll than in the middle, following the profile of a submerged volcano.

**Step 1** A new volcano rises from the sea bed high enough to become an island.

**Step 2** The volcano becomes extinct; meanwhile a coral reef forms around its coast.

**Step 3** As the island erodes and sinks, the coral grows to stay near the water's surface; a lagoon forms between reef and island.

**Step 4** The old volcano sinks entirely, leaving a ring of coral to mark the ancient coastline.

For most of the islands, economic growth has brought improvements in health, education and infrastructure, but the way of life is still largely unchanged and the environmental impact is not marked. Growth has focussed on the capital city where the environmental effects are most severe.

In the medium term, the greatest environmental problem for the Maldives is global warming, with its potentially catastrophic consequences. This is, of course, a global problem caused overwhelmingly by developed countries. The Maldives is like a canary in a mine – when it starts to suffer from environmental problems, it is a warning to the rest of the world that environmental change may be catastrophic (see the 'Coral Bleaching' boxed text later in this chapter).

## Fisheries

**Ocean Fishing** Net fishing and trawling is prohibited in Maldivian waters, which include an 'Exclusive Economic Zone' extending for 320km beyond the atolls. All fishing is by pole and line, with over 75% of the catch being skipjack or yellowfin tuna. The no-nets policy limits the amount of fish caught and helps to prevent over-fishing. It also protects other marine species, such as dolphins, from being inadvertently caught in nets, and it maintains a high level of employment in the industry.

The local tuna population appears to be holding up despite increased catches, and Maldivian fisheries are patrolled to prevent poaching. But the tuna are migratory, and can be caught without limit in international waters where modern European and Asian ships use long-line techniques and drift-nets.

**Reef Fishing** A problem with reef fisheries is the sudden surges in demand for particular species, which can cause a big depletion in stocks before authorities recognise and deal with the problem. Lobster numbers declined rapidly around Male' when resorts began serving them, and they are now protected in that area. Sea cucumbers were over-fished, but a ban on scuba divers collecting them should allow regeneration in deeper waters. Giant clams were much more common before commercial divers began collecting them – export of clam meat was banned in 1991.

There has been a decline in shark numbers at some popular dive sites in recent years, especially when the price for shark fins rose to US$70 per kg. When it became possible to export live grouper to Asia, or air freight it out on ice, there was a huge increase in the catch and there are signs it is being over-fished.

A recent case was the large and handsome Napoleon wrasse, which seemed in danger of extinction when it was selling for US$50 per kg. The government has now banned all exports following protests from many dive operators and tourism interests. Collecting tropical fish for the aquarium trade is a growth industry and quotas have been imposed on the export of various species to ensure it is sustainable in the long term.

## Tourism

Tourism development is also strictly regulated and resorts can only be established on uninhabited islands that the government makes available for commercial leases. Corporations bid for the leases, and the bid proposal must conform to certain minimum standards. Resort buildings cannot cover more than 20% of an island's area, or be higher than the surrounding vegetation. The resort developer must provide all the necessary infrastructure, from electricity and water supply to effective sewage treatment and garbage disposal. Resorts cannot take water from any other island. These and many other regulations are designed to ensure that adverse environmental impacts are minimised. In addition, the bidding process is competitive, and environmental impact is a criterion in selecting the successful bid.

Overwhelmingly, the regulations have been effective in minimising environmental costs and the World Tourism Organisation has cited the Maldives as a model for sustainable tourism development. In 1998, the number of tourist arrivals was 396,000 – more than the Maldives own population. On a per capita basis, it has more tourists than Bali, but away from the capital, the airport and the resorts, tourists and tourist facilities are barely noticeable.

Construction and operation of the resorts does use resources, but the vast majority of these are imported, so the impact is not local. Large amounts of diesel fuel are used to generate electricity and desalinate water. The progressive improvement in standards means that more resorts are providing hot water, swimming pools and air-conditioning, raising the overall energy cost per guest (see Energy later in this chapter).

**Waste Disposal** Sewage must be effectively treated on the island itself – it cannot be pumped out to sea. Efficient incinerators must be installed to dispose of garbage that can't be composted, but many resorts request that visitors take home plastic bottles, used batteries and other items which may present a disposal problem.

With only about 90 resorts spread over 20,000 sq km of sea, air pollution from boats and generators can be easily dispersed. Traffic fumes are occasionally noticeable on Male', on days when there is no wind.

**Coastal Environment** When the first resorts were developed, jetties and break-waters were built, and boat channels cut through reefs, without much understanding of the immediate environmental consequences. In some cases unexpected natural erosion and deposition patterns were disrupted. More structures were built to prevent beach erosion, and sand had to be brought in to restore the damage. Obviously this was expensive and it marred the natural appearance of the island. Developers are now not so quick to alter coasts and reefs, and environmental studies are required before major works can be undertaken.

**Marine Environment** A high proportion of visitors come principally for diving and snorkelling – underwater eco-tourism. Preserving the underwater world in a pristine state is a high priority for the government, the tourism industry and the vast majority of visitors. The dive operators at resorts have taken a leading role in promoting en-

vironmentally sensitive diving practices. Anchors are not used over reefs, spear fishing is forbidden, garbage is kept on boats, it's 'not done' to touch fish or coral and even wearing gloves is discouraged. Some feel that the sheer number of divers could become a problem, though this is more a threat to the quality of the diving experience than the environment.

The crown-of-thorns starfish has appeared on Maldivian reefs, but is not in anything like plague proportions. These animals can devastate large areas of reef, but little is known about what causes infestations or what can be done to eliminate them. Some believe they occur as a result of human interference or environmental change, but others suggest that they come and go as part of a natural cycle.

The government has designated 15 Protected Marine Areas, which are all popular dive sites in tourism zones. Fishing is now banned in these areas, as are certain damaging diving practices such as the use of anchors, which most operators were avoiding anyway. Another 10 Protected Marine Areas were nominated in September 1999.

## Rubbish

Traditionally, Maldivians have thrown their rubbish from boats or beaches into the sea. When this stuff was biodegradable it wasn't a problem, but with increasing use of products and packaging made of metal and plastic, rubbish can now be found washed up on beaches or accumulating on reefs. You won't see it on resorts, where the beach is cleaned every morning, but it's there on other islands. There are steps to raise awareness and educate the people, but it will take time. Tourists can contribute by disposing of their personal rubbish responsibly and ensuring that the dive dhonis, safari boats and resorts they use do likewise. If the operator of a boat or resort does dispose of rubbish irresponsibly, a letter of complaint to the Ministry of Tourism can be very effective.

## Reef Mining

Coral has long been mined in the Maldives, to make cement and to use in coral-stone walls. Some islands, in south Ari Atoll for example, have made an industry of coral mining. With new resorts being built, rapid growth in Male' and greater affluence in many islands, the amount of mining and the extent of damage has increased greatly. The government has now banned the use of coral as a building material, and cement bricks are being used instead. Cement is now being made at a plant on Thilafushi island, near Male'.

Nevertheless, most materials for new resorts and other buildings are imported, including timber, glass, stone, and even soil. To a great extent the Maldives avoids environmental problems by importing so many of its needs. It could be asked whether this is in fact environmentally friendly, or whether it just moves the environmental problems offshore.

## Growth in Male'

Nearly all the problems of rapid growth in the Maldives have been concentrated in Male'. As in many developing countries, there has been a population movement from regional areas to the main city. People come to continue their education, to find employment or to join family members who have already moved. Male' is absorbing nearly all the country's population growth.

The resultant problems include housing shortages, overbuilding, traffic congestion, unemployment and depletion of the natural ground-water supply. Bore water in Male' smells horrible and is scarcely useable for gardening, much less for washing or drinking. Urban sprawl is not an option – the island is full to the edges.

Solutions are being sought. Schools and facilities are being developed in the outer atolls, so young people will have less reason to move to Male'. The neighbouring island of Viligili is being developed as a satellite community, as will be the new island of Hulhu-Male' (see the Male' chapter). Because of the increasingly fragmented pattern of land ownership on Male' – when a landholder dies, their land is often divided between several family members, so the lots become smaller – it's difficult to develop an effective urban planning strategy or to make good use of high-rise buildings. Urban planning may be more effective on the neighbouring islands, where the government has control of the land.

In the longer term, the country needs to limit its population growth, in spite of lower infant mortality and longer life expectancy. In conservative Muslim communities, where women marry at 17 and traditionally don't work outside the home, this will not be easy, but a family planning education program is under way.

## Global Warming

The environmental consequences of global warming are far from certain, but so potentially catastrophic that they can't be ignored, especially in the Maldives. Predictions from very reputable studies are that global warming might result in average sea level rises of between 5mm and 10mm per year. At that rate it would take one or two centuries to submerge most of the country, but it is extreme conditions, rather than average sea levels, that pose the more immediate threat. The concern is not so much a gradual increase in ocean depth, but the infrequent but inevitable combinations of storm and high tide, which will cause major catastrophes. The dangers were highlighted in 1987 when severe storms inundated much of Male' and washed away a third of the recently reclaimed land.

The official Maldives policy has been well articulated by President Gayoom in international forums. Climate change is seen as a global problem that requires a global solution. If the Maldives is at risk in the medium term, then many other places will be at risk very soon afterwards, so there is no room for complacency. Recognising that lack of information and understanding is a major part of the problem, the country is committed to ongoing research and monitoring of all aspects of its environment.

## Energy

With its relatively small number of private cars and lack of industry, the Maldives is not a very energy-hungry nation. Most people and goods move between the islands and atolls by slow boats, which are quite an energy efficient form of transport.

Tourist resorts, however, use surprisingly large amounts of fuel to run the generators supplying power for water desalination, air-conditioning, lighting and so on – a big resort will use several thousand litres a day. Some new resorts are being built with energy-conserving features such as solar hot water systems. Another innovation uses the tag on a room key to activate the power in the room – when you leave the room, you take the key with you and the air-con, TV, fan and lights all turn off automatically. One simple step is asking guests to hang up towels that do not need to be laundered.

## FLORA & FAUNA
### Flora
Most islands have poor, sandy soil and vegetation ranges from thick to sparse to none at all. The vegetated islands have mangroves, breadfruit trees, banyans, bamboo, pandanus, banana, heliotrope, caltrop, hibiscus, tropical vines and numerous coconut palms. Larger, wetter islands have small areas of rainforest.

Sweet potatoes, yams, taro, millet and watermelon are grown. The most fertile island is Fuamulaku in the extreme south, which supports a wider variety of crops, including mangoes and pineapples.

### Fauna
Giant fruit bats or flying foxes are widespread on many islands; you'll see them cruising past at dusk. Colourful lizards are quite common and there is the occasional rat.

Domestic animals include cats, a few chickens and the odd rabbit. A few islands rear goats, but cows are rare.

The mosquito population varies from island to island but tends not to be too bothersome in Male' and the villages. Other invertebrates include ants, centipedes, scorpions and cockroaches. None of these is a problem.

Birdwatchers will do better than wildlife spotters. Land birds include crows, the white-breasted water hen and the rose-ringed parakeet. Migratory birds drop in

too, like harriers and falcons, but waders like plover, snipe, curlew and sandpiper are more common. Several types of heron can be seen in the shallows and there are terns, seagulls and two species of noddy.

### Marine Life
The underwater plant life is vital to the ecosystem, but is not conspicuous to the diver or snorkeller. It consists of seaweeds and hard coralline algae, which grow on the reefs, but are continuously eaten by various herbivores; plankton, which are minute organisms that float in the water (most plankton photosynthesise and are true plants, but many are in fact animals); and the tiny single-celled plants called zooxanthellae, which live symbiotically within the tissues of coral polyps.

As well as the many types of coral, there are various shells, starfish, crustaceans and worms inhabiting the reef. Then there are the more than 700 species of fish in the Indian Ocean, which can be divided into two types: reef fish, which live inside the atoll lagoons, on and around coral reef structures; and pelagics, which live in the open sea, but may come close to the atolls or into channels for food. These include some large animals, such as turtles and cetaceans, which are very popular with divers.

**Coral** These are coelenterates, a class of animal that also includes sea anemones and jellyfish. A coral growth is made up of individual polyps – tiny tube-like fleshy cylinders, which look very much like anemones. The top of the cylinder is open and ringed by waving tentacles (nematocysts), which sting and draw any passing prey inside the open cylinder constituting the polyp's stomach. Coral polyps secrete a calcium-carbonate deposit around their base, and this cup-shaped skeletal structure is what forms a coral reef – new coral grows on old dead coral and the reef gradually builds up.

Most reef-building is done by *hermatypic* corals, whose outer tissues are infused with a tiny algae called zooxanthellae, which can photosynthesise to make its food from carbon dioxide and sunlight. It is an important food-source for the coral, while the coral surface provides a protected environment for the algae, so they live in a symbiotic relationship, each dependent on the other. The zooxanthellae gives coral its colour, so when a piece of coral is removed from the water, the zooxanthellae soon dies and the coral becomes white. If the water temperature rises, the coral expels the algae, and the coral loses its colour in a process called 'coral bleaching' (see the boxed text 'Coral Bleaching').

Polyps reproduce by splitting to form a colony of genetically identical polyps – each colony starts life as a single polyp. Although each polyp catches and digests its own food, the nutrition passes between the polyps to the whole colony. Most coral polyps only feed at night; during the daytime they withdraw into their hard limestone skeleton, so it is only after dark that a coral reef can be seen in its full, colourful glory.

**Hard Corals** These take many forms. One of the most common and easiest to recognise is the staghorn coral, which grows by budding off new branches from the tips. Brain corals are huge and round with a surface looking very much like a human brain. They grow by adding new base levels of skeletal matter and expanding outwards. Flat or sheet corals, like plate coral, expand at their outer edges. Some corals take different shapes depending on their immediate environment.

**Soft Corals** These are made up of individual polyps, but do not form a hard limestone skeleton. Lacking the skeleton that protects hard coral, it would seem likely that soft coral would fall prey to fish, but in fact they seem to remain relatively immune either due to toxic substances in their tissues or to the presence of sharp limestone needles. Soft corals can move around and will sometimes engulf and kill off a hard coral. Attractive varieties include fan corals and whips.

Some corals can give a painful sting and the fern-like stinging hydroid, which looks feathery, like a fern, should be given a wide berth. It's quite common in places where soft corals thrive (reef edges washed by strong currents).

**Molluscs** Invertebrate creatures that inhabit shells are all in the group Mollusca, although not all molluscs have visible shells. There are three groups of molluscs, which include all the sea shells, octopus, sea slugs and even garden snails.

The **gastropods**, or univalves, include most of the shells of interest to observers, including the cowrie, noted for its gently rounded shape, beautiful patterns and glossy surface. Living examples are mainly seen at night, when they come out in search of food. The shell-less sea slug is also a gastropod.

The **bivalves** group includes all the creatures with a two-part shell, such as oysters, clams and scallops. Some bivalves embed themselves in rocks, but most live in mud or sand. Giant clams are a common sight on reef flats in the Maldives. Stories of divers being trapped when a huge clam snaps shut are mythical – the clams shut slowly and none too tightly. Their adductor muscles are certainly strong, however, and persuading a closed clam to reopen is not easy.

Finally there are **cephalopods**, which include octopus, squid, the pearly nautilus and cuttlefish.

**Crustaceans** This group includes shrimp, lobsters and crabs. The most interesting shrimp are the cleaners, which have a symbiotic relationship with larger fish, removing parasites from moray eels, starfish and other reef fish. Lobsters live in small reef crannies and are nocturnal and seldom seen. Not traditionally eaten in the Maldives, lobster numbers fell dramatically when tourist resorts created a demand for them, and harvesting is now banned in the Male' area. (Lobster sold in resorts is expensive because lobster is now bought and sold on an international market – whether it is locally caught or imported, it attracts an international market price.) Hermit crabs live in old sea shells, and these shells can often be seen scurrying across the sand. Other crabs are common on the shoreline, often wonderfully camouflaged with fascinating patterns, and are well worth looking for. Underwater, crabs are also common, but even harder to spot.

## Coral Bleaching

In March 1998, the waters of the Maldives experienced a temporary rise in the sea temperature associated with the El Niño effect. For a period of about two weeks, surface water temperatures were above 32°C, resulting in the loss of the symbiotic algae that lives within the coral polyps. The loss of this zooxanthellae algae causes the coral to lose its colour ('coral bleaching'), and if the algae does not return, the coral polyps die. Coral bleaching has occurred, with varying degrees of severity, in shallow waters throughout the Maldives archipelago. When the coral dies, the underlying calcium carbonate is exposed and becomes more brittle, so many of the more delicate branch and table structures have been broken up by wave action. Mainly hard corals have been affected – soft corals and sea fans are less dependent on zooxanthellae algae, are less affected by the sea temperature changes and recover more quickly from damage.

Some corals, particularly in deeper water, recovered almost immediately as the symbiotic algae returned, while in other areas the old coral has died and it will take some years before it is completely recolonised by new coral growth. Marine biologists are watching this re-colonisation process with interest.

In the meantime, the Maldives dive industry is emphasising that there is lots of healthy, living coral below 6m and that, even in shallow waters, the huge number and variety of reef fish appear to be unaffected. One description is of technicolour fish against a monochrome background. In some places, an unsightly brown algae has grown over the bleached coral, so the number of algal grazers like parrot fish has actually increased. The past year has also seen an exceptionally large number of manta rays and sharks, though this may not be related to the coral bleaching. Recreational divers and snorkellers should also look for the new coral formation. For example, regrowth on old coral blocks is most noticeable around the base and in crevices, where it is difficult for fish to get at.

There is still great scuba diving in the Maldives, and even snorkellers will be impressed by the marine life and by the size and shape of the coral formations, but those who have seen the reefs in their full splendour might be disappointed. Many other coral reefs around the world were also affected by the 1998 El Niño, so alternative diving destinations may be no better, especially those in Indonesia, Thailand, Papua New Guinea and the northern parts of Australia's Great Barrier Reef.

There is evidence that coral bleaching has occurred at many times in the past, and that the reefs have always recovered. The crucial question is whether El Niño events are becoming more severe and more frequent as a result of human-induced global warming. If so, the next El Niño may well cause another bout of coral bleaching before the reefs have recovered from the last one. It's a question of whether coral bleaching is a natural process, a natural disaster, or a man-made disaster.

**Reef Fish** There are many fascinating fish to be seen, with hundreds visible to anyone with a mask and snorkel. They're easy to see and enjoy, but people with a naturalist bent may want to identify the various species and should look for one of the field guides to reef fish, or check the attractive posters which are often displayed in dive schools. Some you're sure to see are the several types of butterfly-fish, angelfish, parrotfish and rock cod, unicornfish, trumpetfish, bluestripe snapper, Moorish idol and oriental sweetlips. For more on fish see the special section 'Common Fish of the Maldives' in the Facts for the Visitor chapter.

**Sharks** These are a primitive form of fish with a cartilaginous skeleton, but they are superbly practical creatures with a sleek and highly streamlined shape, and are a wonderful sight in their natural habitat. Shark species found within atolls and around reefs in the Maldives include grey reef sharks, black-tip reef sharks, white-tip reef sharks and nurse sharks. The white-tip reef shark is a small, non-aggressive, territorial shark rarely more than 1.5m long and is often seen over areas of coral or off reef edges. Grey reef sharks are also timid, shallow-water dwellers and often grow to over 2m in length.

Other species are more open-sea dwellers, but do come into atolls and especially to channel entrances where food is plentiful. These include the strange-looking hammerhead shark and the whale shark, the world's largest fish species, which is a harmless plankton eater.

Sharks are not a problem for divers in the Maldives – there's simply too much else for them to eat. Usually, sharks will simply ignore divers as harmless intruders. Just about every dive base in the Maldives has a shark-spotting dive on their itinerary.

**Stingrays & Manta Rays** Rays are also cartilaginous fish, like flattened sharks. Stingrays are sea-bottom feeders, equipped with crushing teeth to grind the molluscs and crustaceans they sift out of the sand. They are occasionally found in the shallows, often lying motionless on the sandy bottom of lagoons. A barbed and poisonous spine on top of the tail can swing up and forward, and will deliver a very painful injury to anyone who stands on a stingray.

Manta rays are among the largest fish found in the Maldives and a firm favourite of divers. They tend to swim along the surface and pass overhead as a large and silent shadow, gliding smoothly and gracefully through the water. They are quite harmless, feeding only on plankton and small fishes, and in some places seem quite relaxed about divers approaching them closely. Manta rays are sometimes seen to leap completely out of the water, landing back with a tremendous splash. The eagle ray is a close relative of the manta and is also often seen by divers in the Maldives.

## Endangered Species

Local populations of some marine animals have suffered severe declines at times and the government has usually responded with effective restrictions, which have prevented total extinction (see Fisheries earlier in this chapter). Maldivian fishing regulations are actually enforced, unlike the ineffectual window dressing that passes for environmental protection in many other countries and regions.

**Turtles** Worldwide, most turtle species are endangered. Four species are known to nest in the Maldives: green, olive ridley, hawksbill and loggerhead. Leatherback turtles visit Maldivian waters, but are not known to nest. Turtle numbers have been in decline in the Maldives, as elsewhere, but they can still be seen by divers at many sites. Some of this decline was caused by capturing turtles to use the shells for jewellery and decorative objects. The catching of turtles, and the sale and export of turtle shell products, is now totally prohibited in the Maldives, but this alone will not restore turtle numbers.

Turtles are migratory and can be threatened by circumstances many miles away. Accidental capture in fishing nets, depletion of sea-grass areas, plastic waste, oil spills and other toxic pollutants are known causes of decline in turtle numbers. Widespread collection of eggs and the loss of nesting sites are two factors which need to be addressed in the Maldives. It is difficult to assess the extent of these problems because the effects do not show up in the adult turtle population for 10 to 20 years.

Turtle eggs are a traditional food and used in *velaa folhi*, a special Maldivian dish. Without banning egg collection altogether, it would be possible to reduce the problem by making protection of nesting sites a condition of future leases of uninhabited islands. Development of resorts has reduced the availability of nesting sites. One interesting aspect is that artificial lights confuse hatchling turtles, which are instinctively guided into the water by the position of the moon. Beach chairs and boats can also interfere with egg laying and with hatchlings. Resorts occupy only a relatively small number of islands, but the number will certainly increase and they will be on islands with wide beaches.

There are technical means to limit the adverse effects of resort development on turtle breeding. It may even be possible to artificially improve the survival chances of hatchlings in the short term – hatching ponds are used to protect baby turtles and are sometimes stocked with babies taken from beach nesting sites – without harming their survival instincts in the long term. (This could become an eco-tourist attraction in itself.) The ban on turtle products is a positive step, but without protection of nesting sites and eggs, turtle populations cannot be maintained.

## GOVERNMENT & POLITICS
The Maldivian parliament, the Majlis or Citizens' Council, has 48 members. Male', which is the capital island, and each of the atolls have two representatives each, elected for five-year terms. All citizens over 21 years of age can vote. The president chooses the remaining eight parliamentary representatives, has the power to appoint or dismiss cabinet ministers and appoints all judges who administer justice under the broad tenets of Islam.

The Majlis considers candidates for the presidency for each five-year term, and makes a nomination, which is put to a national vote. Only one candidate is put forward, so the vote is not so much an election as a national referendum – a strong vote of support for the president is seen as a show of loyalty to religious authorities, local political leaders and the country as a whole. In recent votes, the current president Mr Gayoom has always received over 90% support.

In 1998, for the first time, any adult male was eligible to put himself up to the Majlis as a presidential candidate, and several people did so. There was never any doubt that the Majlis would nominate Gayoom again, but the candidates were making themselves known on the political scene, and using the chance to express alternative points of view. Some of them were later sanctioned for speaking out, indicating that the Maldives is still some way from the European notion of multi-party politics and complete freedom of political expression. In any case, Mr Gayoom was re-elected with another huge vote. The main constraints on his power are powerful business interests, which try to influence government decisions, and Muslim fundamentalists keen to maintain traditional values.

Local government of the 19 administrative atolls is in the hands of each *atolu verin*, or atoll chief. The *gazi* is the religious head of the atoll and joins the atoll chief in deciding legal matters. Each island also has its own chief, or *kateeb*, who is appointed by the atoll chief in consultation with the Ministry of Atolls Administration.

## ECONOMY
The Maldives has a developing economy based on fishing, tourism and shipping. Statistically, it is still one of the poorest countries in the world, but growth averaged over 9% per annum for much of the 1980s and 1990s. The rate of growth slowed in the late 1990s, but was still a healthy 6.5%. GDP is estimated at about US$300 million, or US$1000 per person. Much of the population lives and works outside the money-based economy, so activities like subsistence fishing, coconut gathering and agriculture are not well accounted for in the figures.

Statistically, it may be a poor country, but life in a Maldivian fishing village may seem almost idyllic, with none of the squalor associated with poverty in other parts of south Asia. In fact, some islands do have problems with nutrition because of a shortage of fresh vegetables, and many people in Male' live in very crowded conditions. In terms of income distribution, it's clear that economic growth has made some people in Male' very wealthy, while people on less populated islands outside the tourism zones have benefited much less. There are deliberate government policies to promote development in the outer atolls, with every island now connected to the phone network, and most now having electricity and adequate rainwater tanks. Unemployment was never seen as a problem in the atolls, where men could always go fishing to earn a living, and women could always do craft work like ropemaking or fish preparation. In the monetised economy of Male', however, there are people who have trouble finding suitable work, especially those who have come to the city for their education, and who have higher expectations. There is no visible begging in the Maldives, and no-one living on the streets,

Despite efforts to increase agricultural output, nearly all the food for the increasing population is imported. Agriculture accounts for less than 8% of GDP and this proportion has actually declined over the last decade. Manufacturing and construction make up 15% of GDP, with small boat yards, fish packing, clothing and a plastic pipe plant, but mostly it's cottage industries and handcrafts producing coconut oil, coir (coconut-husk fibre) and coir products such as rope and matting. Local craft industries are encouraged to expand with assistance from the United Nations Development Program (UNDP).

Many of the new industrial activities are outside Male' proper; several are on nearby islands. Other new plants (eg fish packing) are being established in the outer Atolls.

## Fishing

Fishing, the traditional base of the economy, is still an important export earner, but is declining in relative importance. It now accounts for around 14% of GDP and employs 22% of the labour force, but contributes nearly 40% of export earnings. Skipjack tuna is the principal catch, followed by yellowfin tuna, little tuna and frigate mackerel, as well as reef fish such as sharks.

The fishing industry was dealt a blow in 1972 when the rich Sri Lankan market for 'Maldive Fish' (smoked and dried skipjack tuna) collapsed as Sri Lanka slapped on foreign-exchange controls. The government strategy was to improve productivity by mechanising the fishing fleet, to introduce new packing techniques and to develop new markets. The government took control of a tuna-canning factory in Lhaviyani Atoll and export markets for canned, frozen and salted fish were opened in Japan, South Korea, Singapore and some European countries.

Nevertheless, the fishing industry is vulnerable to international market fluctuations. Towards the end of 1981, for example, a glut of tuna on the international market sent the price plummeting. Most of the fish catch is now bought by the government at controlled prices.

Most adult males have some experience in fishing, and casual employment on fishing boats is something of an economic backstop. Men are unlikely to take on menial work for low pay when there is a prospect that they can get a few days or weeks of relatively well-paid work on a fishing dhoni.

## Tourism

It was an Italian tour operator, George Corbin, who saw the tourism potential of the Maldives when he visited the islands in 1971. The following year, he brought a group of travel writers to the country for a promotional tour. They were enthusiastic, but experts from the UNDP warned that tourism could never succeed in the Maldives – there was no infrastructure, no cultural attractions, no local supplies of suitable food, it was too remote and the people had no experience.

Kurumba Island opened as a resort in 1972 with 30 huts made of local materials. Visitors came on a side trip from Sri Lanka, and they loved it. The word spread around Europe and other islands close to Male' were turned into resorts. By 1977 were 11 resorts, most pretty basic and many were run by foreign investors out for a quick dollar. There were no controls or regulations and soon there were impecunious hippy types renting houses for a few dollars a month, cavorting naked near conservative Muslim villages and using drugs that had never been a part of Maldivian life.

There were environmental problems too, but the real pressure for change came from the offence to traditional values and the fact that so few economic benefits were being realised. In 1978 there were 17 resorts and nearly 30,000 visitors. President Gayoom came to power that year, determined to make the industry generate real benefits for the country. He introduced the bed tax of US$6 per night which was an immediate boon to the treasury.

A Danish consultancy firm was employed to prepare a 10-year master plan for the industry. The study identified scuba diving and the 'Robinson Crusoe' appeal as the major attractions – the former was not a cheap activity and the latter was not compatible with mass tourism. It recommended a strategy of developing 'quality tourism', rather than promoting the country as a cheap seaside destination. The first Tourism Law was enacted in 1979 and it set the model for Maldivian tourism. All resorts were to be registered with the government, confined to uninhabited islands and required to conform to strict environmental and quality standards.

Part of the strategy is the progressive upgrading of facilities and the general standard of the tourism industry. This enabled the local industry to become established when finance was hard to obtain, but ensured that it moved steadily towards the quality end of the market. When the lease on an island expires, the government can require a major renovation and upgrade as a condition of renewal. The average cost of developing a resort, per bed, was US$900 in 1979, US$21,000 in 1985 and US$33,000 by 1993. New leases are subject to a competitive tendering process, where the developer with the best plan *and* the highest bid will get the rights to the island. The new Sun Island resort is one of the largest (350 rooms) and most fully equipped – it cost about US$47 million.

The rate of tourism growth has been stunning. The annual number of visitors was 1097 in 1972, 60,358 in 1981, 196,112 in 1991 and 396,000 in 1998. The industry accounts directly for 18% of GDP and contributes indirectly to growth in construction, transport and distribution. It provides over 60% of export earnings.

Most of the tourists (77%) are Europeans, especially Italians (20%), Germans (19%), British (14%), French (5%), Swiss (6%) and Austrians (4%). The Asian market was the fastest growing sector in the mid-1990s, but growth stalled with the Asian economic 'meltdown', and the proportion of tourists from Asian countries dropped from 21% to 18%, of which most were Japanese (10%). Various countries contribute the remainder, including India (3%), Sri Lanka (1.5%), South Africa (2%) and Russia (1.1%). Fewer than 2% are from Australia and only 1% are from the USA. The industry has proved quite robust, surviving the scare of the Gulf War, economic slowdowns in Europe and Asia, and even the bad publicity about coral bleaching. An expansionist tourism strategy encouraged the opening of

more than a dozen new resorts in the late 1990s, and there is a possibility that the growing number and size of resorts might outstrip the growth in tourist numbers, at least for a short time.

## Shipping

The national shipping line, Maldives Shipping Ltd (MSL), forms the basis of the country's important shipping industry, but this is also vulnerable to international events. In 1981 there was a glut of shipping in the Indian Ocean region and freight prices crashed. Then the Iran-Iraq war affected trade to the extent that the Maldives Shipping Ltd was reduced by two-thirds.

Transport has grown significantly as a proportion of GDP (to about 8%), but much of this is transport within the country.

## POPULATION & PEOPLE

The most recent census, in 1995, put the population at 244,650, with about 65,000 in Male'. The annual rate of population growth is about 3.4%, and the July 1999 population estimate was 300,220.

This growth rate may not seem unmanageable, especially with a national income growing at nearly twice that rate. On the other hand, this is a nation of tiny islands and it's hard to imagine where another 45,000 people will go. There is a family planning program and birth control is available, officially to married couples only, but in fact to most people in the capital and on the larger islands. Some couples still do have large families and the youthful population means a high proportion are about to enter child-bearing years. Also, Maldivians have their families at a young age, accelerating the rate of increase.

A recent publication gives an estimate of life expectancy at 70 years for females and 66 for males, which seems very high for a developing country. Another source from 1991 puts life expectancy at 52 years, while a 1977 publication quotes an estimate of 46 years. This suggests a remarkable improvement, or a statistical aberration.

It is thought that the original settlers of the Maldives were Dravidian and Sinhalese people who came from south India and Ceylon. There has also been a great deal of intermarriage and mixing with Arabian and African people. Maldivians are generally of smaller stature than Indians or Sri Lankans.

The most obvious character trait of the Maldivian people is their generally non-aggressive nature. They laugh a lot and anger is rarely expressed. Although the people are openly friendly to outsiders and very helpful, they don't have a servile attitude towards visitors. Foreigners doing business find it can take quite a long time before they have the trust and confidence of their Maldivian counterparts.

You can address Maldivians by their first or last name. Since so many men are called Mohammed, Hassan or Ali, the surname is more appropriate. In some cases an honorary title like Maniku or Didi is used to bestow respect. Among friends and family, many Maldivians have a nickname, for example, an Ibrahim is often called Ibbie or Ibbay.

## Social Class & Status

Not so long ago, the sultans and their families were the aristocracy, courtiers and local chiefs were the upper classes, and everyone else was part of a peasantry. Though the country is now a republic, and business can be a source of wealth and status, there is still a sense of social hierarchy, but it's nothing like a Hindu caste system.

The upper class of privileged families is called the *befalu* and often bare the names Manik or Didi. At the other end of the scale are the Giraavaru people, descended from early settlers from southern India. They are the Maldives aborigines and only a small community survives in Male' (they were moved from their home island of Giraavaru when their numbers fell below the 40 adult males required for a functioning mosque).

The traditional social structure can be reflected in business and government, where it's important to know the right people and have the right connections. Organisations are often hierarchical and those down the ladder don't make decisions. If you want something done, you have to go to the top.

## Marriage & Divorce

Maldivians marry early and often. Most women marry before the age of 20 to a slightly older man. The woman must agree and the woman's parents must consent and name a *rhan* (bride price). The man must pay the woman this amount and she keeps it if the marriage breaks up. It acts as a sort of insurance. In the past this has often been a nominal amount, but now a woman may ask a higher price, maybe to discourage a suitor she is not too keen on, or because she thinks he is very likely to divorce her. The wedding ceremony is a low-key affair, with the couple and two witnesses and the local *gazi* officiating.

A married woman retains her name and can acquire her own property. The couple commonly live with her parents and have children early. It is often the woman who makes the important family decisions – historically, men may have been away for months at a time fishing or trading. Sex outside marriage is illegal and adultery can be punished by beating.

A man can divorce his wife simply by telling her so and notifying the *gazi*. That's the end of the marriage, but the man must pay maintenance for all the couple's children. The woman is not permitted to remarry for three months to ensure that she is not pregnant to her ex-husband. If a woman wants a divorce, she must have the husband's consent or go through a difficult administrative procedure.

A man can have up to four wives at a time, but few can afford to have more than one. On the other hand, a fisherman or a travelling boatman might have wives on a number of islands. It is not uncommon to find men who have been married more than 20 times and no surprise to learn that the Maldives has the highest rate of divorce in the world. Officially, about 59% of marriages end in divorce.

In theory, a couple can be married one day and divorced the next. There are lots of stories about passing travellers taking temporary wives, and castaways contributing to the local gene pool. These stories may have more to do with male banter on long boat trips than what really happens in Muslim villages. Gossip is rife, but promiscuity is not. Religion, the family and the lack of anonymity make sure of that – no secrets can be kept for long.

## EDUCATION

There are no pre-schools or kindergartens, but children start learning the Quran at a non-government religious school called a *maktab* from about the age of three. There are government primary schools *(madrasa)* on every inhabited island, but some are very small and do not go past fourth or fifth grade. For grades six and seven, children may have to go to a middle school on a larger island or the atoll capital. Atoll capitals have an Atoll Education Centre (AEC) with adult education and sometimes lower secondary schooling (grades eight to 10). Children must often move to another island to continue their education, which is very competitive with a necessarily high drop-out rate.

Only the best students can go on to a higher secondary school which teaches up to the British GCE 'A level' – there is one in Male' and one in Hithadhoo in the far south of the country. In Male' there are four primary schools, two lower secondary schools and one higher secondary school. There are also private secondary schools in Male', catering mostly for those who have been unable to keep up with the standards required to stay in the government system. Students coming to Male' to study often survive by taking live-in domestic jobs, which detract from their study time, especially for girls who are always expected to do more.

Post-secondary education in Male' is limited to a Science Education Centre, Teachers College, Institute of Health Sciences, Institute of Islamic Studies, some vocational training centres and the School of Hotel & Catering Services. For university studies, young Maldivians go abroad, usually to Sri Lanka, India, Britain or Australia.

There is a system of bonded labour under which people must work for the government at a meagre wage for a period which depends on the length of their education in government schools. For many this means a period in the National Security Service or in a government office, where the service can be less than enthusiastic. They may pursue another occupation part time to establish their career or to make ends meet. Many people in Male', particularly young people, have two jobs.

The adult literacy rate is about 93%. English is taught as a second language from grade one and is the usual teaching language at higher secondary school – Maldivians with a secondary education will speak excellent English. Most official forms and publications are printed in both Divehi and English.

## ARTS

Though performances of traditional music and dance are not everyday events, a contemporary Divehi culture is strong and adaptive despite foreign influences, which range from Hindi movies and Oriental martial arts to Michael Jackson and Muslim fundamentalism.

Western and Indian fashions, pop music and videos are highly visible, but on public occasions and festivals, like the beginning and end of Ramadan, the celebrations always have a distinctly Maldivian touch. Three daily newspapers and several magazines are published in the unique national language, rock bands sing Divehi lyrics and multistorey buildings echo traditional village houses. It's remarkable that such a tiny population maintains its own distinctive, living culture.

### Song & Dance

A *bodu beru* means a big drum and gives its name to the best-known form of traditional music and dance. It is what tourist resorts put on for a local culture night and it can be quite sophisticated and compelling. Dancers begin with a slow, nonchalant swaying and swinging of the arms, and become more animated as the tempo increases, finishing in a rhythmic frenzy. In some versions the dancers enter a trance-like state. There are four to six drummers in an ensemble and the sound has strong African influences.

This is also the entertainment at private parties, where a few guys will play the drums and everyone else dances, more and more frenetically as the night goes on.

Contemporary local rock bands often perform at resorts where they do credible covers of the usual old favourites. Performing for a local audience they may incorporate elements of bodu beru in their music, with lots of percussion and extended drum solos. Two bands popular with locals are Freeze and Zero Degree – cassettes and CDs from both bands, and quite a few others, are sold in Male' music shops.

## Literature

Despite a unique script, which dates from the 1600s, most of the Maldivian myths and stories are from an essentially oral tradition and have only recently appeared in print. Many are stories of witchcraft and sorcery, while others are cautionary tales about the evils of vanity, lust and greed, and the sticky fates of those who transgressed. Some are decidedly weird and depressing, and don't make good bed-time reading for young children. Novelty Press has published a small book called *Mysticism in the Maldives*, which is widely available, and a series of booklets called *Finiashi – heard in the islands*, most of which are out of print.

## Architecture

A traditional Maldivian village is notable for its neat and orderly layout, with wide streets in a regular, rectangular grid. Houses are made of coral-stone joined with mortar, and the walls line the sides of the streets. Many houses will have a shaded courtyard in front, enclosed by a chest-high coral wall fronting the street. This courtyard is an outdoor room, with *joli* seats and *undholi*, where families sit in the heat of the day or the cool of the evening. A more private courtyard behind, the *gifili*, has a well and serves as an open-air bathroom.

At intersections, the coral walls have rounded corners, which considerably soften the streetscape. These corners are seemingly designed to facilitate turning vehicles, but they are like this in small island villages that never see a vehicle. The same style is used in Male', where it does make turning

### Sitting in the Maldives

The Maldives has two unique pieces of furniture. One is the *undholi*, a wooden platform or a netting seat that's hung from a tree or triangular frame. Sometimes called a bed-boat, the undholi is a sofa, hammock and fan combination – swinging gently creates a cooling movement of air across the indolent occupant.

The *joli* is a static version – a net seat slung on a rectangular frame, usually made in sociable sets of three or four. Perhaps they were once made of coir rope and wooden sticks, but steel pipes and plastic mesh are now almost universal – it's like sitting in a string shopping bag.

easier for cars and trucks, but it is also a feature of big, modern buildings, and appears to be a deliberate adaptation of a traditional feature. On other buildings, like the president's palace and the police headquarters, the rounded design may derive more from the design of fortresses, especially as these have circular sentry posts on the corners.

The architecture of resorts is more eclectic, imitative of anything from a Balinese *bale* to an African *rondavel*. Some have a natural style, with thatched roof buildings, that blends unobtrusively into the landscape. However, many modern resorts have tiled roofs and stark white walls, and look more like suburban motel blocks than tropical hideaways. The only part of a tourist resort with any identifiably Maldivian character is the open-air bathroom, a delightful feature popular with guests. An exception is the new Reethi Beach resort on Baa Atoll, which has used an exterior concrete moulding, styled after Male's old Friday Mosque.

## Visual Arts

There's no tradition of painting but it has been developing in recent years – many Maldivians do seem to have a talent for graphic design, which is most often seen in advertising, printed matter and locally designed Web sites. A number of contemporary artists exhibit their work at Esjehi Gallery in Male', which is worth a look.

Some islands were once famous for carving, of both calligraphy and the intricate intertwining patterns still seen on old gravestones. A little of this woodcarving is still done, mainly to decorate mosques, and the facade of the new Majlis building in Male' is decorated with intertwined carvings.

## Crafts

The different islands have historically specialised in different crafts, like the silversmiths of Ribudhoo, the lacquer workers of Eydafushi or the weavers of Gadhoo. This might relate to the availability of certain materials, like the special reeds and grasses used for weaving mats, but mainly it seems to be a matter of tradition.

**Mats** The fine woven mats known as *kunaa* are now made only in Gaaf Dhaal, but it seems to be a dying art. A Danish researcher in the 1970s documented the weaving techniques and the plants used for fibre and dyes, and noted that a number of traditional designs had not been woven for 20 years. Collecting the materials and weaving a mat can take weeks and the money that can be made selling the work is not much by modern Maldivian standards. Tourist demand for this superb craft is limited, especially as tourists cannot go to the source, see the work being done or buy directly from the artisans. On the other hand, many of the best pieces are snapped up by local government officials or wealthy business people, so there is an appreciation of the work.

**Lacquer Work** Many types of wood are used to make boxes, bowls, vases and other turned objects. Traditionally the lathe is hand-powered by a cord pulled round a spindle, though electric motors will no doubt replace that method soon. Several layers of lacquer are applied in different colours and allowed to harden, then the design is incised with sharp tools, exposing the bright colours of the underlying layers. Designs are usually floral motifs in red, yellow and green, with a background of black. The patterns are a little abstract and do not usually resemble native Maldivian

**A turned vase decorated with incised lacquer work.**

flora, but may be based on designs seen in Chinese ceramics.

Traditionally, lacquer work was for containers, bowls and trays used to present gifts to the sultan, and some fine examples can be seen in the National Museum in Male'. Vases and small boxes are the most common lacquer-work items in tourist shops, and the designs use traditional colours and styles, though the items themselves are a response to tourist demand. Production of lacquer work seems to be a viable cottage industry and is concentrated in Baa, particularly the islands of Eydafushi and Thuladhoo.

**Jewellery** Ribudhoo Island in Dhaalu (South Nilandhoo Atoll) is famous for making gold jewellery, and Huludeli, in the same atoll, for silver jewellery. According to local belief, a royal jeweller brought the goldsmithing skills to the island centuries ago having been banished to Ribudhoo by a sultan. It's also said that the islanders plundered a shipwreck in the 1700s, and reworked the gold jewellery they found to disguise its origins.

## SOCIETY & CONDUCT
### Traditional Culture

Fishing villages away from the tourist resorts are almost totally unaffected by contact with the outside world. Though most villages have acquired a telephone connection in the last few years, and radios have been present for a while, the amount of personal contact is negligible. Young people may leave the island for education or employment, and men may leave for fishing or trading, but most of the people have no reason to travel and few travellers have any reason or opportunity to visit.

Fishing is the main economic activity and fish is traded for other necessities at the nearest big island. Attending the mosque is the main religious activity and probably the main social and cultural activity as well. There are no guesthouses or restaurants, and minimal modern medical facilities. Motorcycles, taxis, pick-up trucks and televisions are starting to appear on even quite remote islands, video games and the Internet are coming, and one wonders how long a sense of isolation can last.

Amateur anthropologists and cultural voyeurs would love to visit such places, but it's hard to think of any benefits they would bring and it's easy to imagine the potential for problems. In any case, the national government is not keen to explore the possibility, and access to inhabited islands outside the tourism zone is by invitation only.

Within the tourism zone, access is limited to day-time trips with resort-based excursions. Inhabited islands that are frequently visited have souvenir shops with enthusiastic sellers and, while no-one should suggest they are 'ruined', the impression is far from pristine. Even on these islands, visitors are asked to dress respectfully and behave responsibly, but an insensitive few seem incapable of doing so. While responsible travellers may resent the restrictions on access to more isolated islands, they should at least appreciate that there are good reasons for those restrictions.

### Dos & Don'ts

Maldivian resorts make it quite clear what guests should and shouldn't do. Guests must respect the environment (no damage to fish or coral). They must respect Muslim sensibilities. Nudity is strictly forbidden and women must not go topless; bikinis and brief bathers are quite acceptable in resorts, though most prefer that you cover up in the bar, dining and reception areas. In Male' and on other inhabited islands, however, travellers should make an effort not to offend the local standards. Men should never go bare chested and women should avoid low-cut tops and tank tops. Long pants or long skirts are preferable, but shorts are OK if they cover the thighs.

It's best to dress neatly and conservatively when dealing with officials and business people. A suit is unnecessary – Maldivian professional men always wear long trousers, clean shoes (often slip-ons), a shirt and usually a tie. Women usually wear dresses below the knee and covering the shoulders and arms.

Those who spend time outside the resorts should be aware of a few more points:

**Remove your shoes** Maldivians can slip off their footwear without breaking step, but visitors may find it inconvenient. Slip-on shoes are easier than lace-ups, and thongs (flip flops) are easier than sandals.

**The guest doesn't pay** If you ask someone to lunch, that means you'll pay for it; and if someone else asks you, don't reach for the bill.

**Be patient and polite** Government offices can be painfully slow and frustrating.

**Respect the religion** Islam is the state religion, so be aware that prayer times take precedence over business and pleasure, and that Ramadan, a month of fasting, places great demands on local people. Visiting a mosque requires long pants or a long skirt and no shoes. No-one should have alcohol or pork outside resorts.

## RELIGION

Islam is the religion of the Maldives and those who practise it are called Muslims. All Maldivians are Muslims of the Sunni sect, as opposed to the Shi'ia sect. There are no other religions or sects present or permitted in the country.

Islam in the Maldives is fundamental to all aspects of life; there's no getting away from it unless you go to a resort. It is, how-

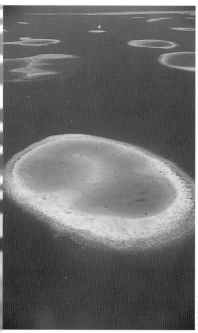

**Top:** Sit atop a mountain! Maldivian atolls are the peaks of a submerged mountain range. **Left:** Land area in the Maldives is only 0.4%, the rest is reef, water and sunshine. **Middle Right:** There isn't a square metre to spare on Male'. **Bottom:** Male's airport has its own island, Huhule.

Maldivian people share a mixed Indian, Arabic and African ancestry.

ever, Islam of a more liberal nature than that adhered to in some of the Arab states; comparable, rather, to the faith practised in India and Indonesia. Maldivian women, for example, do not have to observe purdah, which is the custom of keeping women in seclusion, with clothing that conceals them completely when they go out.

Children are taught the Arabic alphabet and, until their mid-teens, attend a *maktab*, one of the traditional Islamic schools where the reading and reciting of the Quran is taught.

There are mosques for the men and for the women. Most are of simple, unadorned design, both inside and out and, apart from the new Islamic Centre in Male', they are generally not much to look at.

Islam shares its roots with two of the other major religions, Judaism and Christianity, and its teachings correspond closely with the Torah, the Old Testament and the Gospels. Adam, Abraham, Noah, Moses and Jesus are all accepted as Muslim prophets, but Jesus is not recognised as the son of God. According to Islam, these prophets all received the word of Allah (God), but only Mohammed received the complete revelation. The essence of Islam is the Quran and the Prophet Mohammed.

## The Prophet Mohammed

Mohammed was born in Mecca (now in Saudi Arabia) in AD 570 and had his first revelation from Allah in 610. He began to preach against the idolatry that was rampant in the region, particularly in Mecca, and proved to be a powerful and persuasive speaker attracting a devoted following. His teachings appealed to the poorer levels of society and angered the wealthy merchant class.

By 622, life for Mohammed and his followers became so unpleasant that they were forced to migrate to Medina, 300km to the north. This migration, known as the *hejira*, marks the start of the Islamic Calendar: AD 622 became year 1 AH.

In AD 630 Mohammed had gained enough followers to return and take Mecca. Within two decades of Mohammed's death most of Arabia had converted to Islam. With seemingly unlimited ambition and zeal, the Prophet's followers spread the word, using force where necessary, and the influence of the Islamic state soon extended from the Atlantic to the Indian Ocean.

## The Five Pillars of Islam

*Islam* is the Arabic word for submission and underlies the duty of all Muslims to submit themselves to Allah.

*Shahada*, the profession of faith that 'There is no God but Allah and Mohammed is his prophet', is the first of the Five Pillars of Islam – the tenets that guide Muslims in their daily life.

The second pillar, *salath*, is the call to prayer, and Islam decrees that Muslims must face Mecca and pray five times each day. In the Maldives, salath is also called *namadh*.

The third pillar is *zakat*, the act of giving alms to the needy. Some Islamic countries have turned this into an obligatory land tax which goes to help the poor.

The fourth pillar is the fast during the day for the month of *Ramadan*, the ninth month of the Islamic calendar.

The fifth pillar is the *hajj* or pilgrimage to Mecca, the holiest place in Islam. It is the duty of every Muslim who is able, to make the hajj at least once in their life.

## Prayer Times

The initial prayer session is in the first hour before sunrise, the second around noon, the third in mid-afternoon around 3.30 pm, the fourth at sunset and the final session in the early evening.

The call to prayer is delivered by the *mudhim* or muezzin. In former days, he climbed to the top of the minaret and shouted it out. Now a cassette recording, relayed by loudspeakers on the minaret, announces the call and the mudeem even appears on TV.

Shops and offices close for 15 minutes after each call. Some people go to the mosque, some kneel where they are and others do not visibly participate.

## Ramadan

Called Ramazan in the Maldives, this is the month of fasting, which begins at the time of a new moon and ends with the sighting of the next new moon. The Ramadan month gets a little earlier each year because it is based on a lunar calendar of twelve 28-day months (see Public Holidays & Special Events in the Facts for the Visitor chapter for dates over the next few years).

During Ramadan Muslims should not eat, drink, smoke or have sex between sunrise and sunset, and working hours are restricted. Exceptions are granted to young children, pregnant or menstruating women and those who are travelling. It can be a difficult time for travel outside the resorts, as tea-shops and cafes are closed during the day and everybody is generally on edge. The evenings, however, are long and lively.

### Local Beliefs

In the islands people still fear *jinnis*, the evil spirits that come from the sea, land and sky. They are blamed for everything that can't be explained by religion or education.

To combat jinnis there are *fandhita*, which are the spells and potions provided by a local *hakeem* or medicine man. The hakeem is often called upon when illness strikes, if a woman fails to conceive or if the fishing catch is poor.

The hakeem might cast a curing spell by writing phrases from the Quran on strips of paper and sticking or tying them to the patient. Another method is to write the sayings in ink on a plate, fill the plate with water to dissolve the ink and make the patient drink the potion. Other concoctions include *isitri*, a love potion used in matchmaking, and its antidote *varitoli*, which is used to break up marriages.

## LANGUAGE

The language of the Maldives is Divehi, also written as 'Dhivehi'. It is related to an ancient form of Sinhala, a Sri Lankan language, but also contains some Arabic, Hindi and English words. On top of all this, there are several different dialects throughout the country.

English is widely spoken in Male', in the resorts, and by educated people throughout the country. English is also spoken on Addu, the southernmost atoll, where the British employed many of the islanders on the air base for 20 years. On other islands, especially outside the tourist zone, you'd be very lucky to find an adult who speaks anything other than Divehi.

For a brief guide to Divehi and some useful words and phrases, see the Language chapter at the back of this book.

# Facts for the Visitor

## HIGHLIGHTS

If your idea of paradise is a hassle-free holiday on an unspoilt tropical island, then strolling on soft white sand, sitting under a coconut tree, and swimming in a sapphire-like lagoon will be all the highlights you'll need. The brilliant blue of the water is a highlight in itself.

For many, the highlights are under the water, especially the amazing number of fish, which completely surround you with fantastic shapes and lurid colours. It's like swimming in an aquarium.

For scuba divers accustomed to these delights, a highlight is the larger marine life – turtles, napoleon wrasse, mantas and morays, whale sharks, nurse sharks, hammerheads and rays. In the Maldives, so one slogan says, even the sharks are friendly.

Another underwater highlight is the shipwrecks, such as the *Maldive Victory*. It's not that divers like to see a watery graveyard, but more because the wrecks are alive with new coral growth, and a home to trevally, snapper, squirrelfish and cod.

For a different sort of highlight, take a flight over the atolls and watch the free-form patterns of sea, sandbank, reef and island unroll in a panorama of blue, white, turquoise and green.

Finally, for the Maldives' most elusive highlight, find a small fishing village and walk back between the white coral walls, where children play and old people smoke a hookah in the shade of a breadfruit tree. This is a world of its own – traditional, unhurried and almost unchanged for centuries, as simple and well ordered as the straight village streets or the tenets of Islam.

## SUGGESTED ITINERARIES

The vast majority of visitors have a very simple itinerary – they arrive, transfer to their resort island, perhaps make some excursions, transfer back to the airport, and depart. A few people combine two resorts in one holiday, or combine a safari boat trip with a resort stay. Some arrange to spend a day in Male' at the start or end of their trip – this may be unavoidable if you're staying in a more distant resort and your flights arrive in the evening or depart in the early morning. Independent travellers should start with at least a few days in Male', both for interest and to make arrangements for visiting some islands.

## PLANNING
### When to Go

If you're looking for a few extra hours of sunshine then you should go between December and April, which is the dry season, with less rain and lower humidity. February to April is the hottest time and the most popular, when resorts can be fully booked and prices are higher. The period from mid-December to early January, is the highest of the high season and prices are even higher.

From May to November is the period when storms and rain are more likely. It's still warm, but skies can be cloudy and the humidity is higher. This is the low season, with fewer people and lower prices, but August can be more expensive because many Europeans take their holidays then.

There are amazingly complex descriptions of Maldivian weather patterns (see Climate in the Facts about the Maldives chapter) and the pricing patterns of the tourist resorts are equally complex – some seem to have a different price for every week of the year.

### What Kind of Trip?

The vast majority of visitors to the Maldives will be looking for a holiday in an island resort, and might find some help in the following section on Choosing a Resort. A substantial minority will be taking a trip through the islands on a live-aboard boat – see the section on Safari Cruises in the Getting Around chapter for more information. In both cases, it's more than likely that they will make all the arrangements in advance through a travel agent at home.

**Independent Travel** Fully independent travellers, or FITs, are a rare species in the Maldives. If you arrive at Male' airport without a hotel reservation, the immigration authorities will ask you to go outside and make some arrangements with one of the tour operators there. There used to be independent tour operators who would latch on to any arriving FITs and help them book into a resort or get on a safari trip – some were helpful and trustworthy, others were not. These days, virtually all the agents at the airport are representing resorts or resort operators, and are there to meet guests who have bookings.

It's best for arriving FITs to give the name of a hotel in Male', and allow a few days in the capital to shop around, make some phone calls, and arrange their onward travel. FITs who want to get on a safari boat will certainly have to make arrangements in Male' (see Safari Cruises in the Getting Around chapter).

Even the most resolutely independent traveller determined to see untouristed areas will benefit from the help of a good travel agent or operator. Most 'resort operators' in Male' are just a sort of front office, but some are actually the owners and operators.

Travel agents are typically contracted to fill a certain number of rooms at a resort and usually do so in conjunction with a foreign tour operator, but they often have contacts at many resorts and up-to-the-minute information about availability and prices. Especially outside high season, resorts may occasionally be desperate to fill some rooms, and will offer a special price through Male' tour operators and agents.

**AAA Hotels & Resorts** (☎ 324933, fax 324943, ✉ trvlntrs@aaa.com.mv), STO Trade Centre; operators of several quality mid-range resorts.
**Capital Travel & Tours** (☎ 315089, fax 320336, ✉ info@capitaltravel.com), Bluekiya Magu; inbound tour operator booking a number of mid-range resorts and safari boats.
**Champa Trade & Travels** (☎ 314149, fax 314150, ✉ ctnt@dhivehinet.net.mv), Champa Building; is the Male' office for Kuredu and Meeru, two of the biggest budget resorts in the country.

**Inner Maldives** (☎ 326309, fax 330884, ✉ intermal@dhivehinet.net.mv), Ameer Ahmed Magu; small independent agency but very well informed and helpful.
**Lif-Sham Travel & Tours** (☎ 325386, fax 320381, ✉ lift23@dhivehinet.net.mv), Gulisthaanu Magu; small inbound operator which handles some inexpensive resorts.
**Picasso Travels** (☎ 330626, fax 3141003); very small agency that might be able to help independent travellers.
**Paradise Holidays** (☎ 312090, fax 312087, ✉ parahol@dhivehinet.net.mv), 3/9 Fareedhee Magu; very big inbound tour operator, not cheap and not really set up to help FITs, but with access to so many resorts it just might have something.
**Sun Travel & Tours** (☎ 325977, fax 320419, ✉ suntrvl@dhivehinet.net.mv), 8 Boduthakurufaanu Magu (Marine Drive); has arrangements with quite a few resorts and safari boats, often deals with FITs.
**Voyages Maldives** (☎ 325349, fax 325366, ✉ voyages@dhivehinet.net.mv), Chandanee Magu; well-established and efficient safari tour operator which also quotes quite low rates on a number of resorts.

Other small, independent tour operators or travel agents (at the airport or elsewhere) may offer great deals and may also overcharge you. If you decide on a resort, or an agent recommends one, call the resort, or its Male' office, and ask what they'd charge if you booked directly with them.

**Travel Outside Resorts** It's government policy to have tourists stay on island resorts or on boats within the 'tourism zone'. You need a permit to visit islands outside the tourism zone or to stay overnight on any non-resort island. To get a permit you need a sponsor to invite you to the island concerned (see Visas & Documents later in this chapter). There is no commercial accommodation on non-resort islands, so the sponsor will have to arrange a place to stay, and is not allowed to charge for doing so. If you want to visit islands that are occupied by locals rather than tourists, you still have a few options.

Firstly, you can stay in a resort and make day trips. Most resorts offer 'island hopping' trips that visit local fishing villages, though these villages often have conspicuous souvenir shops and persistent sellers. Some resorts are quite close to village islands; you can charter a dhoni to visit the village without a big group. If you do this, it's good protocol to find the *kateeb* (island chief) as soon as you can, introduce yourself and explain your interests. However, the dhoni will probably have to wait for you, and this can get expensive if you stay for most of the day. Resorts won't allow you to use catamarans, windsurfers or canoes to visit nearby islands, but if you explain what you want and you find a sympathetic ear, you may get help, particularly if the island you're visiting is pleased for you to come. You won't be allowed to stay in any village after 6 pm, but you should be able to find some local food for lunch.

Without doubt the best place to stay if you want to visit local villages is the Equator Village Resort on Gan, in the far south of the country. Gan is linked by causeways to five other islands with several large villages, and you can cycle or walk through all of them. See the Southern Atolls chapter for more information.

The second option is to arrange a safari boat trip to the areas you're interested in and make it clear to the operator that you want to visit fishing villages. The operator will arrange permits for all the people on the boat, and because you stay overnight on the boat, the accommodation problem is solved. The catch is that you will have to charter the whole boat, so you'll need at least another five like-minded passengers to share the expense.

The third option is to spend a couple of weeks in Male'. It is, after all, a Maldivian island. It has over a quarter of the country's population, relatively few tourists and it's quite an interesting place in its own right. If you eat in local tea shops, spend time browsing in the craft and souvenir shops, go to the cinema and walk around in the evenings, you'll meet lots of locals. English is widely spoken and people will be more than willing to chat. It's a lot less expensive to stay in Male' than in a resort and you're allowed to make day trips to other islands in the atoll if you're accompanied by someone

from your guesthouse. There are a few inhabited nonresort islands which you could reach and return from in a day – Himmafushi, Huraa, and perhaps Gulhi would be the main possibilities. You might get lucky and meet someone from an outer island who will sponsor you on a visit to their village, but you can't count on it.

## Maps

Maps of the Maldives look pretty confusing – there's a lot more water than land, and on most maps it's hard to spot the islands among the maze of reefs. It can also be hard to figure which names go with which tiny spots of land. One of the problems is scale – the country is over 800km from north to south, but the largest island is only about 8km long. Some of the best maps available are the 1:300,000 British Admiralty charts. At this scale, the whole country covers 3m of paper while Male', the capital island, is about six mm long! There are four sheets for the Maldives (numbers 1011, 1012, 1013 and 1014) and more detailed charts of the areas around Male' (number 3323), Addu (2067) and Thuraakunu (2068). You may be able to receive these at a marine chart specialist or at Art Palace Number 1 (in the MHA building in Male') for around US$50 per sheet.

Several different tourist maps are available in Male' and in resort shops, but some of them are misleading because they try only to show the atolls in the tourism zone. Other maps shade in the whole area of the atolls, giving the impression that they are quite large land masses rather than reefs and lagoons with tiny spots of dry land. The positions of the resorts are sometimes incorrectly marked too, but this doesn't matter much as you'll never have to find your own way to a resort.

For divers and anyone else interested in the exact location of reefs, thillas, channels etc, the best source is the book *Dive Maldives*, the associated sheet map *Maldives Travellers & Divers Map*, and an atlas/directory called *Malways*. All are published by Atoll Editions and available at shops in Male' and most resorts, or from www.atolleditions.com.au. These maps are very accurate, but are not intended for navigation purposes.

## What to Bring

Light clothing is all you'll need, plus a shady hat, sunglasses and sun block. A waterproof cape or jacket may be useful, especially in the wetter months or if you'll be spending much time on boats. Some plastic bags may help protect clothes, cameras and documents if you're out on the water in rough weather. A small bag is enough – a backpack is of limited value since it's unlikely that you'll do a lot of walking or have to carry your luggage far.

Even if you stay on a basic safari boat or a low-budget guesthouse you won't need a sleeping bag, but a sarong is a good idea. Other useful items are a torch with spare batteries, toilet paper, a Swiss army knife or the like, a first-aid kit (see the Health section in this chapter), a sewing kit and a small padlock for locking luggage. Condoms are not readily available in resorts, so bring your own supply.

Bring your own mask, snorkel and fins because most resorts charge extra to rent them. You'll save some money, you'll be sure you have equipment you know is suitable and you'll be able to go out at any time with a minimum of hassle.

## CHOOSING A RESORT

The vast majority of visitors book into a single resort for their entire stay, and their choice is probably determined by the packages and prices presented by their travel agent, rather than by any real knowledge of what the various resorts have to offer. Judging by the brochures, all the resorts are beautiful, with white sand, blue sea and swaying palm trees; they all promise great diving, and they all look very similar. In fact they differ considerably in their comfort, cuisine, clientele, character and their suitability for various excursions and activities.

The quality of accommodation and food is pretty much related to price – the least expensive resorts can have very plain rooms and very ordinary food, but none of them are really bad. Air conditioning and hot water are the main comforts you may require, and they are now standard in most resorts (if you're offered a very cheap rate, ask about air-con and hot water). In fact, every room should have a ceiling fan which will keep you cool enough to sleep, and a 'cold' shower will be at least tepid, and quite refreshing.

You can choose between resorts with modern, motel-style rooms and facilities (TV, minibar and all), or those with thatched roofs, sand floors in the restaurant, and a natural island feel. The modern-look resorts are more likely to have gyms and other recreational facilities. Most resorts don't have pools, especially not the natural style ones which have good beach swimming. Tennis courts are even less common. If you want top-quality cuisine, go for the mid-range to top-end price range, the larger resorts, or for one of the resorts that caters to the Italian market. The meals can be unexciting at smaller, cheaper resorts which are a long distance from Male', but the food is generally good, and the standard is getting better all the time.

The clientele, character and cost of resorts are also related. The larger, cheaper resorts attract younger people, more singles, and are more casual in style, with a lot of people out to have a good time. Smaller resorts are more intimate and cosy, and may appeal to couples and honeymooners, but a single visitor could feel left out. Some resorts cater more or less exclusively to certain nationalities – notably Italians. Italian resorts feature excellent food and lots of group activities, often aided by 'animators' whose job is to ensure that everyone is involved in the fun. If you enjoy Italian style and speak a little of the language you might enjoy these resorts. Some resorts are overwhelmingly patronised by German speakers and others can have, at least at certain times, a high proportion of French or Japanese guests. All resorts offer scuba diving, but some appeal especially to hardcore divers, who dive all day, talk diving at dinner and collapse early into bed – at these places the nondiver may feel like a fish out of water.

Location is also a factor. Some resorts have better access to specific dive sites, local Maldivian villages or to the capital city. If you're keen to visit villages and meet Maldivians, the best place is Equator Village on Gan Island, but any resort close to an inhabited island will be convenient for short trips. You could also arrange to spend a couple days in Male' at the start or the end of your trip.

When you start thinking of a Maldives holiday, get brochures and prices from as many of the tour companies as you can, then read the suggestions in this section on choosing a resort (see also the Choosing a resort table later in this chapter). Check the resorts offered in the various brochures and decide which ones interest you most. Read the descriptions in this book which highlight their particular features and attractions, and check the location on one of the maps.

Once you've narrowed it down to a couple of resorts, look at the prices in the brochures. If the same resort is offered by a couple of companies, check the price of a holiday at the time you want to go, but make sure it includes the same meal plans, extras and number of nights. If a resort described as mid-range to top-end in this book is one of the cheapest packages in your brochure, it's probably a good deal.

If you need more specific information about a resort, call, fax, write or email its office in Male' – addresses and numbers are given in the text.

## RESPONSIBLE TOURISM

The whole structure of the Maldives' tourism industry is geared to minimising its social and environmental impact. Those visiting Male' and/or local islands on resort excursions should be aware of Muslim sensibilities, the tour guide will make this clear. Those who are fortunate enough to travel and stay outside the resort islands should be especially careful to dress and behave appropriately, both to avoid embarrassing their sponsor, and to ensure that access is not made even more restrictive in future.

Care of the marine environment is the responsibility of every diver and snorkeller – see the Snorkelling & Diving special section later in this chapter for guidelines on responsible diving.

## TOURIST OFFICES

The Maldives doesn't have many official tourist offices because most tourism promotion is done by private travel agents, tour operators and resorts (see the Getting There & Away chapter). The official Maldives Tourism Promotion Board does have a good Web site at www.visitmaldives.com.

### Local Tourist Offices

The Maldives Tourism Promotion Board (☎ 323228), on the 4th floor of the Bank of Maldives building on Marine Drive (Boduthakurufaanu Magu), Male', has maps and other printed material, and can answer specific inquiries. The tourist information desk at the airport is sometimes open when flights arrive. Generally, the best sources of information about resorts and safari trips are the various travel agents and tour operators, though they're not exactly objective.

### Tourist Offices Abroad

The Maldives Tourism Promotion Board has an office in Germany (☎ 69-2740 4420, fax 2740 4422, ✉ maldivesinfo.ffm@t-online.de), München er Strasse 48, Frankfurt/Main 60329, Germany. In France, La Maison des Maldives (☎ 01 42 21 44 55), Passage des Panoramas, 75002 Paris, is a kind of unofficial tourist office. Elsewhere, you might get some information from the diplomatic representatives (see Embassies & Consulates later in this chapter).

## VISAS & DOCUMENTS
### Passport

You need a valid passport that is current for the duration of your stay.

### Visas

Visas are not required. Most foreigners are given a free 30-day visitors' permit on arrival; citizens of India, Pakistan, Bangladesh or Nepal are given a 90-day permit. Officially, a visitor must have at least US$25 for every day of their intended stay. In practice the authorities are unlikely to check, especially if you are booked into a resort and you look respectable. Israelis and South Africans are now permitted to visit the Maldives.

**Visa Extensions** To apply for an extension, go to the Immigration Office (☎ 323913) in the Huravee Building next to the police station in Male' (open from about 8 am to 1 pm Sunday to Thursday). You must first buy an Extension of Tourist Visa form (Rf 10) from the ground floor desk. You'll need a local to sponsor, and because the main requirement is evidence that you have accommodation, it's best to have your resort, travel agent or guesthouse manager act as a sponsor and apply on your behalf. Have your sponsor sign the form, and bring it back to the office between 7.30 and 9.30 am, along with your passport, a passport photo, the Rf 350 fee and your air ticket out of the country. The air ticket is a bit tricky, because you have to have a confirmed booking for the new departure date *before* you can get the extension – fortunately, the airlines don't ask to see a visa extension before they'll change the date of your flight. Proof of sufficient funds (US$25 per day) or a credit card may also be required. You'll be asked to leave the documents there and return in a couple of days to pick up the passport with its extended visa (make sure you get a receipt for your passport when you leave it at the Immigration Office).

Extensions are for a maximum of 30 days, but they only give you until the date on your ticket – the cost is the same, for one day or 30. Overstaying your visa (or extension), even by an hour, can be a major hassle as they may not let you board your flight, and you will have to go back to Male', book another flight, get a visa extension, and pay a fine before you can leave.

**Visas for India** An application for an Indian visa can be made at the High Commission in Male'. See Embassies & Consulates in the Maldives later in this chapter. An Indian visa takes four to five days to issue, and costs about US$30, depending on your nationality.

**Visas for Sri Lanka** Most nationalities can get a visa on arrival in Sri Lanka, but check the latest requirements at the High Commission in Male'. See Embassies & Consulates in the Maldives later in this chapter.

## Travel Permits

Foreigners must have an Inter-Atoll Travel Permit to stay on any inhabited island other than Male' or a resort island, and permits are also required to visit uninhabited islands outside the tourism zone. You don't need a permit for a day trip organised by a resort.

Permits are issued by the Ministry of Atolls Administration on Marine Drive in Male', and cost Rf 10. All foreigners must have a local sponsor who will guarantee their accommodation and be responsible for them. Note also that it is illegal for anyone to request payment for accommodation on an inhabited island.

Permit applications must be in writing, and include applicant's name, passport number, nationality, the name of the island/atoll to be visited, dates of visit, name and address of sponsor, the name and registration number of the vessel to be used, and the purpose of the visit.

If you are going on a diving or sightseeing safari trip through the atolls in a registered vessel with a registered safari company, the company will obtain the necessary permits before you start. In effect, the company is acting as your sponsor and supplying accommodation on the boat. If it's to be a diving safari visiting dive sites of historical importance, additional permission may need to be obtained from other government departments.

Your sponsor should be a resident of the island you wish to visit, and must be prepared to vouch for you, feed you and accommodate you. This support must be given in writing, preferably with an OK from the kateeb and submitted with your application. It's best to have the sponsor submit the application on your behalf.

The most straightforward way to visit the outer atolls is with a registered safari boat, but a reputable tour company, travel agent or guesthouse proprietor may be able to help you make the necessary contacts to get a sponsor. Many Male' residents have friends or family in various outer atolls, but as they will be responsible for you when you visit the island, a great deal of trust is involved. Also, getting a letter of support-cum-invitation back from the island can take a couple of weeks if it's isolated from the capital.

The Atolls Administration can be slow and discouraging, so perseverance and patience are necessary. The stated purpose of the visit can be something like visiting friends, sightseeing, photography or private research. A genuine purpose will help your application, but if it sounds like very serious research or professional filming, they may require additional permission from other government authorities. If you obtain a permit, it will specify which atolls or islands you can visit, so it may be best to apply for an atoll approval that will permit you to visit any island within the specified atoll, though this must be consistent with the purpose of the application and the domicile of the sponsor. Permits are issued only between 8.30 and 11 am on all days except government holidays.

As soon as you land on an island you must go to the island office to present the permit. Don't land without one because the island chiefs will enforce the law, and can get into trouble if they don't. A foreigner travelling in the outer atolls without a permit, or breaching any of these conditions, can be fined Rf 100, but the consequences for a Maldivian could be much more serious.

Finally, the most obvious condition applied to, and printed on, a permit is also the most important:

It is prohibited for foreigners on inter-atoll trips to conduct or participate in any activity that might jeopardise the peace and harmony prevailing in the country. Legal action shall be taken against persons known to conduct such activities.

## Onward Tickets

An onward ticket is technically a condition of entry to the country, but you won't be asked to show it unless you apply for an extension of your stay. Tickets are no cheaper in the Maldives than anywhere else, so there's no reason *not* to have an onward or return ticket.

## Travel Insurance

A travel insurance policy to cover theft, loss and medical problems is highly recom-
mended. Some policies offer lower and higher medical-expense options; the higher ones are chiefly for countries which have high medical costs, and this would be a good idea for a Maldives trip. There is a wide variety of policies available, so check the small print. You may prefer a policy which pays doctors or hospitals directly rather than you having to pay on the spot and claim later. If you have to claim later, make sure you keep all documentation. Some policies ask you to call back (reverse charges) to a centre in your home country where an immediate assessment of your problem is made.

Some policies specifically exclude 'dangerous activities', which can include scuba diving. You should ensure that your policy covers air ambulances, helicopter evacuation and an emergency flight home. If you are injured on a Maldivian resort, the closest emergency facilities will be in Male', which can be hours away by boat, but most are within reach of a landing site for a seaplane. An injured person may need extra seats to stretch out on a plane and somebody has to pay for them.

Even if the policy does not exclude diving accidents, it may not cover all the expenses associated with hyperbaric treatment in a recompression chamber. The recompression chambers at the Bandos clinic in the North Male' Atoll and the new one on Kuramathi in Rasdhoo Atoll are set up to provide emergency treatment to any diver who needs it, but they are commercial facilities. Re-compression treatment usually involves between three and eight hours in the chamber and can cost thousands of dollars. A regular travel insurance policy may not cover this and divers may need additional cover that is specially tailored to their needs. DAN (Divers Alert Network) provides specialised divers' injury and evacuation insurance and is worth considering – your local dive shop or club will have information and application forms. Some dive operators in the Maldives include DAN insurance in their rates, so it may be worth asking if this applies at the dive base you'll be using.

## Driving Licence

You won't need a driving licence in the Maldives. There are no cars or motorbikes to rent and International Driving Licences are not valid in the Maldives.

## Student & Youth Cards

About the only place where a foreigner might get a student discount is the cybercafe in Male'.

## Vaccination Certificates

The only vaccination officially required by the Maldives is for yellow fever. You will need one if travelling from an infected area in Africa or South America.

## Copies

All important documents (passport data page and visa page, credit cards, travel insurance policy, air tickets) should be photocopied before you leave home. Leave one copy with someone at home and keep another with you, separate from the originals.

It's also a good idea to store details of your vital travel documents in Lonely Planet's free online Travel Vault in case the photocopies are lost or you can't be bothered with them. Your password-protected Travel Vault is accessible online anywhere in the world – create it at www.ekno.lonelyplanet.com.

## EMBASSIES & CONSULATES
## Maldives Embassies & Consulates

Maldivian diplomatic representatives overseas include:

**Australia**
  *Honorary Consul*: (☎ 03-9328 4133,
  ✪ linton@eisa.net.au) 213 Flemington Rd,
  Box 135, North Melbourne,
  Vic 3051
**Austria**
  *Honorary Consul*: (☎ 01-319 1426)
  Peter Jordan Strasse 21, A-1190 Vienna
**Belgium**
  *Honorary Consul*: (☎ 010-689 212)
  Clos des Genets 17, 1325 Chaumont Gistoux
**France**
  *Honorary Consul*: (☎ 03 80 37 26 60)
  Zone Artisanale, 5 Rue de Lafontaine, 21560
  Arc Sur Tille

**Germany**
  *Honorary Consul*: (☎ 61-728 6293) Immanuel
  Kant Strasse 16, D-61350 Bad Homburg
**India**
  *Honorary Consul*: (☎ 11-5718590) 202 Sethi
  Bhavan, 7 Rajendra Place, New Delhi
  *Honorary Consul*: (☎ 33-2485400) Hastings
  Chambers, Ground Floor, 7C Kiron Shankar
  Roy Rd, Calcutta
  *Honorary Consul*: (☎ 22-5115111) Nathani
  Estate, Nathani Rd, Vidyavihar, Mumbai
  (Bombay)
  *Honorary Consul*: (☎ 44-8835111) 855 Anna
  Salai, Chennai (Madras)
**Japan**
  *Honorary Consul*: (☎ 03-3942 6222)
  1-26-1 Otowa, Bunkyo-Ku, Tokyo 112
**Singapore**
  *Trade Representative*: (☎ 2258955)
  10 Anson Rd, No 18-12 International Plaza
**Sri Lanka**
  *High Commission*: (☎ 01-586762,
  ✪ maldhc@eureka.lk) 23 Kavirathna Place,
  Colombo 6
**South Africa**
  *Honorary Consul*: (☎ 021-761 5038) Sanlam
  Building, 115 Main Rd, Wyuberg, Cape Town
**UK**
  *High Commission*: (☎ 020-7224 2135,
  ✪ maldives.high.commission@virgin.net) 22
  Nottingham Place, London W1M 3FB
**United Nations**
  *Permanent Mission*: (☎ 212-599 6195,
  ✪ mdvun@undp.org) 820 Second Avenue,
  Suite 800C, New York, NY 10017, USA

## Embassies & Consulates in the Maldives

There are very few foreign representatives in Male' and most of them are honorary consuls with limited powers. There are no representatives for France, Italy or the USA. It may be necessary to contact your country's embassy or high commission in Colombo, Sri Lanka. Even an embassy won't be much help in emergencies if the trouble you're in is remotely your own fault. Remember that you are bound by the laws of the country you are in. Your embassy or consulate will not be sympathetic if you end up in jail after committing a crime locally, even if such actions are legal in your own country. In genuine emergencies you might receive some assistance, but only if other channels have been exhausted. If you need to get home urgently, an embassy or consulate would expect you to have insurance. If all your money and documents are lost or stolen, your embassy or consulate might assist with getting a new passport, but a loan for onward travel is out of the question.

**Denmark, Finland, Norway & Sweden**
*Honorary Consul*: (☎ 315175/6/7) Abdulla Saeed, Cyprea, 25 Boduthakurufaanu Magu
**Germany**
*Honorary Consul*: (☎ 322971) Ibrahim Maniku, Universal Enterprises, 38 Orchid Magu
**India**
*High Commission*: (☎ 323016) Ameer Ahmed Magu
**Sri Lanka**
*High Commission*: (☎ 322845) Medhuziyaarai Magu
**UK**
*Honorary Consular Agent*: (☎ 322802 ext 205) c/o Dhiraagu. The honorary consular agent has very limited powers, and any serious matters are referred to the British High Commission in Colombo.

## CUSTOMS
No alcohol, pornography, pork, narcotics, dogs, firearms, spear guns or 'idols of worship' can be brought into the country. Baggage is X-rayed and searched carefully, and if you have any liquor it will be taken and held for you till you're about to leave the country. This service may not extend to other prohibited items. Magazines such as *Cleo* or *Cosmopolitan* may be regarded as pornographic if they have pictures of women in underwear. Prerecorded video cassettes are subject to censorship and are also prohibited. If you bring blank cassettes for your video camera it would be a good idea to make sure they are sealed in the original packaging. Importing any sort of recreational drugs can land you in big trouble – a young woman caught with half a joint was looking at a 12-year sentence.

Export of turtle shell, or any turtle shell products, is forbidden.

## MONEY
### Currency
The unit of currency is the rufiya (Rf), which is divided into 100 larees. Notes

### Idolatry
Most countries prohibit the importation of things like narcotics and firearms, and most travellers understand such restrictions, but when you're forbidden to bring 'idols of worship' into the Maldives, what exactly does that mean? The Maldives is an Islamic nation, and it is sensitive about objects which may offend Muslim sensibilities. A small crucifix, worn as jewellery, is unlikely to be a problem, and many tourists arrive wearing one. A large crucifix with an obvious Christ figure nailed to it may well be prohibited. The same is true of images of Buddha – a small decorative one, perhaps a souvenir from Sri Lanka, is probably OK, but a large and ostentatious one may not be. A set of rosary beads in one's baggage would probably be overlooked, but several sets may be regarded with suspicion.

In particular, Maldivian authorities are concerned about evangelists and the things they might use to spread their beliefs. Inspectors would not really be looking for a Bible in someone's baggage, but if they found two or more Bibles they would almost certainly not allow them to be imported. In such cases, it's not clear whether your 'idols of worship' would be confiscated altogether or if they would be held in bond storage, to be collected when you leave the country.

It would be unwise to test the limits of idolatrous imports – like customs people everywhere, the Maldivian authorities take themselves very seriously. Even when the theme from Jesus Christ Superstar is being played as airport muzak.

come in denominations of 500, 100, 50, 20, 10, five and two rufiya, but the latter are uncommon. Coins are in denominations of two and one rufiya, and 50, 25 and 10 laree.

### Exchange Rates
The exchange rate is displayed at banks, moneychangers and the cashier's office at a resort. The rate is fixed relative to the US$, and all other currencies are traded relative to their current dollar value.

| country | unit | | rufiya |
|---------|------|---|--------|
| Australia | A$1 | = | Rf 7.03 |
| Canada | C$1 | = | Rf 7.85 |
| euro | €1 | = | Rf 10.55 |
| France | 1FF | = | Rf 1.64 |
| Germany | DM1 | = | Rf 5.39 |
| Japan | ¥100 | = | Rf 10.80 |
| NZ | NZ$1 | = | Rf 5.74 |
| UK | UK£1 | = | Rf 17.93 |
| USA | US$1 | = | Rf 11.72 |

## Exchanging Money

Bring a credit card and/or US dollar travellers cheques. Most hotel and travel expenses will be billed in dollars, so there's no point in incurring extra conversion costs. Some cash in small denomination US dollars is useful for tipping and to change into rufiya for use in local shops. If you're staying in a resort, all extras (including diving costs) will be billed to your room, and you pay the day before departure. Resorts accept cash or travellers cheques in UK pounds, Australian dollars, German marks, Japanese yen, Italian lire, French francs, and Swiss francs, but US dollar cheques are by far the best option.

**Cash** Outside resorts, foreign cash is generally accepted – US dollars are most common, but British pounds, German marks and Italian lira are all pretty acceptable. You won't need Maldivian rufiya unless you're using local shops and services. Even these will usually take dollars, but not at full rate. If you pay US$1 for a Rf 10 taxi trip, you won't get any change. If you pay US$5 you may not get change either – it's better to use local currency in the local economy.

There are no restrictions on changing money into rufiya, but there's no need to change a lot. Rufiya are not readily negotiable outside the country. The best place to reconvert excess rufiya is at the bank counter at the airport. Officially, you may need receipts to prove that you bought the rufiya at the official rate, but you won't usually be asked to show them. The airport bank is usually open, even when flights depart at night, but if you're concerned about it, change your excess rufiya in advance at the Maldives Monetary Authority on Chandanee Magu.

**Travellers Cheques** Banks in Male' are clustered at the harbour end of Chandanee Magu and along Marine Drive (East). They are open Sunday to Thursday from 8 am to 1.30 pm. They'll change travellers cheques and cash in US dollars, and possibly UK pounds, German marks, Japanese yen, Italian lire, French francs, and Swiss francs. Most will change US dollar travellers cheques into US dollars cash with a 1% commission.

There are a few official and unofficial moneychangers in Male'. They stick rigidly to the official rates and usually only buy US dollars cash. Some will change US dollar travellers cheques for a small commission.

**ATMs** The few ATMs in Male' are only for use by local Bank of Maldives account holders.

**Credit Cards** Every resort takes American Express and Visa, nearly all take MasterCard and a few take Diners or JCB. A couple staying for a week of diving and drinking could easily run up a tab over US$2000, so make sure your credit limit can stand it. The cashier may want 48 hours' notice to check your credit. Many resorts apply a surcharge of 5% to credit card payments, so it may be well to have enough travellers cheques to cover the bulk of your extras bill. The American Express representative is Universal Enterprises (☎ 322971) at 39 Orchid Magu, Male'.

**International Transfers** Banks in the Maldives are not noted for their efficiency in international transactions. A transfer using the 'Swift' system seems to be the most efficient way to get money to the Maldives. Habib Bank might be the best bet. Try to have the money handed over to you in US dollars.

## Security

On a resort you don't need to carry money at all – everything will be billed to your room and you settle up before you leave, with either travellers cheques or credit cards. In Male', at the airport and on the islands where tourists visit, you probably won't need to carry much money anyway, and the risk of robbery or pickpocketing is negligible.

## Costs

The very cheapest resorts start at around US$55 per day in the low season for a standard double room with full board (ie, breakfast, lunch and dinner), which is very good value. However, at most resorts for most of the year, a double room and board will cost closer to US$100 a day or more. For most visitors, the cost of accommodation and meals will be part of their holiday package and will generally be cheaper than the independent traveller rates which are quoted in this book. Package prices also include airfares and transfers, so it's hard to calculate the cost of the resort, but most brochures give a rate for extra nights which should give you some idea. In any case, the package will be paid for in advance, so there shouldn't be any surprises.

But it doesn't stop there – extras can add greatly to the cost of a Maldives holiday. Drinks will usually cost extra, apart from coffee or tea with meals and juice with breakfast. Soft drinks cost at least US$2 a can, a beer will be US$3 to US$5, and most resorts even charge for drinking water – US$2 to US$4.50 for 1500 ml. The price of drinks is usually proportional to the cost of the resort, but not always – some cheap resorts charge top prices for drinking water. For water, soft drinks and a beer at dinner, allow US$6 to US$10 per person per day. If you want wine with your meal, allow US$20 per day. If you want to have a serious drinking session with US$7 cocktails, it could cost US$50 or more, depending on your capacity and how much you tip.

If you only take a half-board package, allow at least US$7 for lunch. And even with full board you can pay extra for a special beach barbecue or, at the fancier resorts, a dinner in a specialty restaurant. A short phone call home will add at least US$15 or so to your room bill.

The other big extra is activities. Diving costs vary with the cost of the resort, but keen divers in a mid-price resort should each allow maybe US$430 per week if they have their own equipment and US$520 if they're renting everything. This is based on about US$270 for a 10-dive package (or US$350

with equipment rental), plus US$12 per dive for the use of a boat, plus a little for tips and/or service charges. If you're a keen beginner, allow US$480 to US$580 for an open water dive course. If you're here to dive, you won't count the cost and you won't regret it.

If you won't be content to bask on the beach, allow US$25 to US$35 per day for windsurfing, night tennis, island hopping excursions or snorkel hire. Buying souvenirs, sunscreen and sundry items at the resort shop can also add up.

On a safari trip, the costs can be anything from US$60 to US$160 per person per day, with another US$70 or so for diving, but at least there won't be many extras. Staying in Male' on a budget, you could get by on US$40 per day or even less if you were sharing a room; for an air-con room and European style food, allow maybe US$70 per person per day.

## Tipping & Bargaining

If the service is good, and it usually is, it's quite customary to tip room staff and waiters in your resort at the end of your stay. Restaurant seating is usually organised so that you'll have the same waiter for the whole time, and US$10 per couple per week is a suitable amount. US$8 per week is appropriate for the person who cleans your room. A few resorts add a 10% service charge to your bill, in which case you don't need to tip. Sometimes 10% is only added to the bar bill, but if not, the bar staff can be tipped as well. If you go on a boat trip for diving, it's usual to tip US$1 to the crew for handling the tanks and equipment. Give any tips to the staff personally, not to the hotel cashier – US$ or local currency are equally acceptable. Resort staff are not very well paid and are usually employed on contracts that take them away from their home islands for many months at a time – a little extra from tips can make a big difference to their families at home.

In Male' the fancier restaurants usually add a 10% service charge, so you don't need to tip, and tipping is not customary in local tea shops. Taxi drivers are not tipped, but porters at the airport expect Rf 10 or US$1.

Bargaining is limited to the tourist shops in and around the Singapore Bazaar in Male' and at island village souvenir shops where prices are not fixed. Most tourists come on brief shopping excursions from the resorts and some traders will ask what they feel they can get away with.

## TAXES & REFUNDS

The US$6 per person per night is included in the price of every hotel, resort and safari boat bed used by a tourist.

## POST & COMMUNICATIONS

### Post

Postal services are quite efficient, with mail to overseas destinations delivered promptly; mail *from* overseas, especially packets and parcels, is subject to customs screening and can take considerably longer. The main Male' post office is on Marine Drive, near the airport boat landing, and is open from 7.30 am to 6 pm. There is a poste restante service.

To send a postcard anywhere overseas costs Rf 7 and a standard airmail letter costs Rf 10. A high-speed EMS service is available to many countries. Parcel rates can get quite expensive.

At the resorts you can buy stamps and postcards at the shop or the reception desk. Generally there is a mailbox near reception.

### Telephone

Telephone services are provided by Dhiraagu, a joint venture of the government and the British Cable & Wireless company. Every inhabited island now has a telephone connection, and very modern card-operated telephone boxes can be seen somewhat incongruously on the most traditional island streets. Every business in Male' is on the phone, and cardphones are numerous. Telephone cards are widely available and the service is very reliable.

Calls within the capital cost 30 larees per 51 seconds. To other parts of the country, cost depends on distance – up to Rf 3.25 per 51 seconds. International direct dial (IDD) calls can be made from all cardphones – they are quite expensive, depending on destination, but cheaper from midnight to 8 am.

| zone | areas | normal (Rf/min) | off-peak (Rf/min) |
|---|---|---|---|
| 1 | SAARC & Singapore | 22 | 18 |
| 2 | Asia & UK | 34 | 27 |
| 3 | Europe, Mid East & Africa | 46 | 37 |
| 4 | Australia, NZ, Nth & Sth America | 46 | 37 |

All resorts have IDD phones, either in the rooms or available at reception. Charges vary from high to astronomical, starting around US$15 for three minutes. Some resorts have a cardphone in the staff quarters.

The international country code for the Maldives is 960. All Maldives numbers have six digits and there are no area codes. Operator and directory inquiry numbers are 110 for the Maldives and 190 for international inquiries. To make an international call, dial 00, then the country code, area code and number.

The mobile phone network covers most of North Male', South Male' and Ari atolls, and all mobile numbers start with 78. In late 1999 the network switched to GSM, and your mobile might work in the Maldives if it's a GSM 900 type, and if either your telco has a bilateral deal with Dhiraagu, or if you subscribe to the Dhiraagu service and have them issue a SIM card for use in your handset.

### Fax

Faxes are widely used in business, especially the tourist industry. Every resort will have a fax machine that you may be able to use, for a price. The Dhiraagu office in Male' has a public fax service. To send an A4 sheet internationally costs Rf 66 to Zone 1, Rf 88 to Zone 2, and Rf 112 to Zone 3 or Zone 4. You can receive an incoming fax for Rf 10.

### Email & Internet Access

The Maldives connected to the Internet in 1996 and lots of businesses and individuals went online at once. Many tourist businesses have put up Web pages, as has the national government. Dhiraagu runs the only cybercafe in Male' (always busy) and another one on Hithadhoo in Addu Atoll. Some resorts offer Internet access for between US$10 and US$20 per hour. Others will let you prepare an email offline, and will send it for you for US$1 or US$2.

Dhiraagu (www.dhiraagu.com.mv) is the sole service provider, so if you bring your own PC you'll have to open an account with them or pay international phone charges to access an international service provider. Other difficulties with bringing your own machine to access the net are the need for a compatible modem (buy a reputable 'global' modem before you leave home) and the unreliability of local power supplies (bring a universal AC adaptor, and a plug adaptor).

One option for collecting mail through cybercafes is to open a free eKno Web-based email account online at www.ekno .lonelyplanet.com. You can then access your mail from anywhere in the world from any Net-connected machine running a standard Web browser. Other web-based email services (eg Hotmail) can also be used.

## INTERNET RESOURCES

The World Wide Web is a rich resource for travellers. You can research your trip, hunt down bargain air fares, book hotels, check on weather conditions or chat with locals and other travellers about the best places to visit (or avoid!). There's no better place to start your Web explorations than the Lonely Planet Web site (www.lonelyplanet.com). Here you'll find succinct summaries on travelling to most places on earth, postcards from other travellers and the Thorn Tree bulletin board, where you can ask questions before you go or dispense advice when you get back. You can also find travel news and updates to many of our most popular guidebooks, and the subWWWay section links you to the most useful travel resources elsewhere on the Web.

The Maldives Tourist Promotion Board site, www.visitmaldives.com, has links to just about every resort and tour operator in the country. Two very useful sites are www.themaldives.com and www.theMaldives.net; both have plenty of details about the country and provide links to sites with information on official visits, sports events and development initiatives. To keep in-

formed of President Gayoom's movements, check www.presidencymaldives.gov.mv.

The Maldives' three daily newspapers all have Web sites – www.haveeru.com; www .aafathisnews.com; and www.miadhu.com. The Haveeru is the best, updated daily with lots of pictures and material in English. Aafathisnews has a few interesting English language reports, but a lot less material and fewer pictures.

## BOOKS

If you plan to do a lot of reading, take a few paperbacks and swap them later with other guests. Most resorts have several shelves of dog-eared paperbacks, but 90% of them are in German (apparently any leftover English books are quickly snapped up by the staff).

Quite a lot has been written on the Maldives, but titles can be hard to find. Some interesting titles have been published locally by Novelty Press (☎ 960-322490, fax 327039). Many are available from the Novelty Bookshop on Fareedhee Magu in Male', some are sold in resort shops, but others are out of print.

### Diving

*Dive Maldives*, by Tim Godfrey, is a highly recommended diving guide with detailed descriptions of all the main dive sites in the Maldives tourist zone, a fascinating maritime history and stories of the most famous wrecks. The maps are excellent, and are also available in sheet format and as an atlas/directory called Malways. All are published by Atoll Editions (www.atolleditions.com.au) and are available at shops in Male' as well as most resorts.

*The Dive Sites of the Maldives*, by Sam Harwood & Rob Bryning, is another good dive guide, though the dive site descriptions are not quite as detailed. It's available in many resort shops and in Male'.

*Diving Guide*, by Kurt Amsler, has very detailed dive descriptions, with a very helpful drawing of each one, but it doesn't cover nearly as many sites as the other two books.

### Travel

As well as the explorers, seafarers and several shipwreck victims of days gone by, the odd modern adventurer or two has also bumped into the Maldives. Author and sailor

Alan Villiers tells of his brigantine forays in *Give Me a Ship to Sail*. Sportsman, explorer and former US ambassador to Colombo, Philip K Crowe, has an essay on Male' in his *Diversions of a Diplomat in Ceylon*.

## History & Politics

The most renowned historian of the Maldives is HCP Bell, a former British commissioner in the Ceylon Civil Service who led archaeological expeditions in 1920 and 1922, and who published several accounts including *A Description of the Maldive Islands* for the *Journal of the Royal Asiatic Society*. In 1940, three years after his death, the Ceylon Government Press published his main work, *The Maldive Islands: Monograph on the History, Archaeology & Epigraphy*. Original copies of the book are rare, but the National Centre for Linguistic & Historical Research in Male' has reprinted it and it's available from them for Rf 250.

Much of Bell's research on pre-Muslim civilisation has been supported, challenged and expanded by Kon-Tiki explorer Thor Heyerdahl in *The Maldive Mystery*.

Heyerdahl spent several months during 1982–83 digging around the southern atolls, with the encouragement of the Maldives government. He unearthed evidence of early Buddhist, Hindu and sun-worshipping prehistoric societies, which pre-dated the arrival of Islam in the 12th century. Some of Heyerdahl's finds are exhibited at the National Museum in Male', but his theories have not been embraced by authorities who are less than keen to promulgate observations about a pre-Muslim Maldives. Some non-Maldivian critics have also criticised Heyerdahl's populist tendency to jump to conclusions, and some have even dismissed his work as nothing more than fiction.

For a history of the Muslim period, look at Ibn Battuta's *Travels in Asia & Africa 1325–54*, reprinted in paperback by Routledge Kegan Paul in 1983. Ibn Battuta was a great Moorish globetrotter. Another historical text is *The Story of Mohamed Thakurufaan* by Hussain Salahuddeen, which tells of the Maldives' greatest hero who liberated the people from the Portuguese.

A well-respected work is *People of the Maldive Islands* by US anthropologist Dr Clarence Maloney (Orient Longman, New Delhi, 1980). Covering past and present, this is the best general reference on the country and is not too academic. Unfortunately, it is not readily available and it has been banned in the Maldives.

A more recent work is *A Man for all Islands* by Royston Ellis. It's an uncritical biography of President Maumoon Abdul Gayoom and gives some interesting insights into the development of the country over the last 60 years.

## Natural History

Dr Charles Anderson, a British marine biologist living in Male' since 1983, has put together *Maldives, the Diver's Paradise, Living Reefs of the Maldives* and the *Diver's Guide to the Sharks of the Maldives* – three great pictorials to whet your appetite before heading for the depths. Also by Dr Anderson, in conjunction with Ahmed Hafiz, are the identification guides *Common Reef Fishes of the Maldives* parts one, two and three. All six books are published by Novelty Press and most can be found in resort shops.

Two other fishy field guides are *Reef Fishes of the Indian Ocean* by Dr Gerald R Allen & Roger C Steene and *A Guide to Common Reef Fish of the Western Indian Ocean* by KR Bock.

*Photo Guide to Fishes of the Maldives*, by Rudie Kuiter, is a new and authoritative book covering many, many types of fish, all described in detail and accompanied by a colour photograph. It's published by Atoll editions (www.atolleditions.com.au) and is widely available in resorts and Male' bookshops.

## General

*Maldives: A Nation of Islands*, published by the Department of Tourism in 1983, has plenty of colour plates, though the text is somewhat jingoistic. It would make an attractive gift. Perhaps even better, but hard to find, is *Journey through Maldives* by Mohamed Amin, Duncan Willets & Peter Marshall, which has fine photos from even the remotest parts of the country.

*Male' – Capital of the Maldives*, by Adrian Neville, is a beautifully presented coffee-table book with great photos of Male' and its people. Another pretty picture book is *The Maldives – Home of the Children of the Sea. Maldive Impressions*, by Ismail Abdullah, is also a fine photographic coffee-table book. All are published by Novelty and available in town.

About the only novel set in the Maldives is a sea adventure by Hammond Innes called *The Strode Venturer*. The story ranges from a London boardroom to the RAF base on Addu. The southern atolls' bid for independence in the early 1960s is worked into this rather dated ripping yarn from the last days of the empire.

*Mysticism in the Maldives* documents superstitions, encounters with jinnis and other supernatural phenomena. It's published by Novelty in paperback and hard cover, and it has some weird stuff.

## VIDEOS
Several diving videos (all VHS) are available. *Journey through Maldives* (Aqua Vision) is produced by the same team as the excellent coffee-table book of the same name. *Under the Southern Cross* (Filmitalia) is a 90-minute diving safari documentary, produced in Italy but available in an English version.

## NEWSPAPERS & MAGAZINES
The Maldives has three daily papers, printed in Thaana script with some text in English. They all cost Rf 2.

*Aufathis*, which means 'new morning', comes out every morning and usually has two pages, plus the cinema ads, in English, except on Tuesday when there's an English special edition. *Miadhu*, which means 'today', comes out daily at noon, with one page in English. Then there's *Haveeru* ('evening'), which appears daily except Friday and has one or two English pages.

*Furadhaana* is a weekly government magazine published in Divehi. *Explore Maldives* is a glossy English-language quarterly aimed mainly at tourists and the tourist industry. It has some good photos and interesting articles, but don't expect any critical coverage.

English-language magazines featuring news about Hindi movies, movie stars and celebrities are popular. *Time* and *Newsweek* are available from Novelty and Asrafee bookshops and on resorts.

## RADIO & TV
The Voice of Maldives radio is broadcast to the whole country for 11 hours each day on medium wave, 1400kHz, and also at 104MHz. The news, in English, is read at 6 pm for 10 minutes.

TV Maldives, which started in 1978, broadcasts daily from 9 am to midnight. It has two stations – TVM 1, which has news, education and local drama; and TVM +, which costs Rf 150 per month for a de-scrambler and broadcasts lots of sport and news programming which is lifted from satellite broadcasts. Its transmission range is limited, but repeater stations are planned to extend the coverage. There is a daily 20-minute news bulletin in English at 9 pm and international news from overseas sources, with an emphasis on South Asian stories. Most of the entertainment programming is in English, with various soapies from the US and elsewhere – any sexual content is usually censored. The local programming is very much that of a community TV station, with reports on the school sports, religious and cultural events, news from the islands and coverage of official appearances by the president and senior government leaders. Even if you can't understand the language, these programs give some sense of local concerns and priorities.

Two drama series are produced, both imitative of Hindi TV shows but still very popular. Also popular are the locally produced music videos. Made-for-TV movies have also been locally produced over the last few years. They tend to imitate Hindi movies, and some are exact remakes, with the same characters, plot, music and dance moves, with the dialogue done in Divehi.

Most resorts have a satellite dish and a TV in one of the public areas, but it's hardly ever used. People come here to get away from it all, and most don't want to keep up with world events – the philosophy is 'No shoes and no news'. The most commonly available international networks are CNN and BBC. About the only resorts which have TV in the rooms are those of the Villa group – Fun Island, Sun Island, Holiday Island and Paradise Island. They offer CNN, TNT, RTV, MTV (the Indian version), ABN, OPI, Discovery, ATN and BBC, as well as in-house videos.

## VIDEO SYSTEMS

If you want to record or buy video tapes to play back home, you won't get a picture unless the 'image registration' system is the same. Three systems are used in the world, and each one is completely incompatible with the others. The three formats are NTSC, used in North America and Japan; PAL, used in Australia, New Zealand and most of Europe; and SECAM, used in metropolitan France. Maldives uses VHS videos.

## PHOTOGRAPHY & VIDEO
### Film & Equipment

A good selection of film is available in Male' at reasonable prices. Specialist photo shops, such as Reethi Foto and the three branches of Fototeknik, are the best places. Print film costs around Rf 80 for a roll of 24. Ektachrome slide film is about Rf 110 for a roll of 36. Film is much more expensive in resort shops. It's best to buy what you'll need duty-free before you leave home. Though the sunlight is very bright, you should still use reasonably fast film because many potential subjects will be in the shade (Maldivians never stay in the sun if they can avoid it). Also a polarising filter is highly desirable in the bright glary conditions, and this will reduce light readings by up to two f-stops.

In bright light, a polarising filter is like sunglasses for your camera, and makes colours richer, clouds more dramatic and cuts the glare from sand and water. A lens hood can also be useful. Remember spare batteries for cameras and flash.

Don't leave your camera in direct sunlight, keep it protected from water, dust and sand, and don't store used film for long in humid conditions.

You can buy video cartridges in Male', but not at all the resorts, so buy a few cartridges duty free before you leave, but keep them in sealed packaging so customs won't want to subject them to censorship.

## Technical Tips

The best advice for photography in tropical light is to shoot early or late in the day. The sun is high overhead between around 10 am and 3 pm and photos taken at that time tend to be flat or washed out. It's very easy to end up with overexposed photos and you should beware of back lighting from bright sunlight and of reflected light.

## Restrictions

In Male', don't photograph the NSS (National Security Service) headquarters near the Grand Mosque, the Theemuge (president's residence) or any police or security establishment. Don't take pictures of people while they're praying.

## Photographing People

Photographing people requires patience and politeness. Most Maldivians don't seem to mind being photographed in a general scene – let them know you want a shot and they'll usually give you the nod. They can be more reticent about close-up portraits and you'll need to establish some rapport. Make sure you have the light reading from the subject's face, not the background.

## Underwater Photography

The urge to photograph the underwater wonders is going to come upon many snorkellers and divers in the Maldives. Unfortunately, underwater photography presents a number of technical problems which make it difficult to capture anything like the brilliance you see through your face mask.

Many of the bigger resort dive bases rent underwater cameras, video cameras and lighting equipment, so you can give it a try. Discuss it with the diving instructors and don't set your expectations too high. You can also buy little, disposable cameras which are waterproof to about 5m. They are preloaded with colour print film, you point and shoot the 26 frames, then take the whole thing in to be processed. You can buy these duty free for maybe US$8, in Male' for about US$15, or in resort shops for US$25, and you pay the normal cost for processing and prints. It's easy and fun, but not likely to produce very good photos.

As you go deeper under water, natural colours are quickly absorbed, starting with the red end of the spectrum. The deeper you go the more blue things look, and there's no red at all more than 10m down. With a disposable camera, you'll capture some of the colours snorkelling in a metre of water, but photos taken 2m or 3m down will be monochrome blue-grey.

The human brain fools us to some extent by automatically compensating for the colour change, but the camera doesn't lie. To put the colour back in you need artificial lighting, and to work effectively under water it has to be more powerful than a flash above water. If you buy a Nikonos camera, you may have to spend as much money again for flash equipment to go with it. The delight is that underwater flash photography can reveal colours which simply can't be seen 10m under water.

Although objects appear closer under water, you have to get close to achieve good results. Lenses longer than 28 or 35 mm do not work well under water.

**Environmental Care** Underwater photographers must use great care and skill to avoid damaging live coral. Often they must act quickly to get close to an elusive subject, frame the photo, and operate the camera and lights. To do this without fins, tanks or equipment hitting anything requires perfect buoyancy and control, especially in a confined space or a strong current.

## Airport Security

All passengers have to pass their luggage through X-ray machines. In general, airport X-ray technology isn't supposed to jeopardise lower-speed film (under 1600 ASA). Recently, however, new high-powered machines designed to inspect *checked* luggage have been installed at major airports around the world. These machines are capable of conducting high-energy scans that may destroy unprocessed film. Carry film and loaded cameras in your hand-luggage.

## TIME

The Maldives is five hours ahead of GMT/ UTC; Pakistan shares the same time zone. It is half an hour behind India and Sri Lanka, 2½ hours behind Singapore and five hours behind eastern Australia.

A number of resorts operate one to two hours ahead of Male' time to give their guests extra daylight in the evening and longer to sleep in the morning.

## ELECTRICITY

With no national electricity grid, all resorts use diesel-powered generators which usually operate 24 hours a day (fuel is one of a resort's major expenses). Male' has a central electricity supply that is quite reliable, and most of the inhabited islands also have generators, but in many cases they only run in the evening between 6 and 11 pm. A torch (flashlight) can be very useful.

## Voltages & Cycles

Electricity supply is from 220V to 240V, 50 Hz AC. Most resorts have a multi-use socket in the bathroom which can accept razors using 110V with a variety of pin configurations. For other types of 110V appliances, you'll need a transformer.

## Plugs & Sockets

The most common type of socket accepts a plug with three square pins, but various other types are also in use, so bring a multisocket adaptor.

## WEIGHTS & MEASURES

Although officially converting to the metric system, imperial measures are widely used. Metric measurements are used in this book, but there is a metric/imperial conversion chart at the end of the book if you need it.

## LAUNDRY

Many people do their own washing by hand but some of the stuffier resorts don't like laundry hanging in public. Otherwise, the resort will do it, for as much as US$3.50 for a shirt, US$4.50 for pants. There are two or three laundries in Male' which will charge a lot less – ask at your guesthouse.

## TOILETS

Male's public toilets charge a few rufiya. Local islands that tourists visit will have something, but you may have to ask.

## HEALTH

The Maldives is remarkably free of health problems, especially the resorts, which are subject to high public health standards and have a vested interest in ensuring that their guests experience no problems.

### Predeparture Planning

**Immunisations** The only vaccination officially required by the Maldives is for yellow fever if you're coming from an area where yellow fever is endemic – parts of Africa and South America. Carry proof of yellow fever vaccinations if you're coming from an infected area. The Maldives is not regarded as an area of endemic malaria and malaria prophylaxis is not recommended.

You should plan ahead for getting your vaccinations: some of them require more than one injection, while some should not be given together. Note that some vaccinations should not be given during pregnancy or to people with allergies – discuss with your doctor.

It is recommended you seek medical advice at least six weeks before travel. Be aware that there is often a greater risk of disease in children and during pregnancy.

Discuss your requirements with your doctor, but vaccinations you should consider for this trip include the following (for more details about the diseases themselves, see the individual disease entries later in this section).

**Diphtheria & Tetanus** Vaccinations for these two diseases are usually combined and are recommended for everyone. After an initial course of three childhood injections, boosters are necessary every 10 years.

**Polio** Everyone should keep up to date with this vaccination, which is normally given in childhood. A booster every 10 years maintains immunity.

**Hepatitis A** Hepatitis A vaccine (eg, Avaxim, Havrix 1440 or VAQTA) provides long-term immunity (possibly more than 10 years) after an initial injection and a booster at six to 12 months.

Alternatively, an injection of gamma globulin can provide short-term protection against hepatitis A – two to six months, depending on the dose given. It is not a vaccine, but is ready-made antibody collected from blood donations. It is reasonably effective and, unlike the vaccine, it is protective immediately, but because it is a blood product, there are current concerns about its long-term safety.

Hepatitis A vaccine is also available in a combined form, Twinrix, with hepatitis B vaccine. Three injections over a six-month period are required, the first two providing substantial protection against hepatitis A.

**Hepatitis B** Travellers who should consider vaccination against hepatitis B include those on a long trip, as well as those visiting countries where there are high levels of hepatitis B infection, where blood transfusions may not be adequately screened or where sexual contact or needle sharing is a possibility. Vaccination involves three injections, with a booster at 12 months. More rapid courses are available if necessary.

**Divers' Medical Check** If you plan to do a diving course in the Maldives, you should get a diving medical checkup before you leave. There's a special form for this and a dive school can insist on a diving health certificate before you do your course, especially if you are over 50 years old or if you have any medical conditions which might be affected by diving. A local diving club or dive shop will have a list of doctors who can do a diving medical check. Private clinics in Male' and on Bandos island resort can also do a divers' medical.

**Health Insurance** Make sure that you have adequate health insurance. See Travel Insurance under Visas & Documents in the Facts for the Visitor chapter for details.

**Travel Health Guides** If you are planning an extended stay in the outer atolls, you may consider taking a more detailed health guide.

*CDC's Complete Guide to Healthy Travel*, Open Road Publishing, 1997. The US Centers for Disease Control & Prevention recommendations for international travel.

*Staying Healthy in Asia, Africa & Latin America*, Dirk Schroeder, Moon Publications, 1994. Probably the best all-round guide to carry; it's detailed and well organised.

*Travellers' Health*, Dr Richard Dawood, Oxford University Press, 1995. Comprehensive, easy to read, authoritative and highly recommended, although it's rather large to lug around.

*Where There Is No Doctor*, David Werner, Macmillan, 1994. A very detailed guide intended for someone, such as a Peace Corps worker, going to work in an underdeveloped country.

*Travel with Children*, Maureen Wheeler, Lonely Planet Publications, 1995. Includes advice on travel health for younger children.

There are also a number of excellent travel health sites on the Internet. From the Lonely Planet home page there are links at www .lonelyplanet.com/weblinks/wlprep.htm#heal to the World Health Organization and the US Centers for Disease Control & Prevention.

**Other Preparations** Make sure you're healthy before you start travelling. If you are going on a long trip make sure your teeth are OK. If you wear glasses take a spare pair and your prescription.

If you require a particular medication take an adequate supply, as it will probably not be available on a Maldivian resort. Take part of the packaging showing the generic name rather than the brand, which will make getting replacements easier. It's a good idea to have a legible prescription or letter from your doctor to show that you legally use the medication to avoid any problems.

## Basic Rules

**Food in Resorts** Eating in a resort is as safe as in any modern restaurant in Western Europe. All food is prepared in well-run commercial kitchens and most ingredients are imported from reputable suppliers, in proper packaging or under refrigeration. Because the resort is the sole provider of food to the guests, management has complete responsibility for it. You can assume that vegetables and fruit have been washed and

### Medical Kit Check List

Following is a list of items you should consider including in your medical kit – consult your pharmacist for brands available in your country.

☐ **Aspirin or paracetamol (acetaminophen in the USA)** – for pain or fever
☐ **Antihistamine** – for allergies, eg, hay fever; to ease the itch from insect bites or stings; and to prevent motion sickness
☐ **Insect repellent, sunscreen, lip balm and eye drops**
☐ **Calamine lotion, sting relief spray or aloe vera** – to ease irritation from sunburn and insect bites or stings
☐ **Cold and flu tablets, throat lozenges and nasal decongestant**
☐ **Antifungal cream or powder** – for fungal skin infections and thrush
☐ **Antiseptic (such as povidone-iodine)** – for cuts and grazes
☐ **Bandages, Band-Aids (plasters) and other wound dressings**
☐ **Multivitamins** – consider for long trips, when dietary vitamin intake may be inadequate
☐ **Rehydration mixture** – to prevent dehydration, which may occur, for example, during bouts of diarrhoea; particularly important when travelling with children
☐ **Scissors, tweezers and a thermometer** – (note that mercury thermometers are prohibited by airlines)
☐ **Syringes and needles** – in case you need injections – ask your doctor for a note explaining why you have them.

peeled, and that meat and fish have been appropriately stored and prepared. Fresh shellfish such as mussels, oysters and clams are not available, and any prawns (shrimps) will have been imported frozen. There have been a very small number of stomach problems in a couple of resorts, caused by inadequate kitchen hygiene. These outbreaks have affected several guests at the same time, and both the tour wholesalers and the Ministry of Tourism have taken them very seriously. If you have any doubts about the hygiene standards of food in your resort, contact the representative of your tour organiser.

**Local Eateries** There may be a greater risk in local eateries, where food is prepared in advance and laid out on a counter. (In tea shops, food used to be placed on tables and customers helped themselves, but new regulations require it to be kept behind a counter and served as required in individual portions.) Overwhelmingly, however, these places are very clean, as are the staff and the other patrons. The experience of eating Maldivian food is worth the minimal danger of an upset stomach.

**Nutrition** The traditional local diet consists largely of fish, coconut and rice, with some onions, chillies, bananas and breadfruit. There is some evidence that this diet is deficient in fresh vegetables and iodine, and a dietary supplement might be a good idea for long-term visitors. For holidaymakers, even the least fancy resorts offer a good selection of fruits, vegetables and everything else for a healthy diet.

**Water** The usual, number-one rule is *don't drink the water*, and at most Maldivian resorts the management endorses this rule and suggests you buy bottled water, at around US$2 a litre or more. In fact, the tap water in most resorts is desalinated sea water and probably quite OK to drink (see the Water, Water, Everywhere boxed text later in this chapter). It may be very slightly salty, but is unlikely to contain harmful bacteria, unless it has picked up something in the storage tank or the pipes. Tea, coffee, juice, ice and anything washed in the water will be OK. Some resorts provide jugs of drinking water which is collected straight from the desalination plant. Male' guesthouses provide drinking water from the public supply, which is also desalinated.

Make sure you drink enough – don't rely on feeling thirsty to indicate when you should drink. Not needing to urinate or very dark yellow urine is a danger sign. Carry a water bottle on long boat trips.

**Water Purification** On local islands the water supply is from wells or from rainwater tanks. It should be OK if boiled thoroughly. Long-term visitors to local islands might consider bringing a 'total' water filter (it may be expensive but will take out all parasites, bacteria and viruses), chlorine tablets or iodine. Follow the directions carefully and remember that too much iodine can be harmful.

## Medical Problems & Treatment

Self-diagnosis and treatment can be risky, so seek qualified help if you need it. Some large resorts have a resident doctor, but otherwise it may be necessary to go into Male', to the nearest atoll capital, or have a doctor come to you. This is when that medical insurance really comes in useful!

Although we do give drug dosages in this section, they are for emergency use only. Correct diagnosis is vital. In this section we have used the generic names for medications – check with a pharmacist for brands available locally.

Note that antibiotics should ideally be administered only under medical supervision. Take only the recommended dose at the prescribed intervals and use the whole course, even if the illness seems to be cured earlier. Stop immediately if there are any serious reactions and don't use the antibiotic at all if you are unsure that you have the correct one. Some people are allergic to commonly prescribed antibiotics such as penicillin; carry this information (eg, on a bracelet) when travelling.

## Medical Care in the Maldives

Although it is continually being upgraded, the Maldivian health service is limited and relies heavily on doctors, nurses and dentists from overseas. The country's main hospital is the Indira Gandhi Memorial Hospital (☎ 316647) in Male'. There is also a government hospital or health centre on the capital island of each atoll, and these are being improved, but for any serious problem you'll have to go to Male'.

Male' also has the private AMDC Clinic (☎ 325979) and the ADK Private Hospital (☎ 313553), which are more suitable for foreign visitors. The quality of care is said to be high, but so are the prices.

## Everyday Health

Normal body temperature is 37°C or 98.6°F; more than 2°C (4°F) higher indicates a high fever. The normal adult pulse rate is 60 to 100 per minute (children 80 to 100, babies 100 to 140). As a general rule the pulse increases about 20 beats per minute for each 1°C (2°F) rise in fever.

Respiration (breathing) rate is also an indicator of illness. Count the number of breaths per minute: between 12 and 20 is normal for adults and older children (up to 30 for younger children, 40 for babies). People with a high fever or serious respiratory illness breathe more quickly than normal. More than 40 shallow breaths a minute may indicate pneumonia.

Emergency evacuations from resorts are coordinated by the National Coast Guard and the three seaplane companies. At the time of writing there were no helicopters operating in the Maldives, and seaplanes can only do evacuations during daylight hours from a limited number of landing/takeoff sites.

Though the Male' hospitals can deal with routine operations, the postoperative care may not be up to modern European standards. This basically means that getting seriously ill in the Maldives is not recommended. Cases that require specialist operations must be evacuated to Colombo or Singapore, or taken home.

### Environmental Hazards

**Jet Lag** Jet lag is experienced when a person travels by air across more than three time zones (each time zone usually represents a one-hour time difference). It occurs because many of the functions of the human body (such as temperature, pulse rate and emptying of the bladder and bowels) are regulated by internal 24-hour cycles. When we travel long distances rapidly, our bodies take time to adjust to the 'new time' of our destination, and we may experience fatigue, disorientation, insomnia, anxiety, impaired concentration and loss of appetite. These effects will usually be gone within three days of arrival, but to minimise the impact of jet lag:

- Rest for a couple of days prior to departure.
- Try to select flight schedules that minimise sleep deprivation; arriving late in the day means you can go to sleep soon after you arrive. For very long flights, try to organise a stopover.
- Avoid excessive eating (which bloats the stomach) and alcohol (which causes dehydration) during the flight. Instead, drink plenty of noncarbonated, nonalcoholic drinks such as fruit juice or water.
- Avoid smoking.
- Make yourself comfortable by wearing loose-fitting clothes and perhaps bringing an eye mask and ear plugs to help you sleep.
- Try to sleep at the appropriate time for the time zone you are travelling to.

**Heat Exhaustion** Dehydration and salt deficiency can cause heat exhaustion. Take time to acclimatise to high temperatures, drink sufficient liquids and do not do anything too physically demanding.

Salt deficiency is characterised by fatigue, lethargy, headaches, giddiness and muscle cramps; salt tablets may help, but adding extra salt to your food is better.

Anhidrotic heat exhaustion is a rare form of heat exhaustion caused by an inability to sweat. It affects people who have been in a hot climate for some time, rather than newcomers. It can progress to heatstroke. Treatment involves removal to a cooler climate.

**Heatstroke** This serious, occasionally fatal, condition can occur if the body's heat-regulating mechanism breaks down and the body temperature rises to dangerous levels. Long, continuous periods of exposure to high temperatures and insufficient fluids can leave you vulnerable to heatstroke.

The symptoms are feeling unwell, not sweating very much (or at all) and a high body temperature (39° to 41°C or 102° to 106°F). Where sweating has ceased, the skin becomes flushed and red. Severe, throbbing headaches and lack of coordination will also occur, and the sufferer may be confused or aggressive. Eventually the victim will become delirious or convulse. Hospitalisation is essential, but in the interim get the victim out of the sun, remove their clothing, cover them with a wet sheet or towel and then fan continuously. Give fluids if they are conscious.

**Motion Sickness** Eating lightly before and during a trip will reduce the chances of motion sickness. If you are prone to motion sickness try to find a place that minimises movement eg, near the wing on aircraft. On a large boat or a traditional Maldivian dhoni, try to sit close to the middle. On a modern speed boat, there is usually less movement towards the back. If you start to feel queasy, try standing up, watching the horizon, and using your legs to absorb the movement of the boat. Fresh air usually helps; reading and cigarette smoke don't. Commercial motion-sickness preparations, which can cause drowsiness, have to be taken before the trip commences. Ginger (available in capsule form) and peppermint (including mint-flavoured sweets) are believed to be natural preventatives.

**Prickly Heat** Prickly heat is an itchy rash caused by excessive perspiration trapped under the skin. It usually strikes people who have just arrived in a hot climate. Keeping cool, bathing often, drying the skin and using a mild talcum or prickly heat powder or resorting to air-conditioning may help.

**Sunburn** In the tropics you can get sunburnt surprisingly quickly, even through cloud. Use a sunscreen, a hat, and a barrier cream for your nose and lips. Calamine lotion or a commercial after sun preparation are good for mild sunburn. Protect your eyes with good-quality sunglasses, particularly when you're near water and sand which reflect UV radiation. It's easy to burn while snorkelling.

## Infectious Diseases

**Diarrhoea** A change of water, food or climate can all cause a mild bout of diarrhoea, but a few rushed toilet trips with no other symptoms is not indicative of a serious problem. Dehydration is the main danger with any diarrhoea, particularly for children or the elderly, for whom dehydration can occur quite quickly. Fluid replacement remains the mainstay of management. Severe diarrhoea is most unlikely.

**Fungal Infections** Fungal infections occur more commonly in hot weather and are usually found on the scalp, between the toes (athlete's foot) or fingers, in the groin and on the body (ringworm). You get ringworm (which is a fungal infection, not a worm) from infected animals or other people. Moisture encourages these infections.

To prevent fungal infections wear loose, comfortable clothes, avoid artificial fibres, wash frequently and dry yourself carefully. If you do get an infection, wash the infected area at least daily with a disinfectant or medicated soap and water, and rinse and dry well. Apply an antifungal cream or powder like tolnaftate. Try to expose the infected area to air or sunlight as much as possible and wash all towels and underwear in hot water, change them often and let them dry in the sun.

**Hepatitis** Hepatitis is a general term for inflammation of the liver. It is a common disease worldwide. Several different viruses cause hepatitis, and they differ in the way that they are transmitted. The symptoms are similar in all forms of the illness, and include fever, chills, headache, fatigue, feelings of weakness and aches and pains, followed by loss of appetite, nausea, vomiting, abdominal pain, dark urine, light-coloured faeces, jaundiced (yellow) skin and yellowing of the whites of the eyes. People who have had hepatitis should avoid alcohol for some time after the illness, as the liver needs time to recover.

**Hepatitis A** is transmitted by contaminated food and drinking water. You should seek medical advice, but there is not much you can do apart from resting, drinking lots of fluids, eating lightly and avoiding fatty foods. **Hepatitis E** is transmitted in the same way as hepatitis A; it can be particularly serious in pregnant women.

There are almost 300 million chronic carriers of **hepatitis B** in the world. It is spread through contact with infected blood, blood products or body fluids, for example through sexual contact, unsterilised needles and blood transfusions, or contact with blood via small breaks in the skin. Other risk situations include having a shave, tattoo or body piercing with contaminated equipment. The symptoms of hepatitis B may be more severe than type A and the disease can lead to long-term problems such as chronic liver damage, liver cancer or a long term carrier state. **Hepatitis C** and **D** are spread in the same way as hepatitis B and can also lead to long-term complications.

There are vaccines against hepatitis A and B, but there are currently no vaccines against the other types of hepatitis. Following the basic rules about food and water (hepatitis A and E) and avoiding risk situations (hepatitis B, C and D) are important preventative measures.

**HIV & AIDS** Infection with the human immunodeficiency virus (HIV) may lead to acquired immune deficiency syndrome (AIDS), which is a fatal disease. Any exposure to blood, blood products or body fluids may put the individual at risk. Transmission is often through sexual contact or dirty needles – vaccinations, acupuncture, tattooing and body piercing can be potentially as dangerous as intravenous drug use. HIV/AIDS can also be spread through infected blood transfusions. The Maldives has a very limited blood supply, though it is screened for AIDS. (The blood supply is not for general use, and people who need operations are asked to bring a compatible blood donor with them.)

If you do need an injection, ask to see the syringe unwrapped in front of you, or take a needle and syringe pack with you.

Fear of HIV infection shouldn't preclude treatment for serious medical conditions.

**Sexually Transmitted Infections** HIV/AIDS and hepatitis B can be transmitted through sexual contact – see the relevant sections earlier for more details. Other STIs include gonorrhoea, herpes and syphilis; sores, blisters or rashes around the genitals and discharges or pain when urinating are common symptoms. In some STIs, such as wart virus or chlamydia, symptoms may be less marked or not observed at all, especially in women. Chlamydia infection can cause infertility in men and women before any symptoms have been noticed. Syphilis symptoms eventually disappear completely but the disease continues and can cause severe problems in later

years. The treatment of gonorrhoea and syphilis is with antibiotics. The different sexually transmitted infections each require specific antibiotics. While abstinence from sexual contact is the only 100% effective prevention, using condoms is also effective. Remember to bring a supply of condoms with you, as they are not readily available in the Maldives.

## Insect-Borne Diseases

Mosquitoes are not a great problem in Maldivian resorts because there are few areas of open fresh water where they can breed. On some resorts, the whole island is sprayed regularly at times when mosquitoes might breed, typically after heavy rain. If you're in a room with air-conditioning, or there's a ceiling fan to keep the air moving, mosquitoes are unlikely to trouble you. If they do, use repellent or burn mosquito coils – both are available from resort shops.

**Malaria** This serious disease is spread only by mosquito bites. Maldives is not regarded as an area of endemic malaria and prophylaxis is not recommended.

**Dengue Fever** This viral disease is transmitted by mosquitoes and is fast becoming one of the top public health problems in the tropical world. There have been some instances of dengue fever in isolated Maldivian villages, but it is not a significant risk on resort islands or in the capital.

## Cuts, Bites & Stings

Skin punctures can easily become infected in hot climates and may be difficult to heal. Treat any cut with an antiseptic such as povidone-iodine. Where possible avoid bandages and Band-aids, which can keep wounds wet.

Though scuba diving has its own health considerations, there are certain dangers that anyone snorkelling, swimming or even wading in Maldivian waters should be aware of.

The basic rules of reef safety are:

- Don't walk on reefs or in the shallow water between reefs.
- Don't swim in murky water; try to swim when there's bright sunlight.

**Coral Cuts** The most likely marine injury is the simple coral cut. Coral is sharp stuff and brushing up against it is likely to cause a cut or abrasion. Since coral kills its prey with poison you're likely to get some of that poison in the wound, and tiny grains of broken coral are also likely to lodge there. The result is that a small cut can take a long, long time to heal and be very painful in the process. The answer is to wash any coral cuts very thoroughly with fresh water and then treat them liberally with antiseptic.

An even better solution is not to get cut by coral in the first place. Don't walk on reefs, don't swim over coral flats to go snorkelling, and maintain correct buoyancy and control when diving. In cutting yourself you've probably damaged the coral as well, so exercise care, avoid coral cuts and help preserve the environment at the same time.

**Stonefish** Stonefish lie on reefs and the sea bottom, and are well camouflaged. When stepped on, their 13 sharp dorsal spines pop up and inject a venom that causes intense pain and can cause death. Stonefish are usually found in shallow, muddy water, but also on rock and coral sea beds. They are another good reason not to walk on coral reefs.

Shoes with strong soles give the best protection, but if you are unlucky, bathing the wound in very hot water reduces the pain and effects of the venom. An antivenene is available and medical attention should be sought as the after effects can be very long lasting.

**Sea Urchins** Don't step on sea urchins as the spines are long and sharp, break off easily and once embedded in your flesh are very difficult to remove.

**Sea Lice** You may encounter these tiny creatures when swimming or snorkelling. They are too small to see, but they cause annoying little stings on exposed skin – they feel like mosquitoes but you can't swat them. They don't cause any lasting discomfort.

**Stingrays** Stingrays lie on sandy bottoms, and if you step on one its barbed tail can whip up into your leg and cause a nasty poisoned wound. Sand can drift over stingrays so they can become all but invisible while basking on the bottom. Fortunately, although they may be invisible to you, you are certainly not invisible to them and stingrays will usually wake up and glide away as you approach. If you're out walking on the sort of shallow sandy surface which rays like, try to shuffle along and make some noise. If stung, bathing the affected area in hot water is the best treatment; medical attention should be sought to ensure the wound is properly cleaned.

**Cone Shells** The white-banded cone shell *(Conus omaria)* is found in Maldivian waters and can sting dangerously or even fatally. Other fish and sea creatures can sting or bite or are dangerous to eat. See the Diving Health section below for more information.

## Food-Borne Diseases

**Fish Poisoning** Ciguatera is a poison which accumulates in fish which graze on certain types of algae. It concentrates in other fish further up the food chain. The original algae-eating fish doesn't pose the danger, rather the fish which eats the fish which eats the algae-eating fish. Chinaman-fish, red bass, large rock cod and moray eels have all been implicated, but the danger is remote. Maldivian cooks should know which fish are safe to eat.

## Diving Health

If you intend taking a diving course while in the Maldives, you should have a full diving medical checkup before you leave home. In the Maldives, you can have it done at AMDC Clinic or the ADK Hospital in Male', or at the diving clinic at Bandos Resort. In practice, most dive schools will let you dive or do a course if you're under 50 years old and complete a medical questionnaire, but the checkup is still a good idea. This is especially so if you have any problem at all with your breathing, ears or sinuses. If you are an asthmatic, have any other chronic breathing difficulties, or serious inner-ear problems, you will not pass the test and should not do any scuba diving.

*[Continued on page 71]*

# SNORKELLING & DIVING

## Snorkelling

The marine life in the Maldives is incredibly rich and beautiful, and much of it can be seen by snorkellers at depths of just a few metres. Because the water absorbs so much red and yellow light, most of the underwater world is a monochrome blue below about 5m, so snorkelling gear is all you need to see some of the best of it. Unfortunately, the coral in shallow water has been worst affected by bleaching, though the number and variety of fish will still astound you. It's also interesting to look for new coral growth, which indicates that the reefs are recovering. Some islands are much better than others for snorkelling, so if this is a big attraction for you, select your resort with this in mind.

### Islands, Reefs & Resorts

Usually, an island is surrounded firstly by a sand-bottomed lagoon, then by the 'reef flat', a belt of living coral covered by shallow water. At the edge of the reef flat is a steep, coral-covered slope that drops away into deeper water. These 'reef slopes' are the best areas for snorkelling – around a resort island this is often called the 'house reef'. The slope itself can have interesting features like cliffs, terraces and caves, and there are clearly visible changes in the coral and other marine flora as the water gets deeper. You can see both the smaller fish which frequent the reef flats and sometimes much larger animals that live in the deep water between the islands, but come close to the reefs to feed.

The best islands for snorkelling have narrow reef flats with lots of channels through to the outer reef slope. Some resort islands, however, have very wide lagoons and extensive reef flats – you may have to swim hundreds of metres to get out there, and you still won't be able to get across the shallow reef flat to the edge where the reef slope is. (Remember that you're not allowed to walk on the reef or damage the coral, and it's so sharp that you wouldn't want to anyway.) In some cases there will be entrance channels that you can swim through – these are usually natural channels, sometimes widened and deepened to permit boats and snorkellers to get in and out of the lagoon. You should always use these channels rather than try to find your own way across the reef flat. Another option is to walk out on a jetty to the reef edge – all resorts have at least one jetty, though sometimes they don't extend right to the edge of the reef.

If you're keen on snorkelling, choose a resort where the deep water is not far offshore, at least around part of the island. Remember, too, that the 'inner reef slopes' – those that face the sheltered water inside an atoll – are much more suited to snorkelling than the 'outer reef slopes', which face the open sea. Resorts that don't have a reef just offshore usually provide a couple of boat trips per day to a good snorkelling site, but this is a lot less convenient. Also, many resorts offer boat trips or island-hopping excursions which stop at really superb

**Inset:** All you need is a mask, and maybe fins and a snorkel to see some of the best colours.
Photo: James Lyon

snorkelling sites, typically at a giri or near some uninhabited island. These usually cost around US$15 or so, but are definitely worth it. Kuredu Island Resort has the most comprehensive snorkelling program, with night snorkelling and guided snorkelling trips to many interesting sites, including a shipwreck.

## Starting Snorkelling
If you've never tried snorkelling before, you'll soon pick it up – many resorts give brief, free snorkelling lessons in swimming pools or in shallow parts of the lagoon. Every resort will have snorkelling equipment that you can rent, but this will cost up to US$10 per day or US$15 per week. It's definitely better to have your own – it's cheaper in the long run and you can be sure that it suits you and fits properly. You can buy good quality equipment at reasonable prices at the airport shop and in Male'. Most resort shops sell them too, but the range is smaller and the prices are higher. Ideally, you should bring your own set from home.

## Mask
Human eyes won't normally focus in water, but a face mask keeps an air space in front of your eyes so that you can focus under water. Masks cost anything from $10 to hundreds of dollars and, as with most things, you get what you pay for. Any mask, no matter how cheap, should have a shatterproof lens. Ensure that the mask fits comfortably onto your face – for some, oval masks fit better, but others prefer square ones. To check if it fits well, press it gently onto your face without the strap around the back of your head. Breathe in through your nose and the suction should hold the mask on your face if the fit is good.

If you're shortsighted you can get the mask lens ground to your optical prescription, but this is expensive. Alternatively, get a stick-on optical lens to attach to the inside of the mask lens, or simply fold up an old pair of spectacles and wedge them inside the mask. You can wear contact lenses with a mask, but there is the risk of losing them if the mask is flooded – many people now use soft disposable contact lenses under the mask.

## Snorkel
When you dive below the surface, the snorkel tube will fill with water, but you can clear it by blowing out forcefully once the snorkel is back above the water. The snorkel tube has to be long enough to reach above the surface of the water, but should not be either too long or too wide. If it is too big then you have more water to expel when you come to the surface and it's not pleasant to find that first gulp of fresh air is mostly seawater. Also, each breath out leaves a snorkel full of used air. Normally, this only slightly dilutes the fresh air you breathe in, but if the snorkel is too big you will breathe in a larger proportion of carbon dioxide.

## Fins
Fins are not absolutely necessary, but they make swimming easier and let you dive deeper. Fins either fit completely over your foot or have

an open back with a strap around your heel. The former type must fit well, while the latter type can be adjusted, and can be designed for use with wet-suit boots. Boots will make the fins more comfortable and are useful for walking over rocks and rough surfaces, but remember not to walk on coral reefs even if your feet are protected.

# Diving

Scuba diving is the main attraction in the Maldives and it's estimated that over 60% of visitors do some diving. Some resorts are hard-core divers' centres where up to 90% of guests will dive. Even among honeymoon couples, up to 50% will go diving, which must say something about how good the diving is. An alternative to resort-based diving is to charter a live-aboard boat and do a diving safari trip, diving at sites which are beyond the reach of any resort.

## Diving Sites

There are hundreds of recognised and named dive sites, and dozens accessible from nearly every resort, but some resorts may be better located for particular types of diving or at different times of the year. In general there are four types of dive sites in the Maldives:

**Reef Dives** The edges of a reef, where it slopes into deep water, are the most interesting part of a reef to dive. Outer reef slopes, where the atoll meets the open sea, often have interesting terraces, overhangs and caves, and are visited by pelagics (open-sea fish). Visibility is usually good, but surf and currents can make for a demanding dive. Inner reef slopes, in the sheltered waters inside an atoll, are generally easier dives and feature coral formations and numerous smaller reef fish.

**Kandus** A kandu is a channel between islands or reefs on the outer edge of an atoll, or a channel between atolls. Obviously, kandus are subject to currents and this makes them suitable for drift dives. The current also provides an environment in which attractive soft corals thrive. Water inside an atoll is a breeding ground for plankton, and where this water flows out through a kandu into the open sea, the rich supply of plankton attracts large animals such as manta rays and whale

**Right:** Videoing can show richer colours of coral and fish than the naked eye.

sharks. During the south-west monsoon (May – November), currents will generally flow out of an atoll through kandus on the eastern side, while in the north-east monsoon (December – October), the outward flow is on the western side.

**Thillas** A thilla is a coral formation that rises steeply from the atoll floor and reaches to within five to 15m of the water surface – often it's a spectacular underwater mountain which divers fly around like birds. The top of a thilla can be rich in reef fish and hard coral, while the steep sides often have crannies, caves and overhangs which provide shelter for many small fish, while larger fish come, in turn, to feed on the smaller fish.

**Wrecks** While many ships have foundered on Maldivian reefs over the centuries, there are few accessible wrecks with any historical interest. Most were on outer reef slopes and broke up in the surf long ago leaving remnants to be dispersed and covered in coral. Any wreck sites of historical significance will require special permission to dive – the government is anxious that wrecks are not plundered, so that they can be preserved until marine archaeological work can be done. The diveable wrecks are mostly inside the atolls and are not very old. They are interesting for

MICHAEL AW

the coral and other marine life which colonises the hulk within just a few years. Quite a few of the wrecks have been sunk deliberately, to provide an attraction for divers.

Some of the better-known dive sites are described in the chapters on the various atolls and are marked on the maps. Dive Maldives, by Tim Godfrey, describes all of the established dive sites in detail and is a good investment and souvenir for any diver. It's available in Male' and at most resorts. The Dive Sites of the Maldives, by Harwood & Bryning, is also good.

## Marine Environment Protection

The waters of the Maldives may seem pristine but, like everywhere, development and commercial activities can have adverse effects on the marine environment. The Maldivian government recognises that the underwater world is a major attraction, and has imposed many restrictions and controls on fishing, coral mining and tourist operations. Twenty-five Protected Marine Areas have been established, and these are subject to special controls.

Dive operators throughout the country are overwhelmingly conservation-minded too. Diving techniques have been modified to protect the environment, and operators now use drift diving or tie mooring

**Left:** The Halaveli wreck in Ari Atoll was deliberately sunk for diving.

ropes by hand rather than drop anchors. The practice of feeding fish has been abandoned, and most operators are careful to ensure that un-skilled divers are not taken on dives where they may accidentally dam-age coral.

Visiting divers must do their best to ensure that their activities don't spoil the experience of those who will come in the future. The follow-ing rules are generally accepted as necessary for conservation:

- Do not use anchors on the reef, and take care not to ground boats on coral. Encourage dive operators and regulatory bodies to establish permanent moorings at popular dive sites.
- Avoid touching living marine organisms with your body or dragging equipment across the reef. Polyps can be damaged by even the gentlest contact. Handling fish can remove the slimy coating which protects the animal's skin.
- Never stand on corals, even if they look solid and robust. If you must hold on, to prevent being swept away in a current, hold on to dead coral.
- Be conscious of your fins. Even without contact the surge from heavy fin strokes near the reef can damage delicate organisms. When treading water in shallow reef areas, take care not to kick up clouds of sand. Settling sand can easily smother the delicate organisms of the reef.
- Practise and maintain proper buoyancy control. Major damage can be done by divers descending too fast and colliding with the reef. Make sure you are correctly weighted and that your weight belt is positioned so that you stay horizontal. If you have not dived for a while, have a practise dive in a pool or lagoon before taking to the reef. Be aware that buoyancy can change over the period of an extended trip: initially you may breathe harder and need more weight; a few days later you may breathe more easily and need less weight.
- Take great care in underwater caves. Spend as little time within them as possible as your air bubbles may be caught within the roof and thereby leave previously submerged organisms high and dry. Taking turns to inspect the interior of a small cave will lessen the chances of damaging contact.
- Collecting lobster or shell fish is prohibited, as is spearfishing. Removing any coral or shells, living or dead, is against the law. All shipwreck sites are protected by law.
- Take home all your rubbish and any litter you may find as well. Plastics in particular are a serious threat to marine life. Turtles can mistake plastic for jellyfish and eat it.
- Resist the temptation to feed fish. You may disturb their normal eating habits, encourage aggressive behaviour or feed them food that is detrimental to their health.
- Minimise your disturbance of marine animals. Chasing, grabbing or attempting to ride on turtles, mantas or any large marine animal can frighten them and deter them from visiting a dive site.

## Common Fish of the Maldives

### Angelfish (1) (Pomacanthidae family)

Of the many species, there are 14 in the Maldives, mostly seen in shallow water, though some inhabit reef slopes down to 20m. They can be seen individually or in small groups. Small species are around 10cm, largest to 35cm. They feed on sponges and algae. Regal (or empress) angelfish have bright yellow bodies with vertical dark blue and white stripes.The emperor (or imperial) angelfish are larger (to 35cm) and live in deeper water, with almost horizontal blue and yellow lines and a dark blue mask and gill markings; juveniles are quite different in shape and markings. The small, many-spined angelfish are very dark blue with bright blue edging on top and bottom fins.

### Butterflyfish (2) (Chaetodontidae family)

There are over 30 species in the Maldives; they are common in shallow waters and reef slopes, singly, in pairs or small schools. Species vary from 12cm to 30cm, when mature, with a flattened body shape and elaborate markings. Various species of this carnivorous fish have specialised food sources, including anemones, coral polyps, algae and assorted invertebrate prey. Bennett's butterflyfish (illustrated), bright yellow and 18cm long, is one of several species with a 'false eye' near the tail to make predators think it's a larger fish facing the other way. Spotted butterflyfish, which grow to 10cm long, are camouflaged with dark polkadots and a dark band across its real eye.

### Dolphins (3) (Delphinidae family)

Dolphins are mammals, not fish, but common dolphins (Delphinus delphis) are an everyday sight on boat trips through the atolls. Dolphins are almost invariably in groups, and frequently cavort in the bow wave of a boat or leap out of the water in exciting displays. The smaller 'spinner dolphins' are so-named for the spinning trick they perform as they jump from the water.

### Flutemouth (or cornetfish) (4) (Fistulariidae family)

One species of flutemouth is very common in shallow waters in the Maldives, often occurring in small schools. They are very slender, elongated fish, are usually observed at around 60cm, but deep sea specimens are up to 1.5m. Flutemouths eat small fish, often stalking prey by swimming behind a harmless herbivore. The silver colouring seems almost transparent in the water, and it can be hard to spot flutemouths even in shallow sandy lagoons.

### Flying fish (5) (Exocoetidae family)

Several species in the Maldives are commonly seen on boat trips, usually in small groups, leaping from the water and gliding rapidly for maybe 100m or more just a few centimetres above the surface, sometimes changing direction in mid-flight. They are small (up to 15cm), compact, silver fish with pronounced pectoral fins. They fly in order to escape predators, hence they will often surface and fly away from a boat.

### Moorish idol (6) (Zanclidae family)

One species of moorish idol is commonly seen on reef flats and reef slopes in the Maldives, often in pairs. Usually 15cm to 20cm long, the moorish idol is herbivorous, feeding primarily on algae. They are attractive, with broad vertical yellow and black bands, pointed snouts, and long, streamer-like extensions to the upper dorsal fin.

### Sweetlips (7) (Haemulidae family)

Only a few of the many species are found in the Maldives, where they inhabit outer reef slopes. Some species grow up to 1m, but most are between 50cm and 75cm; juveniles are largely herbivorous, feeding on algae, plankton and other small organisms; older fish hunt and eat smaller fish. Oriental sweetlips (illustrated) (which grow to 50cm) are superb looking with horizontal dark and light stripes, dark spots on fins and tail, and large, lugubrious lips. Brown sweetlips are generally bigger, duller and more active at night.

### Parrotfish (8) (Scaridae family)

Over 20 of the many parrotfish species are found in the Maldives – they include some of the most conspicuous and commonly seen reef fish. The largest species grow to more than a metre, but those around 50cm long are more typical. Most parrotfish feed on algae and other organisms growing on and around a hard coral structure. With strong, beak-like mouths they scrape and bite the coral surface, then grind up the coral chunks, swallowing and filtering to extract nutrients. Snorkellers often hear the scraping, grinding sound of parrotfish eating coral, and notice the clouds of coral-sand crap which parrotfish regularly discharge. Colour, pattern and even sex can change as parrotfish mature  – juveniles and females are often drab, while mature males can have brilliant blue-green designs. Bicolour parrotfish start life white with a broad orange stripe, but the mature males (up to 90cm) are a beautiful blue with hot pink highlights on the scale edges, head, fins and tail. Green-face parrotfish grow to 60cm, with the adult male identified by its blue-green body, bright green 'face' and white marks on fins and tail. Heavy-beak (or steephead) parrotfish (illustrated) can be 70cm long, and have a distinctive rounded head.

FACING ILLUSTRATIONS BY ADRIANA MAMMARELLA & TRUDI CANAVAN

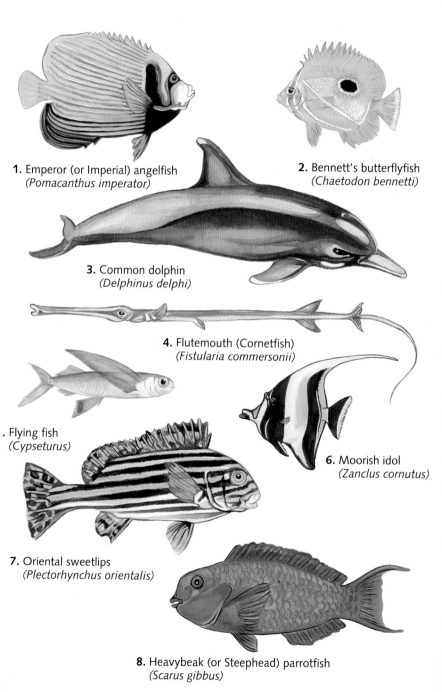

**1.** Emperor (or Imperial) angelfish
(*Pomacanthus imperator*)

**2.** Bennett's butterflyfish
(*Chaetodon bennetti*)

**3.** Common dolphin
(*Delphinus delphi*)

**4.** Flutemouth (Cornetfish)
(*Fistularia commersonii*)

**5.** Flying fish
(*Cypseturus*)

**6.** Moorish idol
(*Zanclus cornutus*)

**7.** Oriental sweetlips
(*Plectorhynchus orientalis*)

**8.** Heavybeak (or Steephead) parrotfish
(*Scarus gibbus*)

MICHAEL AW

JAMES LYON

MICHAEL AW

MICHAEL AW

You can look at the coral. You can even video it. But you can't touch it, not even with a flipper!
Over 60% of visitors to the Maldives do at least some diving. All diving operations are affiliated with
at least one international accreditation organisation and many cater for beginners.

MICHAEL AW

CHRIS MELLOR

CHRIS MELLOR

CHRIS MELLOR

CHRIS MELLOR

Colourful diving – despite damage from El Niño weather patterns, the views are spectacular.

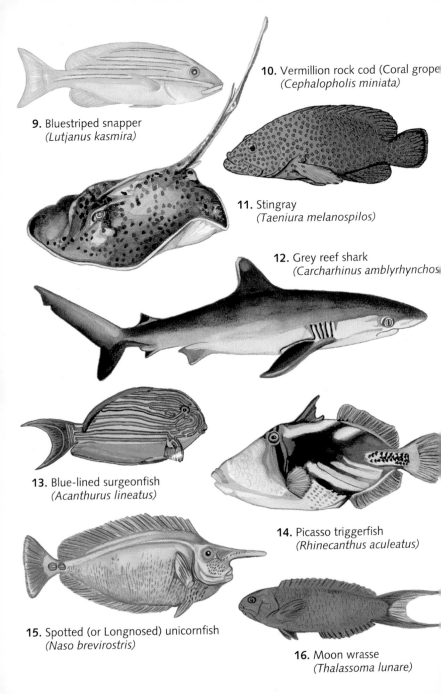

9. Bluestriped snapper
(*Lutjanus kasmira*)

10. Vermillion rock cod (Coral grope
(*Cephalopholis miniata*)

11. Stingray
(*Taeniura melanospilos*)

12. Grey reef shark
(*Carcharhinus amblyrhynchos*

13. Blue-lined surgeonfish
(*Acanthurus lineatus*)

14. Picasso triggerfish
(*Rhinecanthus aculeatus*)

15. Spotted (or Longnosed) unicornfish
(*Naso brevirostris*)

16. Moon wrasse
(*Thalassoma lunare*)

## Common Fish of the Maldives

### Snapper (9) *(Lutjanidae family)*
There are only 28 species in the Maldives, mostly in deep water. Small species are around 20cm and the largest grow to 1m (snapper, themselves carnivorous, are popular with anglers as a fighting fish, and are excellent to eat). Bluestriped snapper (illustrated), commonly seen in schools near inshore reefs, are an attractive yellow with blue-white horizontal stripes. Red snapper (or red bass), are often seen in lagoons.

### Rock cod (10) *(Serranidae family)*
Cephalopholis subfamily. Hundreds of species are currently classified as Serranidae, including rock cod and groper which are common around reefs. Smaller species reach 20cm; many larger species grow to 50cm and some to over a metre. Rock cod are carnivorous, feeding on smaller fish and invertebrates. Vermillion rock cod (or coral groper) ) (illustrated) are often seen in shallow waters and near the coral formations in which they hide; they are a brilliant crimson colour covered with blue spots, up to 40cm long.

### Stingray (11) *(Dasyatidae family)*
Several species are often seen in very shallow water on the sandy bed of a lagoon where they are often well camouflaged. Most rays seen inshore are juveniles, up to about 50cm across; mature rays can be over a metre across, and maybe 2m long including the whiplike tail. A barbed and venomous spine on top of the tail can swing up and forward, and will deliver a painful injury to anyone who stands on it.

### Reef shark (12) *(Carcharhinidae family)*
Several smaller shark species frequent reef flats and reef edges inside Maldivian atolls, often in schools, while larger pelagic species (Rhincodontidae family) congregate around channels in the atoll rim at certain times of the year. Most reef species are small, typically 1m to 2m. Reef sharks hunt small fish (attacks on swimmers and divers are almost unknown). White-tips grow from 1m to 2m long and have white tips on dorsal fins. They are often seen in schools of ten or more in the sandy shallows of a lagoon. Black-tips, distinguished by tips on dorsal fins and tail, grow to 2m. Grey reef sharks (illustrated) are thicker in the mid-section and have a white trailing edge on the dorsal fin.

### Surgeonfish (13) *(Acanthuridae family)*
Over 20 species are found here, often in large schools. The adults range from 20cm to 60cm. All species graze for algae on the sea bottom or on coral surfaces. Blue-lined surgeonfish (illustrated), quite common in shallow waters, have distinctive horizontal blue and yellow stripes and crescent-shaped tails with elongated top and bottom edges; they grow to 30cm, and usually live in large schools in water with strong currents.

### Triggerfish (14) *(Balistidae family)*
There are over a dozen species in the Maldives, on outer reef slopes and also in shallower reef environments. Small species are around 25cm and the largest species to over 75cm. Triggerfish are carnivorous. Orangestriped triggerfish are common in shallow reef waters (30cm). Titan triggerfish have yellow and dark-brown crisscross patterning, grow up to 75cm and can be aggressive, especially when defending eggs, and will charge at divers. Picasso triggerfish (illustrated) have a yellow line which extends from the mouth as a broad smile; the underside has oblique zebra stripes; a black and blue band camouflages the eyes; and the back is black with white patches (40cm).

### Unicornfish (15) *(Acanthuridae family)*
From the same family as the surgeonfish, there are several species of the Nasinae subfamily. They grow from 40cm to 75cm long (only males of some species have the horn for which the species is named). Unicorn fish are herbivores. Spotted unicornfish (illustrated) are very common blue-grey or olive-brown fish with narrow dotted vertical markings (males can change their colours for display, and exhibit a broad white vertical band); their prominent horns get longer with age.

### Wrasse (16) *(Labridae family)*
Some 60 species of this large and very diverse family occur, some on reefs, others on sandy lagoon floors, others in open water. The smallest wrasse species are only 10cm; the largest over 2m. Most wrasse are carnivores; larger wrasse will hunt and eat small fish. Napoleonfish (or napoleon wrasse, or humphead wrasse) are the largest wrasse species, often seen around wrecks and outer reef slopes; they are generally green with fine vertical patterning. Large males have a humped head (2m).

Moon wrasse (illustrated), about 25cm, live in shallow waters and reef slopes, where adult males are beautifully coloured in green with pink patterning and a yellow marking on the tail. Juveniles are plain green or brown with a false eye on the dorsal fin. Cleaner wrasse have a symbiotic relationship with larger fish which allows the wrasse to eat the small parasites and food scraps from their mouths, gills and skin surface. At certain times, large numbers of pelagic species congregate at 'cleaning stations' where cleaner wrasse abound – a great sight for divers.

FACING ILLUSTRATIONS BY ADRIANA MAMMARELLA & TRUDI CANAVAN

## Diving Seasons

January to April are generally considered the best months for diving, and should have fine weather and good visibility. May and June can have unstable weather, and storms and cloudy days are common until September. October and November tend to have calmer, clearer weather, but visibility can be slightly reduced because of abundant plankton in the water. Some divers like this period because many large fish, such as whale sharks and mantas, come into the channels to feed on the plankton. December can have rough, windy weather and rain.

## Dive Schools & Operators

Virtually every resort has a professional diving operation and can run courses for beginners, as well as dive trips and courses that will challenge even the most experienced diver. A couple of dive operations in Male' cater mainly to expatriate workers. The government requires that all dive operations maintain high standards, and all of them are affiliated with one or more of the international diving accreditation organisations – most are with PADI, but some are with Confederation Mondiale des Activities Subaquatique (CMAS) or Scuba Schools International (SSI) as well. Nearly all the operations are run and staffed by foreigners, but there are some Maldivian instructors and divemasters now. You may be required to do a check dive to assess your level of ability.

## Diving Courses

Diving is not difficult, but it requires knowledge and care, and a lot of experience before you can safely dive independently. It doesn't require great strength or fitness and if you can do things with minimum expenditure of energy, your tank of air will last longer. An experienced diver will use much less air than a beginner. Women often have an advantage also, because they don't breathe as much air as men.

There's a range of courses, from an introductory dive in a pool or lagoon, to a 'resort course' (which allows you to dive at that resort only), to an open-water course that gives an internationally recognised qualification. Beyond that, there are advanced and specialty courses, and courses that lead to divemaster and instructor qualifications.

JAMES LYON

**Left:** Many resorts give introductory diving lessons.

Courses in the Maldives are not a bargain, but they're reasonably priced and you are assured of high standards, good equipment and extremely pleasant conditions. On the other hand, if you do a course at home you'll have more time for diving when you get to the Maldives. A compromise is to do the theoretical stuff and introductory dives at home, so you just have to complete the open-water dives when you reach your resort.

An introductory dive will cost about US$30 with all equipment supplied and sometimes this can be credited towards a proper course if you decide you like diving. Some resorts even offer a free introductory dive to get you in.

A resort course is usually a couple of dives in sheltered water (pool or lagoon), plus a couple in open water, with some basic theory and your first logbook. This will cost from US$150 to US$200, depending on how much the course includes. Again, the cost and the training can sometimes be credited towards a more advanced course.

If you're at all serious about diving, you should do an open-water course. This requires about nine dives, usually five in sheltered water and four in open water, as well as classroom training and completion of a multiple-choice test. The cost in the Maldives is around US$380 to US$550. Sometimes the price is all-inclusive, but there are often a few extra charges – US$12 for each boat trip, US$50 for equipment hire, US$80 for log books, certificates, dive tables, course materials, 10% service charge etc. These can really add up. One resort advertised its open-water course for US$455, but by the time you include all the extras, like a US$45 certificate, a US$10 log book and US$48 for boat trips, it would cost you over US$600. You could do the course in as little as five days, but you really should allow six to nine. Don't try it on a one week package – transfers and jet lag will take a day or so, and you shouldn't dive within 12 to 24 hours before a plane flight. Besides, you'll want to do some recreational dives to try out your new skills.

The next stage is an advanced open-water course, which will involve five dives (including one night dive). The cost will be US$250 to US$350, depending on the dive school and the number of extra charges. Then there are the specialty courses in night diving, rescue diving, wreck diving, nitrox diving and so on. Some of the specialty courses don't seem like great value, such as a 'Shark and Ray Diver' course, which costs US$83 and consists of a video tape plus one dive. Ask about the content of the course before you sign up.

## Health Requirements
Officially, a doctor should check you over before you do a course, and fill out a form full of diving health questions. Ideally you should get a diving health certificate before you leave home – a local diving club or dive shop will have a list of doctors. In practice, most dive schools ask you to complete the form yourself and, if you don't admit to any of the diving-related health problems (such as dizzy spells or a history of drug or alcohol abuse), you will be allowed to dive. Some doctors in Male', and also on Bandos resort, can give you the diving medical check up if required.

## Insurance

In addition to normal travel insurance, it's a very good idea to take out insurance which gives specific cover for diving, and which will pay for evacuation to a recompression facility and the cost of hyperbaric treatment in a chamber. Some dive operations insist on this insurance. The most commonly recommended policy is through DAN (Divers Alert Network), which can be contacted through most dive shops and clubs.

## Certificates

When you complete an open-water course, you receive a certificate that is recognised by diving operators all over the world. Certificates in the Maldives are generally issued by PADI, the largest and the best-known organisation, but certificates from CMAS, SSI, the National Association of Underwater Instructors (NAUI), and a number of other organisations are quite acceptable.

## Safety Guidelines

In the Maldives the dive base will ensure you are aware of the following points to ensure a safe and enjoyable experience, whether scuba diving, skin diving or snorkelling:

- If you are scuba diving, you must possess a current diving certification card from a recognised scuba diving instructional agency. The resort dive base will check your card and provide training if you need it. A check dive is often required.
- Obtain reliable information about physical and environmental conditions at the dive site. The dive base will always provide this.
- Be aware of local laws, regulations and etiquette about marine life and the environment. (See Marine Environment Protection later in this special section.)
- Dive only at sites within your realm of experience.
- Be aware that underwater conditions vary significantly from one region, or even site, to another. Seasonal changes can significantly alter any site and dive conditions. These differences influence the way divers dress for a dive and what diving techniques they use.

The following laws apply to recreational diving in the Maldives, and divemasters must enforce them:

- Maximum depth: 30m.
- Maximum time: 6 minutes.
- No decompression dives.
- Each diver must carry a dive computer.
- Obligatory 3-minute safety stop at 5m.
- Last dive no later than 12 hours before a flight.

MICHAEL AW

## Equipment

Dive schools in the Maldives can rent out all diving gear, but most divers prefer to have at least some of their own equipment. It's best to have your own mask, snorkel and fins, which you can also use just for snorkelling. The tank and weight belt are always included in the cost of a dive, so you don't need to bring them – sealed tanks are prohibited on aircraft anyway, and you'd be crazy to carry lead weights. The main pieces of diving equipment to bring with you are:

**Wet suit** The water may be warm (27°C to 30°C) but a wet suit is still necessary for comfortable diving. A 3mm suit, or a Lycra one, should be adequate, but 5mm is preferable if you want to go deep or dive more than once per day. Some resorts don't have a good selection of wet suits for rental, and it's important that it fits well, so this is a good item to bring if you can. Renting a suit will cost about US$5 per day.
**Regulator** Many divers have their own regulator, with which they are familiar and confident, and a 'reg' is not cumbersome to carry. Rental will cost from US$3 to US$7 per dive.
**Buoyancy Control Device (BCD)** These are readily available for rent, at US$3 to US$7 per dive, but bring your own if possible.
**Depth gauge, tank pressure gauge & timer** These are usually available too, but if you have them, bring them.
**Dive computer** Now generally preferred over dive tables, these devices are available for rent, from US$4 to US$7 per dive.
**Log book** You'll need this to indicate to dive masters your level of experience, and to record your latest dives.

Other items you might need include an underwater torch (especially for cave and night dives), waterproof camera, compass and safety buoy, most of which are available for rental. Some things you won't need are a spear gun, which is prohibited, and diving gloves, which are discouraged since you're not supposed to touch anything anyway.

**Right:** Gliding over hard coral.

## Diving Costs

For qualified divers, the cost of diving varies a bit between resorts, and depends on whether you need to rent equipment and whether you get a multi-dive package. Generally, a very upmarket resort will have a more expensive dive program. A single dive, with only tank and weights supplied, runs from US$25 to US$40, but is generally around US$30 (night dives cost more). If you need to rent a regulator and a buoyancy control device (BCD) as well, a dive will be from US$32 to US$47. Sometimes the full equipment price includes mask, snorkel, fins, dive computer and pressure gauge, but they can cost extra. A package of 10 dives will cost from US$220 to US$295, or US$265 to US$355 with equipment rental. Other possibilities are five-, 12- and 15-dive packages, and packages that allow you as many dives as you want within a certain number of consecutive days. In addition to the dive cost, there is usually a charge for using a boat – US$12 for half a day, twice that for a full day. There may also be a service charge of 10% if diving is billed to your room.

Someone planning to do 10 dives in a week should budget around US$400 to US$500, or perhaps a little less if they bring all their own equipment, stay in a less expensive resort, and do the dives as a package.

## Reality Check

Though Maldivian waters are rich in marine life, and some sites are known habitats for certain animals such as whale sharks, manta rays, turtles or tuna, remember that these are wild creatures in a natural environment. There can be no guarantee that you will be able to see them at any given place and time. Dive masters despair of divers who become indignant when no mantas are found at Manta Point. The uncertainty is part of the thrill and one of the things that makes diving so rewarding.

## Fish

You don't have to be a hardcore diver to enjoy the rich marine life of the Maldives. You'll see an amazing variety just snorkelling, walking in the shallows, peering off the end of a jetty, or travelling anywhere by boat. The Common Fish of the Maldives colour isllustrations in this section will help you identify a few of the most colourful and conspicuous varieties, but any keen observer will spot many more, and will find whole books and several large wall charts devoted to the subject. Some smaller charts are printed on plastic, so you can take them with you into the water. Identifying fish species can be surprisingly difficult, as you try to recall the details of some weird creature which doesn't look exactly like anything in the books. A point to remember is that even within the same species, colour and patterning can vary greatly over a fish's life cycle, and also according to gender.

*[Continued from page 58]*

**Decompression Sickness** This is a very serious condition usually, though not always, associated with diver error. The most common symptoms are unusual fatigue or weakness; skin itch; pain in the arms, legs (joints or mid-limb) or torso; dizziness and vertigo; local numbness, tingling or paralysis; and shortness of breath. Signs may also include a blotchy skin rash, a tendency to favour an arm or a leg, staggering, coughing spasms, collapse or unconsciousness. These symptoms and signs can occur individually, or a number of them can appear at one time.

The most common causes of decompression sickness (or 'the bends' as it is commonly known) are diving too deep, staying at depth for too long, or ascending too quickly. This results in nitrogen coming out of solution in the blood and forming bubbles, most commonly in the bones and particularly in the joints or in weak spots such as healed fracture sites.

There are other factors which have been shown to have a causal effect in decompression sickness, including excess body fat; heavy exertion prior to, during and after diving; injuries and illness; dehydration; alcohol; cold water, hot showers or baths after diving; carbon dioxide increase (eg, through smoking); and age.

Avoid flying after diving, as it causes nitrogen to come out of the blood even faster than it would at sea level. It's not a good idea to dive within 24 hours before a flight, and certainly not within 12 hours. Low altitude flights, like a helicopter or seaplane transfer to the airport, may be just as dangerous because the aircraft are not pressurised, though the flights are usually of short duration. Opinions vary as to the risks and the time required to minimise them – a lot depends on the frequency, depth and duration of dives over several days before the flight. Seek the advice of an instructor when planning the dives during the final few days of your stay, and try to finish up with shallow dives.

Even if you take all the necessary precautions, there is no guarantee that you will not be hit by the bends. All divers have a responsibility to be aware of anything unusual about their own condition, and that of their diving buddy, after a dive.

The only treatment for decompression sickness is to put the patient into a recompression chamber. There are several in the Maldives, but the best place is the clinic at Bandos Island Resort, near Male', which has a trained hyperbaric specialist available. A new chamber is being installed at Kuramathi, which will also have qualified staff and be available, at a price, to those who need it. A chamber provides an artificial means of putting a person back under pressure similar to, or often greater than, that of the depth at which they were diving so the nitrogen bubbles can be reabsorbed. The time required in the chamber is usually three to eight hours. The treatment is usually effective, with the main problem being caused by delay in getting the patient to the chamber. If you think that you, or anyone else you are diving with, are suffering from the bends, get to a recompression chamber as soon as possible.

**Ear Problems** Many divers experience pain in the ears after diving, which is commonly caused by failure of the ears to compensate properly for changes in pressure. The problem will usually fix itself, but injuries are often caused when people try to treat themselves by poking cotton buds or other objects into the ear.

**Sharks** Sharks are a negligible danger if they are not provoked. There are many types of shark in the Maldives, but they all have plentiful supplies of their natural food, which they find far tastier and more conveniently bite-sized than humans. Some people have been injured when feeding sharks by hand, and this practice is now banned. Apart from the obvious dangers, it can put future divers at risk because sharks will approach them seeking a handout, sometimes aggressively.

**Fish Bites** Lots of fish will bite if you put your fingers in their mouths. Many scuba divers used to find this out hand-feeding fish, which is strongly discouraged. A bite from most small fish is nothing more than a playful nip, but stingrays, moray eels and many other large fish can give painful bites and cause injuries. You are unlikely to be bitten if you follow the rules of not feeding or touching any fish.

**Butterfly Cod** These fish are closely related to the stonefish and have a series of poisonous spines down their back. The butterfly cod, also known as the lionfish or firefish, is an incredibly beautiful and slow-moving creature – it knows it's deadly and doesn't worry about possible enemies. Even brushing against the spines can be painful, but a stab from them could be fatal. Fortunately it's hard to miss a butterfly cod so, unless you step on one or deliberately hit one, the danger is remote.

**Stings** All coral is poisonous to some extent and brushing against fire coral or the feathery hydroid can give you a painful sting and an itchy rash which takes a long time to heal. Anemones are also poisonous and putting your arm into one can give you a painful sting.

## Women's Health
**Gynaecological Problems** Antibiotic use, synthetic underwear, sweating and contraceptive pills can lead to fungal vaginal infections, especially when travelling in hot climates. Thrush or vaginal candidiasis is characterised by a rash, itch and discharge. Nystatin, miconazole or clotrimazole pessaries are the usual treatment, but some people use a more traditional remedy involving vinegar or lemon juice douches, or yoghurt. Maintaining good personal hygiene and wearing loose-fitting clothes and cotton underwear may help prevent these infections.

Sexually transmitted diseases are a major cause of vaginal problems. Symptoms include a smelly discharge, painful intercourse and sometimes a burning sensation when urinating. Medical attention should be sought and male sexual partners must also be treated. For more details see the section on Sexually Transmitted Diseases earlier in this section. Besides abstinence, the best thing is to practise safer sex using condoms.

**Pregnancy** Vaccinations normally used to prevent serious diseases are not advisable during pregnancy (eg, yellow fever). In addition, some diseases are much more serious for the mother (and may increase the risk of a stillborn child) in pregnancy (eg, malaria).

Most miscarriages occur during the first three months of pregnancy. Miscarriage is not uncommon and can occasionally lead to severe bleeding. The last three months should also be spent within reasonable distance of good medical care. A baby born as early as 24 weeks stands a chance of survival, but only in a good modern hospital. Pregnant women should avoid all unnecessary medication, although vaccinations and malarial prophylactics should still be taken where needed. Additional care should be taken to prevent illness and particular attention should be paid to diet and nutrition. Alcohol and nicotine, for example, should be avoided.

## WOMEN TRAVELLERS
It is almost impossible for a woman (or anyone else for that matter) to travel alone – they will almost invariably need to be accompanied by a Maldivian. Women who do travel outside resorts to local islands should be sensitive to local customs which would usually mean not entering male bastions like a tea shop. However, it is very unlikely that a foreign woman would be harassed or feel threatened on a local island. They are very closed, small communities and the fact that a woman would be associated with a local sponsor should give a high level of security.

Culturally, resorts are European enclaves and visiting women will not have to make too many adjustments. You should be aware, however, that topless bathing and nudity are strictly forbidden in the Maldives, and both the individual and the resort can be fined heavily if this law is broken. Even very brief bikinis, however, seem to be perfectly acceptable in resorts.

In Male' and the inhabited islands visited by tourists, reasonably modest dress is required – shorts should cover the thighs and shirts should not be too low cut. In more out-of-the-way parts of the country, slightly more conservative dress may be in order.

## Attitudes Towards Women

Officially, the status of women is not inferior, and the Maldives has been ruled by women several times (though not in the last few centuries). Women can and do vote, run for public office and have equal rights in law to education, employment and property. They cannot, however, become president of the republic. Nevertheless, traditional Maldivian society has clearly delineated gender roles and expectations, and is strongly influenced by Islamic teachings.

In the villages, men build the boats, go out fishing and do the trading, while women process the fish, gather the coconuts, prepare the food and look after children. Girls are expected to do more domestic work, which disadvantages their education. They marry young and have children early. The average age of marriage is about 17 for females, but 21 or 22 for males. Historically, men were away for long periods, fishing, trading or working on other islands. Women stayed on their home island with the extended family and took care of everything else. These days there may be a similar pattern, with men working in tourist resorts for 11 months of the year, but even when the men are home, women make all the important family decisions.

Under Islamic law, men are responsible for their female relatives, so a son inherits twice as much of a family estate as a daughter. A man must ask a woman's parents for permission to marry her, but the woman must also agree. A married woman retains her name and can acquire her own property, but she has fewer rights if the marriage ends. In Maldivian custom, a husband can divorce his wife simply by telling her so, but if a woman wants a divorce, she must have the husband's consent or go through a difficult administrative procedure. The woman keeps half of their joint property, plus whatever she owns personally, and theoretically the man must pay for the maintenance of his children. In practice, the amount required for maintenance is only Rf 280 per month and may not always be paid, leaving the mother and children in a difficult position.

It is not at all a Muslim-fundamentalist society and women in the capital, particularly women from higher status families, are less likely to conform to traditional norms. Women hold responsible positions in government and business, and serve in the armed forces. No-one is required to wear a veil, though many wear a headscarf. Married women usually dress modestly, covering their legs and arms, but young women in Male' are often bare headed, use make-up and even wear fashionably short skirts. Educated women in particular have a feminist consciousness and are working to improve the general status and welfare of women in the country. They tend not to be confrontational, but have been known to enter male bastions like tea shops to make a point.

## Organisations

Apart from the government Department of Women's Affairs, there are several organisations in Male' which visiting women could contact. All of them can be found in the phone book or by asking around, and all have catchy English acronyms!

**FASHAN** – Foundation for the Advancement of Self Help in Attaining Needs
**MARDOW** – Maldivian Association for Research and Development of Women
**SHE** – Society for Health Education

## GAY & LESBIAN TRAVELLERS

There doesn't seem to be any restriction on what tourists do in resorts in private, but it's unlawful for Maldivians to engage in just about any form of extramarital sex. A gay couple should have no problem booking a resort room with a double bed but public displays of affection may be frowned upon. Use your own discretion. None of the resorts makes any appeal to the gay market or has any noticeable gay scene.

## DISABLED TRAVELLERS

At Male' International Airport, passengers must use steps to get on and off planes, so contact the airline you'll be using to find out what arrangements can be made. The arrivals area is all at ground level, but special arrangements may need to be made for departure, which usually involves going up and down stairs.

Transfers to nearby resorts are by dhoni or speedboat and a person in a wheelchair or with limited mobility will need assistance – a dhoni is probably more accessible than most speedboats. Transfer to more distant resorts is often by seaplanes, which are difficult to access, so it would be better to choose a resort that you can reach by boat.

Most resorts are wheelchair friendly, with few steps, ground-level rooms and reasonably smooth paths to beaches, boat jetties and all public areas. There's no traffic and staff will be on hand to assist disabled guests. Some of the newer resorts have split-level designs and elevated lobbies and bars, but in the more rustic ones, soft sand floors and paths will be a challenge to wheelchairs. If you narrow your options down to a couple of resorts, you can call them directly and ask about the layout. It's usually a good idea for guests to advise the tour agency of any special needs, but if you want to find out about specific facilities, it's best to contact the resort itself.

Quite a few resort activities are potentially suitable for disabled guests, apart from the very popular sitting-on-a-beach-doing-nothing. Fishing trips and excursions to inhabited islands should be easy, but uninhabited islands may be more difficult to disembark on. Catamaran sailing and canoeing are possibilities, especially if you've had experience in these activities. Anyone who can swim will be able to enjoy snorkelling. Scuba diving is a possibility – in the USA, the Professional Association of Diving Instructors (PADI) has a disabled divers group and has developed training standards, so PADI may be a good starting point. A good resort dive school should be able to arrange a special course or program for any group of four or more people with a similar disability.

No dogs are permitted in the Maldives, so it's not a destination for anyone dependent on a guide dog.

## SENIOR TRAVELLERS

Most resorts have a good mix of age groups and some guests are well over retirement age. Once you arrive, there are no special deals or discounts for senior citizens, but when you book your holiday be on the lookout for any tour company promotions aimed at the older market.

## TRAVEL WITH CHILDREN

Younger children will enjoy a couple of weeks on a Maldivian resort island, particularly if they like playing in the water and on the beach. Resorts offer a very safe environment with shallow water, virtually no traffic, no cliffs and no unsavoury characters – the only people on the island will be resort staff or guests. Though exotic cuisine is sometimes on the menu, there are always some pretty standard Western-style dishes that kids will find OK.

Older children and teenagers could find a resort a little confining after a few days and they may get bored. Canoeing and fishing trips may provide some diversion, while a course in sailing or windsurfing could be a great way to spend a holiday. Some resorts have table tennis, tennis, volleyball or badminton. Parents should allow an extra few hundred dollars for these activities. The minimum age for scuba diving is 16 years, but some resorts offer a 'bubble blowers' introduction for younger kids.

Families would probably be better on a larger resort on one of the bigger islands, where children will have more space to explore and will be more likely to find other kids their own age. A few resorts boast a children's playground, and some offer childcare, but none are making a major pitch for the family market. Nevertheless, most resorts are very child-friendly, and will probably be able to arrange a baby-sitter in the evening. Children sharing a room with their parents are charged as a supplement. For children two years and younger, usually just the US$6 bed tax is payable. From two to 12 years, the child supplement with full board will be from US$15 to US$30 in most low to midprice resorts, but much more in expensive resorts. Transfers from the airport are charged at half the adult rate.

The main danger is sunburn, so bring sun hats and plenty of sun block. Lycra swim shirts are an excellent idea – they can be worn on the beach and in the water and block out most UV radiation. Children's swim shoes are also available, like little wet-suit boots, which protect the feet when running in the water or round the island. It's best to bring a kid-sized mask, snorkel and fins – they may be available in a resort, but it's cheaper to have your own and you'll be sure they fit. Also bring some children's games, books and beach toys.

For more advice on travelling with children, pick up *Travel with Children* by Maureen Wheeler, Lonely Planet Publications, 1995.

## USEFUL ORGANISATIONS
For serious students of Maldivian history and culture, the National Council for Linguistic & Historical Research, on Sosun Magu, might be useful.

The British Voluntary Service Overseas (VSO) office (☎ 323167) is in the centre of Male' near Majeedi Magu. Volunteers, based in Male' and in the outer atolls, include teachers, health professionals, agricultural advisers and so on. It's not their job to help foreign visitors, but some have a very good knowledge of what's going on in the country and are happy to talk about it. If you want to visit, it's best to telephone first.

United Nations' agencies include the UNDP (UN Development Program; ☎ 324501), which provides aid to the agriculture, fishing and craft industries, and also UNICEF and WHO.

## DANGERS & ANNOYANCES
Apart from a few marine dangers (see the Health section earlier in this chapter), and any risks associated with diving, surfing or other activities, the Maldives is a particularly safe destination.

Don't touch coral, shells or fish. Beware of the possibility of strong currents and don't swim too far out from an island's fringing reef, or too far from a boat on a snorkelling trip. Don't try surfing unless you know where you are and what you're doing – surf breaks over coral reefs and you could be badly grazed, or even knocked out and drowned.

## Coconuts
If you don't think this is serious, just imagine a 2kg coconut falling 15m onto your head. They don't fall often, and you'd have to be unlucky to be underneath one, but it does happen. It's easy to see if a tree is laden with big heavy coconuts, and they are more likely to fall in windy weather.

## Crime
Crimes of violence are very unusual, but there are burglaries and theft in the capital – bicycle theft is common.

There are very few cases of theft from resort rooms. Nevertheless, it's wise to deposit your valuables with the resort office, to keep your room locked and not leave cash lying around.

## EMERGENCIES
If there's an emergency in a resort, call the duty manager or go to the front desk. See the Male' chapter for emergency phone numbers there.

## LEGAL MATTERS
With a scattered island population and limited resources, the Maldivian authorities rely heavily on delegation. Apart from the police and the military, there is a chief on every atoll and island who must keep an eye on what is happening, report to the central government and be responsible for the actions of local people.

If, for example, a private yacht appears in an atoll, the local fishermen will see it and report it to the village chief. The village chief reports to the atoll chief and the atoll chief reports to the capital. The authorities in the capital will know if the yacht has an Inter-Atoll Travel Permit and whether the permit includes that atoll. They can contact the yacht by radio, or send an aircraft or a boat to watch it or intercept it.

Every foreigner in the country has, in effect, a Maldivian minder who is responsible for him or her. Resorts are responsible for their guests and for what happens on their island. If a guest goes swimming in the nude, the resort can be fined as well as the visitor. If a foreigner lands illegally on an island, the skipper or owner of the boat will be held responsible. If a diver in the outer atolls damages a reef or spears a fish, the operator of the safari boat is liable.

## Police & Military

The Maldives police consists of a civilian and a military force. The latter, the National Security Service (NSS), is involved in guarding the president, airport and other sensitive subjects. They wear olive green camouflage uniforms and berets, and sometimes have Kalashnikov AK47s and M16s, but they maintain a low profile and do not have much to do with visitors.

The civilian police are efficient but unobtrusive. The only uniform apparent on many is a light blue shirt. Unless there's a chevron or two on the sleeve, you can't tell if you're looking at a police officer.

The Maldivian justice system reflects Islamic values and the authorities' desire to prevent activities which may 'jeopardise the peace and harmony prevailing in the country'. Penalties can be both merciful and severe at the same time – there is no summary execution, no chopping off the hands of thieves and no flogging people for drinking whisky. The most common punishments are to put offenders under house arrest or banish them to an island a long way from their home. Banishment to an idyllic island may not seem harsh, but for Maldivians it is a devastating punishment since they are taken away from their families and friends, often for many years (though many are given a reprieve after two years). A house arrest can also be imposed for many years, though it may be just for a few weeks, to prevent someone causing trouble at a certain time.

## Drugs

Illicit drugs are not widespread, and penalties are heavy. 'Brown sugar', a semirefined form of heroin, has become a problem amongst some young people in the capital, and is believed to have increased the number of thefts and burglaries.

The baggage of arriving passengers is X-rayed and searched – mainly for alcohol, but drugs will not be overlooked. Visitors are

### Brought to Justice

One famous (or infamous) case of crime and punishment in the Maldives involved a German traveller who, in 1976, brutally murdered his French girlfriend in a Male' guesthouse. He was convicted in a Maldivian court, and banished for life to an island in the northern atolls. He resigned himself to life on the island, and resisted all attempts by the German government to have him extradited to serve his sentence at home. Some years later he converted to Islam, which is regarded as a total renunciation of one's previous life. He was then pardoned by the Maldivian government, married a local woman, and still lives on the same island with his wife and two children. (The US magazine *New Look* carried a feature on him in the April 1986 edition.)

unlikely to encounter drugs in any resort, and the resort management would be obliged to report any instance of drug use to the authorities. Anyone offering to sell drugs is more likely to be an informant or an undercover cop than a bona fide drug dealer.

## Alcohol

Alcohol is illegal outside resorts. This means, for example, that you're not allowed to take a can of beer out on a boat trip. Some foreign residents in the capital have a liquor permit, which entitles them to a limited amount per month, but they're not allowed to consume it outside their home, and they're not allowed to give it to anyone else. Strictly speaking, they can't even ask someone over for a drink.

## BUSINESS HOURS

Government offices are open Sunday to Thursday from 7.30 am to 2 pm. During Ramadan, hours are from 8 am to 2.30 pm.

Business hours vary. In Male' the shops open between 7.30 and 9 am and close between 9 and 11 pm, except on Friday when they open at 1.30 pm. When prayer is called doors close for about 15 minutes. The streets are pretty quiet in the middle of the day, from about 1 to 3 pm, and also around the time of the last two prayer calls, between 6 and 8 pm.

Some tea shops open very early, while others close very late – there's usually something open. During Ramadan the places where locals go will probably not be open during daylight hours, but will really bustle after dark.

## PUBLIC HOLIDAYS & SPECIAL EVENTS

Most holidays are based on the Islamic lunar calendar and the dates vary from year to year.

**Ramadan** Known as Ramazan or *roarda mas* in the Maldives, the Islamic month of fasting is an important religious occasion which starts on a new moon and continues for 28 days. Expected starting dates for the next few years are 28 November 2000, 17 November 2001, 6 November 2002, 27 October 2003.

**Kuda Id** Also called Id-ul-Fitr, this occurs at the end of Ramadan, with the sighting of the new moon, and is celebrated with a feast.

**Bodu Id** The Festival of the sacrifice, 66 days after the end of Ramadan, is the time when many Muslims begin the pilgrimage *(haj)* to Mecca.

**National Day** A major event celebrating the day Mohammed Thakurufaanu and his men overthrew the Portuguese on Male' in 1578, it is celebrated on the first day of the third month of the lunar calendar.

**Prophet's Birthday** The birthday of the Prophet Mohammed is celebrated with three days of eating and merriment. The dates are: 15 June 2000, 4 June 2001, 25 May 2002, 14 May 2003.

**Huravee Day** The day the Malabars of India were kicked out by Sultan Hassan Izzuddeen after their brief occupation in 1752.

**Martyr's Day** Commemorates the death of Sultan Ali VI at the hands of the Portuguese in 1558.

Fixed holiday dates are:

**New Year's Day** 1 January

**Independence Day** 26 July – the day the British protectorate ended.

**Victory Day** 3 November – celebrates the victory over the Sri Lankan mercenaries who tried to overthrow the Maldivian government in 1988.

**Republic Day** 11 November – commemorates the second (current) republic, founded in 1968. Celebrated in Male' with lots of pomp, brass bands and parades. Sometimes the following day is also a holiday.

**Fisheries Day** 10 December – recognises the importance of the fishing industry in Malidivian society and economy.

## ACTIVITIES

Though many dream of a tropical island holiday where they do nothing but laze on the beach, lots of visitors to the Maldives are keen to pursue water sports, especially scuba diving for which the islands are justly renowned. Even snorkelling around the reefs is a magical experience, as well as being less demanding and a lot less expensive. One activity you can't try is spearfishing, which is not permitted anywhere in the country.

Sailing and windsurfing are available at all resorts, while motorised water sports like water-skiing and parasailing are offered at some of the bigger ones. There are a few areas with good surf, and fishing is available everywhere. Some resorts have tennis, badminton or squash courts, and most will have beach volleyball. The bigger islands have football (soccer) fields where enthusiastic staff teams regularly trounce the guests.

Most resorts also offer 'island hopping' trips, and those close to the capital offer excursions to Male'.

### Sailing

Most resorts have catamarans for rent and will give lessons for beginners, but it's quite expensive – around US$25 per hour for rental, US$40 with lessons. It's cheaper by the day or week, but for a lot of sailing you should budget US$250 per week. Even if you don't need it, you may have to do at least one lesson to convince the staff you're a safe sailor. The boats are usually Hobie Cats or Top Cats, with fibreglass hulls and two sails – no spinnakers.

If you're thinking of cruising around in your own yacht, see the Getting Around chapter for more information.

### Windsurfing

Most resorts offer windsurfers for rent, as well as windsurfing lessons, but the Maldives is not an ideal windsurfing destination. The lagoons around most resort islands are shallow and sheltered, and though this usually makes for a good beginners area, falling off a windsurfer in shallow water over a coral reef can be painful, or even dangerous.

Some of the lagoons are large enough for experienced windsurfers to enjoy, but winds are usually well under 15 knots so it's not super challenging. Mistral, the French windsurfer manufacturer, has a windsurfing school at Reethi Rah resort, in north Male' Atoll. Other resorts that are particularly suitable for windsurfing include Kuramathi and Reethi Beach.

Windsurfer rental usually costs between US$12 and US$18 per hour, depending on the standard of the resort, but it's much cheaper if you take it for a longer period – maybe US$180 for unlimited use for a week. Private lessons can be as much as US$45 per hour, but a 10-hour course, at around US$170, is better value.

## Surfing

There's some great surf in the Maldives, though there are only a small number of accessible breaks in the tourist zone and they only work from March to November. Surfers have a choice of basing themselves at a resort and taking a boat to nearby breaks, or arranging a live-aboard safari cruise which will take them to less accessible areas. In either case, make arrangements in advance with a reputable surf travel operator who knows the area well. The Maldives is definitely not the sort of place where a surfer can just turn up and head for the waves.

The period of the south-west monsoon (May to November) generates the best waves, but March and April are also good and have the best weather. June can have bad weather and storms, and is not great for boat trips, but it is also a time for big swells. Most of the surfing season is a quiet time for Maldivian resorts, so surfers can come when accommodation is cheaper. The best breaks occur on the outer reefs on the southeast sides of the atolls, but only where a gap in the reef allows the waves to wrap around.

Surfing in the Maldives was pioneered by Tony Hussein (aka Tony Hinde), a Sydney surfer who was shipwrecked in the Maldives in the early 1970s. Before the first tourist resorts were opened, he discovered, surfed and named all the main breaks, and had them all to himself for many years. All of the recog-

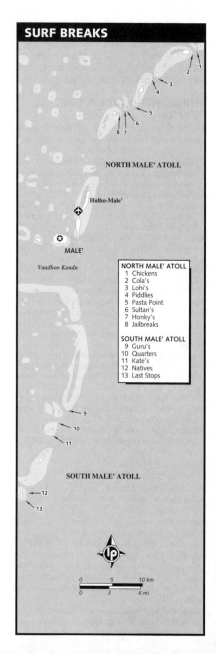

**SURF BREAKS**

NORTH MALE' ATOLL

Hulhu-Male'

MALE'

Vaadhoo Kandu

**NORTH MALE' ATOLL**
1 Chickens
2 Cola's
3 Lohi's
4 Piddlies
5 Pasta Point
6 Sultan's
7 Honky's
8 Jailbreaks

**SOUTH MALE' ATOLL**
9 Guru's
10 Quarters
11 Kate's
12 Natives
13 Last Stops

SOUTH MALE' ATOLL

0      5      10 km
0      3      6 mi

nised and reliable breaks in the tourism zone are in North Male' and South Male' atolls.

**North Male' Atoll** This is where the best and most established breaks are, though working out which will be best on a given day requires some local knowledge. These are listed from north to south.

**Chickens** A left-hander which sections when small, but on a bigger swell and a higher tide it all comes together to make a long and satisfying wave. It's named for the old poultry farm onshore, not because of any reaction to the conditions here.

**Cola's** A heavy, hollow, shallow right-hander; when it's big, it's one of the best breaks in the area. This is a very thick wave breaking hard over a shallow reef, so it's definitely for experienced, gutsy surfers only. Named for the Coca-Cola factory nearby on the island of Thulusdhoo, it's also called Cokes.

**Lohi's** A left-hander which usually breaks in two sections, but with a big enough swell and a high enough tide the sections link up. You can paddle out to this break from the resort island of Lohifushi.

**Piddlies** A slow, mellow, mushy right-hander; a good Malibu wave; also called Ninja's because of its appeal to Japanese surfers.

**Pasta Point** A perfect left which works like clockwork on all tides. There's a long outside wall at the take-off point, jacking into a bowling section called the 'macaroni bowl'. On big days the break continues to another section called 'lock jaws' which grinds into very shallow water over the reef. It's easily reached from the shore at Tari Village resort, whose guests have exclusive use of this break. Tari used to be an all-Italian resort (hence the name of the break), but it now has a more varied clientele and menu.

**Sultan's** This is a classic right-hand break, and the bigger the swell, the better it works. A steep outside peak leads to a super-fast wall and then an inside section which throws right out, and tubes on every wave.

**Honky's** During its season, this is the best wave in the Maldives. It's a super long, wally left-hander that wraps nearly 90° and can nearly double in size by the end section.

**Jailbreaks** A right-hander that works best with a big swell, when the three sections combine to make a single, long, perfect wave. The catch is that there is a prison on the island, and for years the surrounding waters were absolutely off-limits for security reasons. Recently it has been possible to surf the break with a special permit, which is a hassle to obtain independently.

**South Male' Atoll** There are a few breaks in South Male' Atoll, but they are smaller than those in North Male' Atoll and generally more fickle. It will be harder here to find a boatman who really knows the surf scene.

**Guru's** A nice little left off the island of Gulhi; it can get good sometimes.

**Quarters** Another small right-hander, rarely more than a metre.

**Kate's** A small left-hander, rarely more than a metre.

**Natives** A small right-hander, rarely more than a metre.

**Last Stops** This is a bowly right-hander breaking over a channel reef. It's a protected marine area, and can get very strong currents when the tides are running.

**Outer Atolls** Looking at a map, you might think that the Maldives would have hundreds of surf breaks around its many islands and atolls. In fact, there are only a few areas with a combination of the right reef topography and the right orientation in relation to swell and wind direction. These are all in the southern atolls, where named breaks include Beacons (right), Castaways (right), Harbours (right), Love Charms (left), Tigers (left) and Two Ways (left and right). They're all outside the tourist zone and can only be accessed with permits from Atolls Administration. The only feasible way to surf them is with a safari boat, or a combination of a domestic flight and safari boat, arranged through one of the surfing tour operators. These breaks work on specific swell and wind conditions, so an experienced outer atoll guide is essential.

**Resort-Based Surfing** The best and most accessible surf breaks are in the south-eastern part of North Male' Atoll, where there are half a dozen resorts that can access them by a short boat ride. The problem is that boat charters from the resorts can be quite expensive (boats are usually filled with divers happily paying US$50-plus per head), and most resorts don't have any boatmen who really know the surf spots.

Tari Village is the best and most popular resort for surfers – the reliable waves of

Pasta Point are just out the back door, while Sultan's and Honky's are close by. There are frequent boats to other breaks, and they have surf guides who know the area well. Atoll Adventures surfing packages to Tari, which include unlimited boat trips and guides, can be booked through some of the agents mentioned below. As part of the package, they will apply on your behalf for a permit allowing you to surf Jailbreaks – subject to official approval the permit should be ready when you arrive.

Lohifushi, a few kilometres north-east of Tari, is a bigger, more expensive resort with more facilities, but it's not as well set up for surfers. Its surf break is a fair hike from the rooms, and to surf anywhere else you need to book a boat the day before (US$8 per person for three hours, minimum four persons), though the boatmen are not really surf guides, and the boats aren't always punctual. The main innovation for the surfing market is a makeshift bar overlooking the surf break at the south end of the island. Kanifinolhu is another resort island which has a small surf break, but doesn't have any knowledgable surf guides or any surfing program.

**Surfing Safaris** While there are many possibilities for chartering a safari boat in the Maldives, surfers wanting to explore the outer atolls would be well advised to arrange their trip in advance through a reputable surf travel agent. Agents in Male' may promise all kinds of things, but very few safari boat operators have a specialised knowledge of surfing and many have little experience working in the outer atolls. Some operators offer surfing 'surfaris' which in fact just cruise around North Male' Atoll, visiting breaks that are quite accessible from resorts in the area.

Safari boats used by surfers should have guides with a good knowledge of surfing conditions, and they will give you the best chance of getting to the right place at the right time. They should also have a good relationship with Atolls Administration, so that they can get the necessary permits before you arrive. It's important that the safari operator has an understanding of the sensitivities of cruising in the outer atolls, because

attempts to sneak surfs in unauthorised areas, inappropriate behaviour near inhabited islands, or any other breach of regulations or local customs may result in more severe restrictions on surfers in the future.

You need at least six people to make a safari boat affordable; the surfing specialists should be able to put together the necessary numbers. Don't book on to a safari which is primarily for diving or cruising. Allow at least two weeks for the trip or you may spend most of your time chugging to and from the outer atolls. A 14-day surfari will cost from US$1950 per person, not including airfares.

If you had your own yacht, you could theoretically cruise around looking for surf, but in practice this would not be a good option. Apart from the need for local knowledge and special permits, the Maldives is a difficult and dangerous place to cruise in any boat that draws more than a metre or so, and high fees are charged for boats staying more than about a week in Maldivian waters.

**Surf Travel Operators** The following agents specialise in surf travel and book tours and safaris to the Maldives.

**Atoll Travel** (☎ 1800-622310, 03-5682 1088, fax 03-5682 1202, **@** atolltvl@onaustralia.com.au) Box 205, Foster, Victoria 3960, Australia. Australian and international agent for Atoll Adventures. It offers premium surfing safari tours in Male' Atoll (from US$800 for a seven-day trip, including all meals; airfares extra) and to the outer atolls (around US$2000 for a 14-day trip, including all meals, internal airfares, boat transport and accommodation), as well as surfing packages to Tari Village resort (from US$900 per surfer for seven nights with full board, drinking water and unlimited boat access to all the nearby breaks; international airfares extra), and Lohifushi. Web site: www.users.bigpond .com/atolltvl

**Surf Travel Company** (☎ 02-9527 4722, fax 02-9527 4522) 25 Cronulla Plaza, Cronulla Beach, NSW 2230, Australia. A well-known surf travel operator offering tours to anywhere with waves; it books surfers into Lohifushi resort (from US$60 per person day, twin share in low season) and does boat based tours in North and South Male' Atolls (from US$660 per person for a seven night trip). Web site: www .surftravel.com

Waterways Travel (☎ 1800-928 3757, 818-376 0341, fax 818-376 0353) 15145 Califa St, Van Nuys, CA 91411, USA. A well-run agency that does surfing tours to many destinations; US agent for Atoll Adventures surfing safaris and packages to Tari Village. Web site: www .waterways.com

World Surfaris (☎ 1800-611 163, 07-3861 1163, fax 07-3861 1165) Box 91, Wilston, Queensland 4051, Australia. Offering tours to various surfing destinations, it books surfers into Lohifushi resort and also does boat-based trips in the inner atolls, and offers a limited number of 8-day outer atoll surfaris. Web site: www .worldsurfaris.com

## Island Hopping

Every resort offers guests the opportunity to visit some of the nearby islands, usually on a half- or full-day 'island-hopping' trip. In general, a full-day trip will include a visit to a fishing village on an inhabited island, an uninhabited island for snorkelling and a barbecue lunch, and then another resort island where you can have a drink and enjoy the facilities. Costs vary, usually in proportion to the classiness of the resort you're staying at, but are generally between US$35 and US$50 (including lunch). Half-day trips usually just go to a fishing village and an uninhabited island for snorkelling, and cost around US$20.

Though a visit to a village on an inhabited island should be a good chance to see the local way of life, many of the islands visited by tourists have a slew of souvenir shops, and it's very hard to get away from these on the short stop allowed by an island-hopping tour. Moreover, the tours usually visit the island in the middle of the day, when most sensible Maldivians are resting inside or in the shade, so the 'inhabited' island may seem to be pretty much deserted.

As the tourist boat arrives at the jetty, there is a scurry of activity as every second or third house along the main street is converted into a shop selling Balinese T-shirts, Sri Lankan wooden elephants, seashells and coral products to the tourists. If you look hard you will find some locally made handcrafts, especially the lacquer work. There's not as big a selection as you'll find in

Male', but if you haggle gently, the prices can be lower on these islands (see the Things to Buy section later in this chapter).

If you want to see more than this, try to get a trip that will stop longer at the village and get well away from the souvenir shops. You'll probably be accompanied by a souvenir seller, but make it clear that you're more interested in looking around. Look along the waterside for a dhoni under construction and try to find the village office, the school and the mosque. If your resort is close to an inhabited island, you can usually charter a dhoni to take you on a special trip – this is much better than arriving with a group, and you have more time to look around and meet people. Villagers can be reserved at first, but are friendly if you have a little time and a good disposition. Note that some inhabited islands do not allow tourists to visit at all, and in all cases the visitors must leave the island before 6 pm. Some resorts are so close to a village island that you could walk across at low tide, or cross by canoe or windsurfer, but this is usually forbidden.

## Fishing

Most resorts organise regular night fishing trips. About a dozen people go out in a dhoni for two or three hours with a handline each and a bucket full of bait. On a typical evening you would expect over 80% of them to catch something, and everyone would get a few nibbles. Apart from the numerous reef fish which go for the bait, you can catch barracuda and, if you're trolling, tuna may take an interest. Night fishing trips generally cost around US$15 per person, and you can usually arrange to have your catch prepared by the resort's chef.

Some resorts arrange traditional Maldivian fishing trips, which start early in the morning and return in the afternoon. Traditional fishing is for tuna, with a pole, line and unbaited hook. This is a much more authentic experience, but is only offered by a few resorts, including Kuredu and Asdu.

For the high rollers there's game fishing on the open sea between the atolls with a fast modern boat and some specialised equipment. It's an expensive activity, around

US$350 for four hours or US$500 for six hours, with a maximum of four to six fishing passengers to share the cost. The main species of game fish are yellowfin tuna, sailfish, blue and black marlin, barracuda, wahoo, jackfish, shark and dorado. The policy of the Maldives game fishing industry is 'tag and release', especially for bill-fish such as marlin and sailfish. If you plan to make any record-breaking catches, bring a camera along. Resorts that arrange game-fishing trips include Baros, Full Moon, Kurumba, Laguna and Nakatchafushi, which are all operated by the Universal group (☎ 322971, fax 322678), 38 Orchid Magu, Male'.

### Canoeing
Canoes, usually fibreglass touring kayaks, are available at most resorts from about US$8 per hour. It's a great way to look around the lagoon, but you're not usually permitted to take them on a long trip, or to another island. To some extent this is for safety reasons, in case you hit a reef or get caught in a channel, but it's mainly to restrict access to other islands.

At least one tour group has explored the possibility of extended sea-kayak trips through a number of atolls outside the tourist zone, but these would be very much special expeditions requiring approval from the Maldivian authorities.

### Tennis
Quite a few resorts have tennis courts, sometimes included in a package, but usually subject to an extra charge of US$5 to US$10 per hour, often more at night. Sometimes racquets and balls are rented separately, for an extra dollar or two per hour. If you're a keen player, bring your own balls and racquets.

### Other Activities
There are a number of other activities on offer at various resorts. Those involving power boats are pretty pricey. For example, there's the 'banana ride', where eight or so guests climb onto a giant, inflatable banana and scream as they are dragged around the lagoon by a speedboat. At US$10 to US$15 per round, it's not exactly a cheap thrill.

Water-skiing is available on some islands at around US$15 per quarter hour. Parasailing is about US$35 a go, and jetskis cost around US$25 for 15 minutes. Generally, the power boat activities don't seem to be enormously popular, which is a great blessing for those who want to sit quietly on a beach.

## COURSES
Diving courses are a particular attraction in the Maldives. The standard learn-to-dive course is an open water certificate, but the bigger dive centres offer a host of advanced and specialty courses, including advanced open water, divemaster, night diving and so on (see the Snorkelling & Diving special section for more information).

Courses in windsurfing and catamaran sailing are also available. A 10-hour course will cost a minimum of about US$150 for a windsurfer, US$220 for a catamaran.

## WORK
Work permits are issued, but they are mainly for tourism-related employment. This generally means people such as diving and other water-sport instructors, tourist company representatives and pilots. It is the employer's responsibility to obtain the permit. Find a job first, then let the employer sort out the work permits and visas. A number of volunteer aid workers are employed in Male' and outer islands. Contact the volunteer aid organisations in your home country if you have skills which may be needed and you want to contribute.

If you are intending to work in the Maldives, you must advise the immigration authorities of this when you enter the country. If you do organise work while in the Maldives, you will have to leave the country while the employer gets the permit, then re-enter.

## ACCOMMODATION
### Resorts
While all the resorts have certain similarities (nearly every one is on a small island with no other development), there is a range of types or styles. There are the very natural looking, rusticated resorts, which put their guests in

## Choosing a Resort

| resort name | atoll | tel | email/Web site | rooms/OWB[1] | recommended |
|---|---|---|---|---|---|
| Ari Beach | South Ari | 450513 | aribeach@dhivehinet.net.mv | 121/30 | Singles |
| Asdu Sun Island | North Male' | 445051 | info@asdu.com.mv | 30 | Good value |
| Athuruga | South Ari | 450508 | athadmin@dhivehinet.net.mv | 42 | Good value |
| Bandos Island | North Male' | 440088 | www.bandos.com | 225 | All |
| Banyan Tree | North Male' | 443147 | www.banyantree.com | 48 | Luxury |
| Club Med | North Male' | 322976 | www.clubmed.com | 150 | Luxury |
| Coco Palm | SM[2] | 230011 | cocopalm@dhivehinet.net.mv | 86 /14 | Luxury |
| Dhigufinolhu | South Male' | 443599 | www.dhigufinolhu.com | 97 | Diving |
| Ellaidhoo | North Ari | 450514 | mail@travelin-maldives.com | 50 | Diving |
| Embudu Village | South Male' | 444776 | embvil@dhivehinet.net.mv | 124 | Singles |
| Equator Village | Addu | 588019 | kaimoo@dhivehinet.net.mv | 60 | Good value |
| Eriyadu | North Male' | 444487 | eriyadu@aaa.com.mv | 46 | Good value |
| Fihalhohi | South Male' | 442903 | fiha@dhivehinet.net.mv | 128 | Families |
| Filitheyo | NN[3] | 460025 | fili@aaa.com.mv | 109/16 | Diving |
| Four Seasons | North Male' | 444888 | www.fourseasons.com | 106 | Luxury |
| Helengeli | North Male' | 444615 | engeli88@dhivehinet.net.mv | 50 | Diving |
| Hilton | South Ari | 450629 | www.hilton.com | 100/30 | Natural style |
| Ihuru Tourist | North Male' | 443502 | ihuru@dhivehinet.net.mv | 45 | Natural style |
| Kuramathi Island | North Ari | 450527 | www.unisurf.com | 277 | Families |
| Kuredu Island | Faadhippolhu | 230337 | info@kuredu.com | 300 | Families |
| Kurumba Village | North Male' | 442324 | www.unisurf.com | 180 | Business |
| Laguna Beach | South Male' | 445906 | www.unisurf.com | 115 | Families |
| Lily Beach | South Ari | 450013 | lilybech@dhivehinet.net.mv | 68/16 | All inclusive |
| Maayafushi | North Ari | 450588 | maaya@dhivehinet.net.mv | 60 | Diving |
| Makunudu Island | North Male' | 446464 | sunland@dhivehinet.net.mv | 36 | Natural style |
| Meeru Island | North Male' | 443157 | www.meeru.com | 227 | Families |
| Nakatchafushi | North Male' | 443847 | www.unisurf.com | 51 | Good value |
| Nika Hotel | North Ari | 450516 | nika-htl@dhivehinet.net.mv | 24 | Luxury |
| Paradise Island | North Male' | 440011 | paradise@dhivehinet.net.mv | 260 | All mod-cons |
| Reethi Beach | SM[2] | 232626 | info@reethibeach.com.mv | 100 | Natural style |
| Reethi Rah | North Male' | 441905 | rrresort@dhivehinet.net.mv | 50/10 | Good value |
| Rihiveli Beach | South Male' | 443731 | no email | 48 | Natural style |
| Sun Island | South Ari | 450088 | www.villahotels.com | 278/72 | All mod-cons |
| Taj Coral Reef | North Male' | 441948 | tajcr@dhivehinet.net.mvl | 24 | All mod-cons |
| Tari Village | North Male' | 440013 | no email | 30/36 | Surfing |
| Vadoo Diving | South Male' | 443976 | vadoo@dhivehinet.net.mv | -/33 | Diving |
| Vakarufalhi | South Ari | 450004 | vakaru@dhivehinet.net.mv | 50 | Good value |
| Velidhu Island | North Ari | 450018 | velidhu@dhivehinet.net.mv | 87 | Good value |
| Vilamendhoo | South Ari | 450637 | vilamndu@aaa.com.mv | 100 | Good value |

[1] Over-water bungalow        [2] South Maalhosmadulu        [3] North Nilandhoo

thatched bungalows, cabanas, bures, rondavels, units, huts or whatever the brochure wants to call them, with an attached open-air bathroom and a veranda of sorts facing the beach. The bar, reception area and restaurant may also feature a thatched roof, sand floor and open sides, while the gardens have that exuberant tropical lushness that requires careful cultivation, irrigation and imported soil. Natural-style resorts include Bathala, Ihuru, Madoogali, Nika Hotel, Reethi Rah and Sonevafushi, among others. Natural does not mean cheap, and some have gone to great expense to achieve that primitive, rustic look.

At the other extreme are the modern, 'international style' resorts which could just as easily be in the Caribbean, the Pacific or South-East Asia. The rooms are neat and white, with tiled roof, glossy bathroom and air-conditioning. The landscaping tends more to the manicured garden than the tropical jungle. These resorts are usually bigger, with slick dining and entertainment areas, a range of shops and services and often a swimming pool. Examples include Paradise, Full Moon, Laguna, Holiday Island and especially Sun Island. These are not cheap either.

In between in style, and generally cheaper in price, are the resorts with plain, simple rooms and a basic range of facilities, but which don't pretend to be old-fashioned fishing villages. They mightn't be much to look at, with boxy rooms, iron roofs, barn-like buildings and scrubby vegetation, but they get their ambience from carefree clientele and an untidy, unpretentious island feel. Angaga, Asdu, Kuredu, Embudhu Village and Ari Beach are all a bit like this, and may be survivors from a time when tourism was less developed and visitors' expectations were lower.

Most resorts are on leased land and most must be upgraded each time the lease is renewed. In this way the Maldives ensures that the standard of its resorts keeps on rising. But as soon as a place acquires some genuine character, it's in danger of losing it in the next renovation. Soon all rooms will have to have air-conditioning, which may be more comfortable, but it means that most visitors will spend their nights in a sealed room with a humming gadget instead of drifting off to the lapping of the waves and the breeze in the trees.

**Water Supply** Brackish, bore-water showers were once the biggest complaint of Maldives visitors, but now every resort has a desalination plant providing fresh water in every bathroom.

**Prices** The prices quoted for resorts in this book are the FIT (fully independent traveller) rates for a night, with full board in one of the resort's standard rooms, unless otherwise stated. A range of prices is given, from low season to high season (see When to Go earlier in this chapter). Prices are given to convey some idea of the relative cost of resorts, but if you contact a resort directly and book a room yourself, the price they quote for a given week may not be the same as the figures in this book – if only it were that simple.

The pricing structures are enormously complex, with multiple pricing periods; all-inclusive, full-board, half-board, bed & breakfast and room-only options; standard, superior and deluxe rooms; single, double and triple rates; child supplements; Christmas dinner surcharges; repeat customer discounts; and special deals for a second week free (but you still have to pay for meals and taxes). As you will see, the price increases for the high season vary remarkably from resort to resort. In some cases it's only a matter of a few more dollars; in others the rate more than doubles.

Even more complicated is the system of discounts, wholesale prices and special deals given to various international and local agents. A lot of wheeling and dealing goes on, and many resorts and operators are reluctant to reveal their prices because they are trading one agent off against another, and there are commitments not to sell rooms to casual customers for less than the agents are selling them. It's strange to stand at the front desk of a hotel, ask for the price of a room, and be told that they don't know or they won't tell! But Maldivian resorts are for island holidays and they don't get any walk-in trade.

## Water, Water, Everywhere

Ensuring a supply of fresh water has always been imperative for small island communities. Rainwater quickly soaks into the sandy island soil and usually forms an underground reservoir of fresh water, held in place by a circle of salt water from the surrounding sea. Wells can be dug to extract the fresh ground water, but if water is pumped out faster than rainfall replenishes the supply, then salty water infiltrates from around the island and the well water becomes brackish. Decaying organic matter and septic tanks can also contaminate the ground water, giving it an unpleasant sulphurous smell, even if it isn't unhealthy.

One way to increase the fresh-water supply is to catch and store rainwater from rooftops. This wasn't feasible on islands that had only small buildings with roofs of palm thatch, but economic development and the use of corrugated iron has changed all that. Nearly every inhabited island now has a government-supported primary school, which is often the biggest, newest building on the island. The other sizeable building is likely to be the mosque, which is typically a focus of community pride. Along with education and spiritual sustenance, many Maldivians now also get their drinking water from the local school or the mosque.

Expanding tourist resorts required more water than was available from wells or rooftops and, as resorts grew larger, the tourists' showers became saltier. Also, the ground water became too salty to irrigate the exotic gardens that every tourist expects on a tropical island. The solution was the desalination of sea water using 'reverse osmosis' – a combination of membrane technology and brute force.

Now every resort has a desalination plant, with racks of metal cylinders, each containing an inner cylinder made of a polymer membrane. Sea water is pumped into the inner cylinder at high pressure and the membrane allows pure water to pass through into the outer cylinder from which it is piped away. Normally, when a membrane separates fresh water from salt water, both salt and water will pass through the membrane in opposite directions to equalise the saltiness on either side. This process is called osmosis, and it normally means that pure water will permeate the membrane from the freshwater side to the saltwater side. Under pressure, the special polymer membrane allows the natural process of osmosis to be reversed.

A large desalination plant now provides drinking water for all of Male'. Small, reliable desalination plants have been a boon for the resorts, providing abundant fresh water for bathrooms, kitchens, gardens and, increasingly, for swimming pools. Of course it's expensive, as the plants use lots of diesel fuel for their powerful pumps and the polymer membranes need to be replaced regularly. Many resorts ask their guests to be moderate in their water use, while a few are looking at ways to recycle bath and laundry water onto garden beds. Most have dual water supplies, so that brackish ground water is used to flush the toilet while desalinated sea water is provided in the shower and the hand basin.

Is desalinated water good enough to drink? If a desalination plant is working properly, it should produce, in effect, 100% pure distilled water. The island of Thulusdhoo, in North Male' Atoll, has the only factory in the world where Coca-Cola is made out of sea water. Some resorts will run a quantity of water twice through the desalination plant and place it in the rooms as drinking water for guests – it tastes perfect. In most resorts, the water from the bathroom tap tastes just fine, but management advises guests not to drink it. One story is that the water is too pure and lacks the trace minerals essential for good health. Another is that the water is purified in the plant, but in the pipes it can pick up bacteria, which may cause diarrhoea. Usually, the resort and hotel management will suggest that guests buy mineral water from the bar, shop or restaurant, where it will cost between US$2 and US$4 for 1.5 litres. This water is bottled in the Maldives using purified, desalinated water.

You will, almost invariably, get a cheaper rate with a holiday package than the rates quoted here, but you can never tell because the price of accommodation is always combined with an airfare and various extras. Independent tour operators in Male' sometimes have the cheapest room rates of all, but you won't know until you get there, and you won't get the benefit of a discount package-deal airfare or a charter flight. The big travel companies get cheap wholesale prices for everything and pass some of the savings on to the customers – it's a very competitive business.

You might find it more helpful to look at the general description of resort prices in terms of low, medium or high price ranges. This is based on the FIT rate for a double room, with full board, in late February. Those around US$120 and under are classed as inexpensive (and there aren't many of them); from US$120 to US$220 is midrange (under US$150 is low mid-range and above US$180 is high mid-range); and more than US$220 is top end. These general price levels should correspond to the relative costs of various package tour prices. If not, double-check whether meals and extras are included in the deal.

## Hotels & Guesthouses

Apart from the resorts, the only commercial accommodation is available at the hotels and guesthouses in Male'. See the Male' chapter for details.

## Island Villages

If you are fortunate enough to stay in an island village you will be housed where there is room, and not necessarily with the person who invited you and sponsored your permit application. Particularly on smaller islands, where you stay will depend on the *kateeb* (island chief). You are not legally permitted to pay for accommodation in an island village.

Official visitors are usually put up in the kateeb's house, while informal guests will be offered a room with a family. This will usually have coral walls, a palm-thatched or corrugated iron roof, and beds with mattresses and pillows filled with coconut mat-

ting. The *gifili* is the bathroom and toilet, usually a hole in the ground surrounded by shrubs or a thatched fence. Some homes have a well out the front, comparable to the kitchen sink, and another out the back for bathing only. Washing is done around the well, not in it. Water is drawn by a large tin can on the end of a long pole. Use rainwater for drinking, never well water.

All meals will be provided by your host, but you may be expected to dine separately from the family. This could be because they think you would prefer to, maybe for religious reasons, or it might simply signify special treatment along with a special menu.

Most islands have a generator, but the use of electricity may be restricted to between 6 and 11 pm, and only used for radios and lights. Apart from this, lighting is provided by candles and hurricane lanterns.

**Protocol** As a matter of protocol, guests should introduce themselves to the kateeb upon arrival or shortly after. If the island is the atoll capital, guests should also introduce themselves to the atoll chief. The other person to make yourself known to is the *gazi* (champion of the faith), the island's religious leader and judge.

It is always best to dress as smartly as possible when meeting officials. Wear a shirt rather than a T-shirt, shoes not thongs, and long trousers or a skirt instead of shorts. Don't worry about this too much if you arrive by fishing dhoni after spending eight hours at sea, but it helps to justify the respect that is customarily shown to visitors.

## FOOD

For many, the biggest disappointment about the Maldives is the scarcity of luscious tropical fruits and vegetables. Very little is grown, because there is very little arable land and the soil is thin and infertile. The coconut thrives, and almost everything else is imported.

### Resort Food

In recent years there has been a great improvement in the food on most islands, mainly because the process of importing and distributing ingredients has become more reliable. One innovation is the Floating Market, a regular cargo ship that comes to Male' with all types of fresh, frozen and packaged food – fruit, meat, vegetables, pastry, pasta, pickles, dairy foods, eggs and juices. It unloads straight onto dhonis which take the goods directly to resort pantries and cool rooms. Most resort meals are served buffet-style, so you can choose what you want and eat as much as you like.

The quality of the food is generally in proportion to the price of the resort, but even the least expensive Italian resorts serve excellent food. Club Med also has good food for its price. Bigger resorts tend to have a bigger range of dishes, while those a long way from Male' seem to have more trouble getting fresh supplies. On the other hand, a small resort is more likely to do a special dish on request, especially if it's a Maldivian dish.

Some of the big resorts have several restaurants, which may appeal if you want a wider variety of meals. However, the full-board rate at these resorts will only include meals at the main restaurant. Full-board guests can eat in the specialty restaurants, but they only get a small discount to offset the fact that they've already paid for all their meals. If you choose a big resort because you want the choice of several restaurants, a half-board or breakfast-only package may suit you better.

## Maldivian Food

Resorts will rarely serve Maldivian food, apart from a 'Maldivian barbecue buffet', which will be very enjoyable, if not authentic. The opinion is that western stomachs will not cope with the spices. In a small resort you could ask the kitchen staff to make a fish curry or a tray of short eats – they may be making it for the staff anyway. Otherwise, your best bet is to go to the tea shops in Male'.

Fish and rice are the staple foods of the Maldivian people; meat and chicken are saved for special occasions. If you're going to eat local food, prepare your pallet for fish curry, fish soup, fish patties and variations thereof. Any substantial meal, with rice and *roshi* (unleavened bread), is called 'long eats'. 'Short eats' or *hedhikaa* is the selection of little sweet and savoury items displayed on the counter of a local tea shop. Select the ones that look good, and take them to your table. Generally, anything small and brown will be savoury and contain fish, and anything light or brightly coloured will be sweet. The only rude shock is the white cake with a brown top – coconut cream with fried-onion icing.

The Maldivian equivalent of the after-dinner mint is the *areca* nut, chewed after a meal or snack. The little oval nuts are sliced into thin sections, some cloves and lime paste are added, the whole lot is wrapped in an areca leaf, and the wad is chewed whole. It's definitely an acquired taste.

## DRINKS

A reasonable selection of soft drinks is available in Male', including some Coca-Cola products made locally with desalinated water. Mineral water is also available at prices much lower than in resorts. Some places sell Amstel nonalcoholic beer, which is OK if you want a drink that isn't sweet. Foreigners who do not have a liquor permit are not allowed to drink alcohol in Male'. Permits are only issued to foreigners resident in the country, and they aren't supposed to share their monthly entitlements, even in their own homes. The closest bars are in the new airport hotel, and on nearby resort islands.

Alcohol at resorts is available to non-Muslim guests and is a big earner. Expect to pay US$2.50 to US$4.50 for a can of beer, at least US$4 for spirits and US$6 for cocktails, and much more in some resorts. A bottle of ordinary Italian or French wine will cost from US$20 to US$45, or US$4 by the glass. A 1500 ml bottle of mineral water is usually over US$2.50, sometimes US$4.50. A service charge of 10% is often added to your bar bill as well, and drinks from a minibar in your room will be even more expensive. A few resorts offer packages which include beer, basic spirits and sometimes wine. For a moderate drinker this would be worth at least US$10 per day, but don't expect top-quality wine or real scotch whisky.

In resorts, Maldivians are not allowed to pour alcoholic drinks and the bar staff are always foreign workers, usually from India or Sri Lanka. A Maldivian can take your order and bring a drink to your table, but the opening of bottles and preparation of drinks must be done by a foreigner.

Unfortunately, at most resorts only instant coffee is served.

Until recently all safari boats were alcohol free and had to stop in at resorts from time to time so that their passengers could take some liquid refreshment. A new regulation permits safari boats of a certain standard to have a bar, but it must be completely closed and locked when the boat is in port at Male'.

*Raa* is the name for toddy tapped from the crown of the palm trunk at the point where the coconuts grow. Every village has its toddy man or *raa veri*. The raa is sweet and delicious if you can get over the pungent smell. It can be drunk immediately after it is tapped from the tree, or left to become a little alcoholic as the sugar ferments.

## ENTERTAINMENT

Most resorts have some kind of entertainment a couple of evenings a week. Sometimes it's a band or a disco night, and other times a Maldivian cultural show, usually a *bodu beru* (big drum) performance with dancing. Fire dancers from Sri Lanka are popular. Some resorts, especially Italian ones, have 'animators' who organise games and amusements and fun activities almost nonstop. For the less animated there might be table tennis, chess, snooker or *carrom* (board game with counters).

In Male' the options are a night at the movies, hanging out in the tea shops, chess, carrom, or strolling in the cool of the evening. On Thursday nights and special occasions there will be an outdoor concert with the local bands, both modern and traditional.

## SPECTATOR SPORTS

Soccer is the most popular sport and is played all year around. On most islands there's a football pitch, and the late afternoon match among the young men is a daily ritual. There's a league competition in Male', played at the National Stadium on Majeedi Magu between teams with names such as 'Valencia' and 'Victory'. There is also an annual tournament against teams from Sri Lanka.

Cricket is played at the stadium for a few months, beginning in March. Some Maldivians follow the fortunes of Sri Lanka, India and the other cricketing countries. The president is a keen cricket fan and was a good player for his school in Sri Lanka. Volleyball is played indoors and in the waterfront parks. The two venues for indoor sport are the Centre for Social Education, on the west side of Male', and a new facility just east of the New Harbour, used for basketball (men and women), netball, volleyball and badminton.

Traditional games include *bai bala*, where one team tries to tag members of the other team inside a circle, and *wadhemun*, a tug-of-war. *Bashi* is a popular girls game, played on something like a tennis court, where a girl stands facing away from the net and serves a tennis ball backwards, over her head, to a team of girls on the other side who try to catch it. You'll see it in Male' parks in the early evening.

*Thin mugoali* ('three circles') is a game similar to baseball that has been played in the atolls for more than 400 years. The ball was traditionally made of coconut fronds, but these days a tennis ball is used. The bat is still made of the sun-hardened lower part of a coconut leaf stem. The *mugoali* or 'bases' are made by rotating on one foot in the sand through 360 degrees leaving a circle behind. The object, as in baseball, is to accrue as many 'home runs' or *landeh* as possible.

## SHOPPING

There are many skilled artists and craftspeople in the Maldives, but generally it seems to be more profitable to import handcrafts from India, Sri Lanka or Bali. This trend is supported by many undiscriminating tourists who enthusiastically buy the imported stuff and don't take the trouble to look for good-quality local products.

Of the items made in the Maldives, an increasing number are modern souvenirs,

## Turtles, Coral & Conservation

In the interests of conservation, the Maldivian government has now banned the capture of turtles and the import, export and sale of all turtle-shell products. You're unlikely to see any carved tortoiseshell products in any shops. If you're tempted, remember that the import of any turtle products is strictly forbidden to countries who are party to the Convention on International Trade in Endangered Species (CITES) – that includes Australia, USA, the UK and all other EC countries.

It's also forbidden to sell or export any 'unfinished' coral and shell products. This means that shells and mother-of-pearl can be used for craft work, and carvings can be sold and exported, but it's illegal to sell coral branches or shells in their natural state. Most coral carvings and souvenirs are made from dead coral that has been washed ashore – live coral is likely to get very smelly. Many of the painted model fish on sale are not carved coral, but a mixture of ground coral and plastic resin set in a mould. In any case, it's illegal for visitors to remove any shells or coral from beaches or during dives. Hefty fines can be doled out to those who breach these regulations.

Black coral is a special case. There is some concern that natural growths of black coral are in decline due to overexploitation, and in some more accessible areas this is certainly true. There is some talk of banning trade in black coral products, but it is a superb material for carving and has been used for a long time. It is also a renewable resource, so there is a possibility that it can be harvested and used in a sustainable way. Though it is currently legal to buy any 'finished' black coral product, it would be better to avoid buying large chunks or branches that have been polished and nothing more – go for smaller pieces that have been skilfully carved.

such as T-shirts, colourful carved coral fish and carved rosewood manta rays. These can be attractive and well made, but are not as distinctive as the traditional crafts, which are getting harder to find.

Resort shops usually have a limited range of souvenirs and gifts, mostly imported and quite expensive. Male' is the best place for shopping, with lots of tourist shops and some fascinating places selling items that local people use every day in their homes or on their boats. The island hopping trips from resorts will usually include more than enough souvenir shopping opportunities. Shops on these islands often sell craft items cheaper than in town.

### Craft Fair

Every year, but unfortunately not on a predictable schedule, there is a big craft fair in Male', with each atoll sending examples of its best work. The work is judged and there are awards in many categories. Many of the best pieces are sold to dignitaries in advance of the public opening, but remain on display until the end of the exhibition. There is still a large choice left, though the prices are higher than in the shops.

### Mats

The fine woven mats known as *kunaa* are one of the most attractive and uniquely Maldivian crafts, with their elegant, abstract geometrical patterns and subdued natural colourings. They are made only in Gaaf Dhaal (South Huvadhoo Atoll), but a small selection is available in the souvenir shops in Male'. Prices vary from Rf 250 for a small piece (35 sq cm), up to Rf 3000 and more for a full-sized prayer mat. They can be rolled, but not folded, and are easy to carry. It's likely that quality examples of this craft will become increasingly rare.

## Lacquer Work

Turned wooden boxes, lacquered in black with incised red, yellow and green floral patterns, are another attractive and distinctive Maldivian craft product. Traditionally, lacquer work was for containers, bowls and trays used to present gifts and serve food, but vases and small boxes are the most common lacquer work items in tourist shops. They are very colourful and beautifully finished, and range in price from Rf 250 for a small box to Rf 4000 for a top-quality 40 cm vase. Make sure there are no cracks around the edges.

## Jewellery

Though gold and silver work is a traditional craft on some islands, it is almost impossible to find good examples of local work. Antique bracelets, rings, mesh belts, necklaces and decorated boxes are now very rare. Most of the quality jewellery in shops comes from Sri Lanka, which is also a source of fine gem stones, especially sapphires. There are some stunning pieces available at good prices (look in Sifani, on Chandanee Magu), but they are not Maldivian. Most of the local artisans are now working in local materials.

## Shells, Coral & Fish Bone

Beautiful jewellery and decorative items are made from mother-of-pearl and black coral, including rings, bracelets, necklaces and carved model dhonis.

## Dresses

The traditional woman's *libaas*, a silk dress with the collar richly embroidered with concentric patterns of gold thread, can be bought in some souvenir shops. You'll probably only find them in small sizes.

## Drums

You can buy the Maldives' national instrument, the bodu beru, but it is cumbersome to carry. They're made from a hollowed coconut tree trunk and covered with stingray skin. The best ones come from Felidhoo Atoll.

## Music

Quite a few shops in Male' sell cassettes and CDs with Maldivian music, both traditional and contemporary.

## Maldiviana

General household items that can make good souvenirs or gifts are anything made from a coconut shell (such as toddy holders and cups), woven palm leaf baskets and mats *(sataa)*, and folding, carved Quran rests. Hardware and general stores in Male' sell some interesting everyday items, like wooden scoops for bailing boats, fittings for hookahs, woven trays for winnowing rice and an amazing assortment of medicinal herbs and potions.

## Duty Free

The airport duty-free shops have a good range of liquor, perfume, cameras and electrical goods, but Singapore is much better, if you're going home that way. Sifani Jewellers has some beautiful work with sapphires, rubies and other gems from Sri Lanka. Its shop in town could probably arrange for you to pick up duty-free from its airport outlet.

# Getting There & Away

Aside from a few yachties and cruise-line passengers, just about everyone who comes to the Maldives arrives by plane. Most are on holiday packages and use either scheduled or chartered flights. The vast majority are from Europe, and flights are direct or via the Middle East or Colombo (Sri Lanka). Asian and Australian visitors fly in via Singapore, Kuala Lumpur or Colombo.

## AIR

In clear weather, the atolls and islands of the Maldives archipelago look stunning from the air – it's worth getting a window seat.

## Airports & Airlines

**Male' International Airport** There's only one international airport in the Maldives – Male' International Airport (☎ 322075), on Huhule Island, 2km across the water from the capital.

Immigration and health checks are usually straightforward, especially if you are on the way to a resort with all the other passengers. Customs checks are quite thorough and involve an X-ray of all your luggage – if you have any alcohol it will be taken away, but you'll get it back when you leave.

As you leave the arrivals hall, you will see rows of counters with resort representatives and inbound tour operators. They pick out their own clients (the baggage tickets are the obvious indicator), check them off their list and escort them to a boat or seaplane for transfer to the resort. The representative will usually collect all the air tickets from arriving passengers so that outward flights can be reconfirmed; tickets are returned to the passengers before they check out at the end of their stay. This is standard procedure and the tickets are always returned.

If you are a fully independent traveller (FIT) and not on a package tour, your first problem will be the immigration form, which asks for an address in the Maldives. If you have a confirmed hotel booking in Male', give that address. If you plan to stay in one of the hotels listed in this book, especially a more upmarket one, you could use that address. If you don't answer the question to the satisfaction of the immigration officers, your passport will be held while you go outside to the tourist-information desk or tour operators and make a reservation.

The tourist-information desk is usually open for the arrival of incoming flights, as is the airport branch of the Bank of Maldives, but don't count on using it if you are arriving late at night. You can get into town and find a meal and accommodation using low denomination US dollars, but making phone calls will be a problem – you'll need a phonecard, and the airport shop that sells them may also be closed.

If you're heading into Male', go past the resort reps' counters and continue over to the waterfront, where lots of boats will be waiting. Look for a *dhoni* (a Maldivian ferry boat) loaded with lots of locals. They go into town, leave when full and charge Rf 10. However, if it's late and you're the only passenger it will cost Rf 70.

**Airlines** At the time of writing Air Maldives had ceased to operate. But check with your travel agent – by the time you wish to travel they may be flying again. The Maldives can be reached by scheduled carriers, and from Europe, by charter airlines. Emirates Airlines, SriLankan Airlines, Indian Airlines and Singapore Airlines are the main carriers to the Maldives.

Charter flights include Condor, LTU International Airways, Air Europe, Balair, AOM French Airlines, Austrian Airlines, British Caledonian, Finn Air, Lauda Air, Monarch Airlines and Britannia Airways.

**Colombo Connections** Many flights to the Maldives go via Colombo, Sri Lanka, where the airport is subject to very stringent security precautions. It's now probably one of the most secure airports in the world, but if you have any more than a refuel stop here, your flight may experience some delays. Air Lanka flight numbers start with the letters UL, which is said to stand for 'usually late'.

## Buying Tickets

The Maldives is not a major international hub and there is not a huge amount of cut-throat competition on the route. Cheap fares are most likely to be offered in conjunction with a holiday package, especially during low season, and some of the cheapest are charter flights. It is still worth doing some research – start early: some of the cheapest packages have to be bought months in advance, and some agents have discounts for those who book early. Look at the ads in newspapers, magazines and the Internet, and watch for special offers. Then phone travel agents for bargains – they will almost invariably offer cheaper fares than the airlines themselves.

If you plan to travel independently, try the better-known budget travel agents such as STA Travel, which has offices worldwide, Council Travel in the USA, Travel CUTS in Canada or NBBS in the Netherlands.

Once you have your ticket, write its number down, together with the flight number and other details, and keep the information somewhere separate. If the ticket is lost or stolen, this will help you get a replacement.

It's sensible to buy travel insurance as early as possible, to cover the cost of any delays that may occur before your scheduled departure.

**Buying Tickets on the Internet** Fare discounters and even the airlines themselves can offer some excellent fares on the Internet. They may sell seats by auction or simply cut prices to reflect the reduced cost of electronic selling. Many travel agents around the world have Web sites, which can make the Internet a quick and easy way to compare prices. Online ticket sales work well if you are doing a simple one-way or return trip on specified dates. However, online fare generators are no substitute for a travel agent who knows all about special deals, has strategies for avoiding layovers and can offer advice on everything from which airline has

## Warning

The information in this chapter is particularly vulnerable to change: Prices for international travel are volatile, routes are introduced and cancelled, schedules change, special deals come and go, and rules and visa requirements are amended. Airlines and governments seem to take a perverse pleasure in making price structures and regulations as complicated as possible. You should check directly with the airline or a travel agent to make sure you understand how a fare (and ticket you may buy) works. In addition, the travel industry is highly competitive and there are many lurks and perks.

The upshot of this is that you should get opinions, quotes and advice from as many airlines and travel agents as possible before you part with your hard-earned cash. The details given in this chapter should be regarded as pointers and are not a substitute for your own careful, up-to-date research.

the best vegetarian food to the best travel insurance to buy alongside your ticket.

**Round-the-World Tickets** It may be tricky getting a RTW ticket stopping at the Maldives because of the limited number of direct connections. Strictly speaking, if you fly in from Singapore, it would be a backtrack to fly out to Colombo; you'd have to continue westward, maybe to Karachi or Dubai, and this may mean using another airline. Emirates reputedly has a slightly flexible attitude to the 'no backtracking' rule, so check its RTW deals.

## Travellers with Special Needs

If you have special needs of any sort – you've broken a leg, you're vegetarian, travelling in a wheelchair, taking the baby, terrified of flying – you should let the airline know as soon as possible so that it can make arrangements accordingly. You should remind it when you reconfirm your booking (at least 72 hours before departure) and again when you check in at the airport. It may also be worth ringing several airlines before you make your booking to find out how each caters for your particular needs.

Airports and airlines can be surprisingly helpful, but they do need advance warning. Most international airports will provide escorts from check-in desk to plane where needed, and there should be ramps, lifts, accessible toilets and phones. Aircraft toilets, on the other hand, are likely to present a problem; travellers should discuss this with the airline at an early stage and, if necessary, with their doctor.

Deaf travellers can ask for airport and in-flight announcements to be written down for them.

Children under two travel for 10% of the standard fare (or free, on some airlines), as long as they don't occupy a seat. They don't get a baggage allowance either. 'Skycots' should be provided by the airline if requested in advance; these will take a child weighing up to about 10kg. Children between two and 12 can usually occupy a seat for half to two-thirds of the full fare and do get a baggage allowance. Pushchairs can often be taken as hand luggage.

### Departure Tax
The 'passenger service charge' at Male' airport is US$10 and must be paid in US dollars. Pay it at the window just outside the terminal building before you pass through security into the building.

### The UK
There are no direct flights from the UK except with charter companies. The cheapest fares will be as part of a tour package – see the Organised Tours section at the end of this chapter. But you can still get flight-only fares on charter flights. Monarch Airlines has year round return fares for around £520. Emirates and SriLankan offer the best scheduled flight deals from the UK. In the low season the cheapest scheduled fares are just a little less than the cheapest packages. Expect to pay around £600 for a return flight in the low season, either via Dubai with Emirates or via Colombo with SriLankan. Fares to Male' from the UK are more expensive if you travel via Europe, fares start from £1300 to £2000.

Advertisements for many travel agents appear in the travel pages of the weekend broadsheets, such as the *Independent* on Saturday and the *Sunday Times*. Look out for free magazines, such as *TNT*, which are widely available in London – try outside tube and train stations. STA Travel (☎ 020-7361 6161) has an office at 86 Old Brompton Rd, London SW7 3LQ, and other offices in London and Manchester. Check its Web site (www.statravel.co.uk). Usit Campus Travel (☎ 0870 240 1010), 52 Grosvenor Gardens, London SW1W 0AG, has branches throughout the UK. Check its Web site (www.usitcampus.com). Both of these agencies sell tickets to all travellers , but cater especially to young people and students. Other recommended bucket shops include: Trailfinders (☎ 020-7938 3939), 194 Kensington High St, London W8 7RG; Bridge the World (☎ 020-7734 7447), 4 Regent Place, London W1R 5FB; and Flightbookers (☎ 020-7757 2000), 177–178 Tottenham Court Rd, London W1P 9LF.

### Continental Europe
There are two direct flights per week from Germany to Male', one on LTU and the other on Condor. Fares on both airlines start at DM1590 for a return flight. Try one of the STA offices for student or budget fares. STA Travel (☎ 69 430191) Bergerstrasse 118, 60316 Frankfurt is one of the many STA offices throughout Germany. For a cheap deal, try your luck with a 'last minute' (stand-by) flight (these can be organised at most major airports in Germany).

From the Netherlands, Tamair has one flight per week via Muscat. NBBS Reizen (☎ 020-624 09 89), Rokin 66, Amsterdam, is the official student travel agency. They have several other local agencies. Malibu Travel (☎ 020-626 32 30), Prinsengracht 230, Amsterdam, is also recommended. In April 2000, Martin Air of the Netherlands began scheduled flights to the Maldives.

From other European cities, SriLankan flies from Vienna, Rome and Paris, via Colombo.

Agencies in France for good fare deals include OTU Voyages (☎ 01 44 41 38 50), 39

## Air Travel Glossary

**Baggage Allowance** This will be written on your ticket and usually includes one 20kg item to go in the hold, plus one item of hand luggage.

**Bucket Shops** These are unbonded travel agencies specialising in discounted airline tickets.

**Bumped** Just because you have a confirmed seat doesn't mean you're going to get on the plane (see Overbooking).

**Cancellation Penalties** If you have to cancel or change a discounted ticket, there are often heavy penalties involved; insurance can sometimes be taken out against these penalties. Some airlines impose penalties on regular tickets as well, particularly against 'no-show' passengers.

**Check-In** Airlines ask you to check-in a certain time ahead of the flight departure (usually one to two hours on international flights). If you fail to check-in on time and the flight is overbooked, the airline can cancel your booking and give your seat to somebody else.

**Confirmation** Having a ticket written out with the flight and date you want doesn't mean you have a seat until the agent has checked with the airline that your status is 'OK' or confirmed. Meanwhile you could just be 'on request'.

**Full Fares** Airlines traditionally offer 1st class (coded F), business class (coded J) and economy class (coded Y) tickets. These days there are so many promotional and discounted fares available that few passengers pay the full price for economy fares.

**ITX** An ITX, or 'independent inclusive tour excursion', is often available on tickets to popular holiday destinations. Officially it's a package deal combined with hotel accommodation, but many agents will sell you one of these for the flight only and give you phoney hotel vouchers in the unlikely event that you're challenged at the airport.

**Lost Tickets** If you lose your airline ticket an airline will usually treat it like a travellers cheque and, after inquiries, issue you with another one. Legally, however, an airline is entitled to treat it like cash and if you lose it then it's gone forever. Take good care of your tickets.

**No-Shows** No-shows are passengers who fail to show up for their flight. Full-fare passengers who fail to turn up are sometimes entitled to travel on a later flight. The rest are penalised (see Cancellation Penalties).

**On Request** This is an unconfirmed booking for a flight.

**Onward Tickets** An entry requirement for many countries is that you have a ticket out of the country. If you're unsure of your next move, the easiest solution is to buy the cheapest onward ticket to a neighbouring country, or a ticket from a reliable airline, which can later be refunded if you do not use it.

---

Ave Georges Bernanos (5e), Paris, and at another 42 offices around the country. Check its Web site (www.otu.fr). Acceuil des Jeunes en France (☎ 01 42 77 87 80), 119 rue Saint Martin (4e), Paris, is another popular discount travel agency. General travel agencies that offer some of the best services and deals include Nouvelles Frontières (☎ 08 03 33 33 33), 5 Ave de l'Opéra (1er), Paris; check its Web site at www.nouvelles-frontieres.com. Try also Voyageurs du Monde (☎ 01 42 86 16 00) at 55 rue Sainte Anne (2e), Paris.

In Vienna try ÖKISTA, the national student organisation, for student and budget fares. Its head office (☎ 401 48) is at 09, Garnisongasse 7. In Rome, CTS, the national student travel service, (☎ 06 687 26 72) Corso Vittorio Emanuele II 297, is a good place to start looking for cheap flights.

Note that many of the flights from Europe are charter flights and you'll only get on them if you take an accommodation package. Some use obscure airlines like Pinestate, Tamair, Air Nordic and Calmair.

### Eastern Europe & Central Asia

Aeroflot flies once weekly from Moscow to Male' via Dubai. Balkan Airlines flies from Sofia to Male' twice weekly.

## Air Travel Glossary

**Overbooking** Airlines hate to fly empty seats and since every flight has some passengers who fail to show up, airlines often book more passengers than they have seats. Usually excess passengers make up for the no-shows, but occasionally somebody gets 'bumped' onto the next available flight. Guess who it is most likely to be? The passengers who check in late.

**Point-to-Point Tickets** These are discount tickets that can be bought on some routes in return for passengers waiving their rights to a stopover.

**Promotional Fares** These are officially discounted fares, available from travel agencies or direct from the airline.

**Reconfirmation** If you don't reconfirm your flight at least 72 hours prior to departure, the airline may delete your name from the passenger list. Ring to find out if your airline requires reconfirmation.

**Restrictions** Discounted tickets often have various restrictions on them – such as needing to be paid for in advance and incurring a penalty to be altered. Others are restrictions on the minimum and maximum period you must be away, such as a minimum of 14 days or a maximum of one year.

**Round-the-World Tickets** RTW tickets give you a limited period (usually a year) in which to circumnavigate the globe. You can go anywhere the carrying airlines go, as long as you don't backtrack. The number of stopovers or total number of separate flights is decided before you set off and they usually cost a bit more than a basic return flight.

**Stand-By** This is a discounted ticket where you only fly if there is a seat free at the last moment. Stand-by fares are usually only available on domestic routes.

**Transferred Tickets** Airline tickets cannot be transferred from one person to another. Travellers sometimes try to sell the return half of their ticket, but officials can ask you to prove that you are the person named on the ticket. This is less likely to happen on domestic flights. However, on an international flight, tickets are compared with passports.

**Travel Agencies** Travel agencies vary widely and you should choose one that suits your needs. Some simply handle tours, while full-service agencies handle everything from tours and tickets to car rental and hotel bookings. If all you want is a ticket at the lowest possible price, then go to an agency specialising in discounted fares.

**Travel Periods** Ticket prices vary with the time of year. There is a low (off-peak) season and a high (peak) season, and often a low-shoulder season and a high-shoulder season as well. Usually the fare depends on your outward flight – if you depart in the high season and return in the low season, you pay the high-season fare.

## South Asia

There are frequent flights between Male' and its regional neighbours. From Colombo return fares are around US$168 on SriLankan There are no direct flights from Pakistan but Emirates fly from Karachi, via Dubai, for US$384. From India, all flights to the Maldives are via Thiruvananthapuram (Trivandrum), in Kerala. From Mumbai (Bombay) expect to pay US$361, or US$584 from Delhi, for a return fare with Indian Airlines.

## South-East Asia

The best connections to Male' are from Singapore, which has daily flights with Singapore Airlines. There are also flights from Kuala Lumpur with Malaysia Airlines and from Colombo with SriLankan.

Flights from other centres, including Hong Kong, Tokyo and Bangkok, will go via Singapore, Kuala Lumpur or Colombo. The best places to buy tickets are discount travel agents in Bangkok, Singapore or KL.

## Australia

The most convenient flights from Australia to the Maldives are with Singapore Airlines and involve a short stop at Singapore airport. A discount three-month excursion fare from Melbourne, Sydney, Brisbane or Adelaide via Singapore to Male', is around A$1600 in the low season but only as much as A$2050 in the high season (22 November to 31 January).

The cheapest flights are with SriLankan Airlines, which has introduced direct flights from Sydney to Colombo. A three-month excursion fare to Male' in the low season is about A$1265, though you may have to spend a few hours, or even a whole day, in Colombo before you make the connection to Male'.

Some travel agents, particularly smaller ones, advertise cheap air fares in the travel sections of weekend newspapers, such as the Melbourne *Age* and the *Sydney Morning Herald*.

For cheap tickets, give Flight Centre a try (☎ 131 600), which has dozens of offices throughout Australia. Check its Web site at www.flightcentre.com.au for details. Try also STA Travel (☎ 03-9349 2411, 131 776), 224 Faraday St, Carlton, VIC 3053, with offices in all major cities and on many university campuses. It also has a Web site at www.statravel.com.au.

### New Zealand

The most convenient route from New Zealand is a direct Singapore Airlines or Air New Zealand flight from Auckland or Christchurch to Singapore, changing there for a Maldives flight. A SriLankan flight from Sydney via Colombo might work out cheaper. The *New Zealand Herald* has a travel section in which travel agents advertise fares. Flight Centre (☎ 09-309 6171), National Bank Towers, Queen and Darby Sts, Auckland, has many branches throughout the country. STA Travel (☎ 09-309 0458), 10 High St, Auckland, has other offices in Auckland, Hamilton, Palmerston North, Wellington, Christchurch and Dunedin. Check its Web site (www.sta.travel.com .au) for details.

### Middle East

Dubai has the most frequent connections from the Middle East to Male' on Emirates and SriLankan (via Colombo).

### The USA & Canada

There are no direct flights from North America to the Maldives, which is almost exactly half a world away, hence the relatively small number of American visitors. The best fare deals from the west coast are via Singapore or Colombo. Low season return fares start from US$1600 to US$2170. From the east coast, the best fare deals are via Europe, generally London or Zurich, and Dubai. In the low season return fares start from US$3090 to US$3245.

## SEA
### Boat

The occasional cruise ship drops by, but there are no regular passenger boats travelling to and from the Maldives. It might be possible to get on a cargo ship, but you'll have to be keen, and lucky.

### Private Yacht

The Maldives is not a popular stop for cruising yachties. The maze of reefs makes it a hazardous area, the fees for Cruising Permits can be high, the officialdom is a hassle, there are restrictions on where yachts can go, and no lively little ports with cheap cafes and waterfront bars.

The three points where a yacht can get an initial 'clear in' are Uligamu (Ihavandhippolhu Atoll) in the north, Hithadhoo (Addu Atoll) in the south, and Male'. Call in on VHF channel 16 to the NSS Coastguard, and follow his instructions. If you're just passing through and want to stop only briefly, a 72-hour permit is usually easy to arrange. The northern and southern ports will give you a security clearance, but if you want to stay longer than 72 hours in Maldivian waters, or to stop and re-provision, you'll have to go to Male' to do the full clear-in bit and get a Cruising Permit.

Arrive at Male' well before dark, go to the east side of Viligili Island, between Viligili and Male', and call the coastguard on channel 16. Follow carefully the coastguard's instructions on where to anchor, or you may find yourself in water that's very deep, or too shallow. Then contact the port agent, FIFO, on channel 16 (if it hasn't already

Dhonis are built in many shapes and sizes. The tall curved prow is often removable on modern dhonis to allow for loading; in shallow water a sailor stands at the prow, navigating through the reefs and channels. Other boats which ply Maldivian waters include tourist safari boats **(bottom right)**.

Dhonis are the main public transport between atolls.

contacted you). FIFO (☎ 318646, fax 317642, ✆ fifo@dhivehinet.net.mv, Box 2012), Ship Plaza, 1st floor, Orchid Magu, Male', will arrange for port authority checks, and immigration, customs and quarantine checks, and can give lots of other helpful advice – for a fee of about US$90. It would be a nightmare trying to do it without FIFO's help.

After the initial checks you'll be able to cross to the lagoon beside Hulhu-Male', the reclaimed land north of the airport. This is a good anchorage. To get from there into town, take your tender to the east side of the airport island, and leave it near the Maldivian Air Taxi seaplane port. From there you can use MAT's minibus to the airport terminal, and from there get a regular airport dhoni across to Male'.

The bigger stores, like STO People's Choice and Fantasy, have quite a good range of provisions at reasonable prices. FIFO can advise on other necessities like radio repairs, water and fuelling. Diesel fuel is about US$0.30 per litre.

The cost of a Cruising Permit increases greatly with the length of stay – the first two weeks are free, the first month is US$200, the second month is US$300. There is also an atoll permit fee, as well as customs, port and inspection charges, which increase with the size of the boat. If you go cruising in the tourism zone you'll be able to stop at many of the resorts to eat, drink, swim, dive and spend your money, but you should always call the resort first. Usually you have to be off the island by sunset. FIFO can advise on which resorts are the most welcoming. It can also explain the conditions for visiting those local islands without resorts, also known as 'fishing islands' or 'village islands'.

Before you leave Maldivian waters, don't forget to 'clear out' at Uligamu, Hithadhoo or Male'.

## ORGANISED TOURS

About 90% of visitors to the Maldives go to just one resort on a seven- to 14-day package holiday, with absolutely everything arranged for them. Most Maldives packages are sold by a limited number of large travel companies, but there are some excellent small operators, particularly for specialist diving, surfing and safari trips. The big tour-company packages will cost the same from any travel agent, but it's worth comparing a few different tour companies. Some travel agents may be more creative in what they can add on before and after a standard holiday package, and this can be worth considering if you want to stay a day or two in Male', or maybe stop over in Sri Lanka or Singapore.

If you just want to spend one or two weeks in a resort, it's most unlikely that you could save any money by booking into the resort directly yourself, or by travelling independently and making a booking when you arrive in Male'. The big operators can get special airfares, cheap charter flights and wholesale deals at the resorts.

On a package, the best ways to cut costs are to travel at off-peak times and stay at cheaper resorts. It's no cheaper getting a bed & breakfast package unless you're a really light eater – snacks or meals bought at the resort will cost more than you'll save on the tour price and there's nowhere else to buy food. Some people find that half board is the least expensive option, because they can really fill up on buffet breakfasts and dinners, and get by with a light snack at lunch time. Packages that include windsurfing, sailing or some dive costs can save you money if you're keen on these activities. Likewise if they include drinks.

The tour companies' brochures will offer packages at various resorts at various prices – you can check the location and description of the resort in this book, to see if it suits you. The resort prices in this book may not bear much resemblance to the cost of a package, but remember that the package price includes airfares and transfers, and is always per person, not per room. Also, look at the sections on Choosing a Resort, Accommodation and Food in the Facts for the Visitor chapter.

### The UK

Some of the biggest tour operators to the Maldives are:

Hayes & Jarvis Travel Ltd (☎ 0870 89 89890, ✉ res@hayes-jarvis.com) Hayes House, 152 King St, London W6 0QU

Kuoni Travel Ltd (☎ 01306 743000, ✉ india.sales@kuoni.co.uk) Kuoni House, Dorking, Surrey RH5 4AZ
Web site: www.kuoni.co.uk

Thompson Tour Operations Ltd (☎ 0990 502 590) Greater London House, Hampstead Rd, London NW1 7SD

Some advertised packages (with prices per person, twin share) include:

**Budget resort** 14 nights, half board at Meerufenfushi for UK£695 in June, UK£1033 in August, and UK£1690 over Christmas; a full-board supplement is US$5 per person, per day.

**Mid-Range resort** 14 nights, half board at Vilamendhoo for UK£932 in June, UK£1142 in August, and UK£1755 over Christmas; full-board supplement US$5 per person per day; an all-inclusive supplement is US$20 per person, per day.

**Top-End resort** 14 nights, half board at Four Seasons for UK£1695 in June, UK£2053 in August, and UK£2859 over Christmas.

These include airfares from London, and transfers between Male' International Airport and the resort.

It's also worth checking with Maldive Travel (☎ 020-7352 2246), Esher House, 11 Edith Terrace, London, SW10 OTH. This agency is run by Toni de Laroque, known as 'The Maldive Lady'.

## Continental Europe

**Austria** Look for packages from Meridian Reisen und Touristik, Jumbo Touristik or Kuoni.

**Belgium** Jetair and Odysseus Travel do Maldives packages.

**France** Packages are arranged by Voyages Kuoni, Planet Voyages, MVM Paris, Air Tour, AOM and Nouvelles Frontières.

**Germany** The second biggest source of tourists to the Maldives is Germany, and many companies arrange packages. Some of the biggest are Neckermann, Transair, ITS, LTU, Air Tour International, Tjaeborg, Jet Reisen and Jahn Reisen.

**Italy** There are more visitors to the Maldives from Italy than anywhere else, with packages arranged by Turisanda, Club Vacanzi, Intravco, Valtur and Viaggi Kuoni, among others.

**The Netherlands** Try Sportreizen Service, Globas or Eis Bruijstens.

**Norway** Try Travel Club, in Oslo.

**Sweden** Lloyd Tours, Fritids Resor and Vingressor have Maldives packages.

**Switzerland** This is another country with lots of Maldivés packages, including those from Kuoni, Balair, Imholz, Manta Reisen, Esco Reisen, Airtour Suisse and Tropic Tours.

## Asia
**Hong Kong** Try Kwan's Travel.

**Japan** Inpac, Miki Tourist Co, Sun Travel and Play Guide Tours all arrange packages.

**Singapore** Club Med, Tradewinds and Singapore Airlines have a few options.

## Australia & New Zealand
The Maldives is not a big destination for Aussies and Kiwis, but the best-known packages are the 'Island Affairs' from Singapore Airlines. From the east-coast capitals, a five-night affair at a mid-range resort, with full board, will cost from A$1729 to A$2309 per person depending on the season. Prices are about A$200 cheaper from Perth and a bit more expensive from New Zealand. Club Med holidays are quite popular, too, and though the dollar price is higher, the inclusion of some drinks and activities makes them good value. Atoll Travel (☎ 03-5682 1088) is primarily for surf tours, but also does regular holiday packages.

## South Africa
Interest from South Africa has stalled a little since the South African Airways flights

via Mauritius ceased, but for a package tour, try Logans Tours.

## Israel

The Maldives has only recently opened up to Israelis. Divers who have done the Red Sea to death might check out diving packages with Route Tours (☎ 5162443) in Tel Aviv.

## North America

The Maldives is so far away that the only people who might be interested would be divers – who should check the offerings in diving magazines – or surfers, who could try Waterways Travel (☎ 1800 928 3757) in California. Singapore Airlines might be worth checking out, too.

# Getting Around

Apart from a few air services, there are no regular, scheduled transport links between the Maldives' atolls and islands. Transfers between the airport and the resorts are arranged by agents as part of the resort package and are by seaplane, local boat (called a *dhoni*), speedboat or launch.

Boats and aircraft can be chartered for special trips, though this is expensive. Not many people need to travel between resorts, but the most straightforward way to do so is usually to go via the airport, taking the same boats or aircraft which carry arriving and departing guests.

Transport to and from nonresort islands can be arranged on cargo boats, but only by those who have the requisite travel permit. The other option is a 'safari', cruising around the atolls on a live-aboard boat, with whatever stops for diving and sightseeing that the operator can arrange.

## AIR
### Domestic Air Services

At the time of going to print Air Maldives' (☎ 314808) internal flights were frequently being cancelled or rescheduled. (The flights linked five airfields throughout the country, though only Male' and Gan are accessible to visitors without an Inter-Atoll Travel Permit.) Seaplane transfers between Male' and the resorts are not scheduled – they're more like little charter flights arranged by the resorts and travel agents.

**Air Maldives** Daily afternoon flights from Male' to Gan were in a 37-seat Dash-8 jet. Check the airline for details. The fare for foreigners was US$119 one way, US$238 return, but if booking a package to the Equator Village resort on Gan, you could get a better rate.

Other internal flights are in a Dornier 228 turbo-prop 16 seater. The only connection to the northern atolls is to Hanimaadhoo Island in Haa Dhaal Atoll (airport code HAQ), which has daily flights (one hour, US$64

one way). To the southern atolls, there is the Gan connection, plus flights on Tuesday, Thursday, Friday, Saturday and Sunday to Kadhoo Island (KDO) in Laamu Atoll (one hour, US$64 one way) and flights daily except Saturday to Kaadedhoo island (KDM), near Thinadhoo in Gaaf Dhaal Atoll (80 minutes, US$94 one way).

### To/From Resorts

**Seaplane** Three companies are now making transfers by seaplane. Maldivian Air Taxi (☎ 315201, fax 315203, ✆ mataxi@dhivehinet.net.mv) is a Maldivian company managed by Danes, using seaplanes made in Canada. Its standard aircraft is a 16-seat De Havilland Twin Otter. They take off from the lagoon just east of Male' airport and fly mainly to resorts in Ari Atoll. Usually they 'land' in a lagoon, tie up to a pontoon and passengers are ferried to their resorts by dhoni. Note that cargo capacity is limited. All passengers and baggage are weighed before loading, and some heavy items may have to wait for a later flight or be transferred by boat.

Hummingbird Island Airways (☎ 325708, fax 323161, ✆ humbird@dhivehinet.net.mv) uses De Havilland Twin Otters, and also eight-seat amphibious Cessna Caravans, which can land on runways as well as on the water. The operation is essentially the same, except that in Male' the Cessnas land and take off from the airport runway. A third seaplane company, Sunexpress Airlines (☎ 320001, fax 320007, ✆ info@sunexpressair.com) has just two De Havilland Twin Otters.

Flights are chartered by resorts and tour agents and don't usually take individual passengers. A seaplane transfer will cost from about US$185 return, but the price varies depending on the distance and the arrangements the resorts and agents make – some deals include the flight at minimal cost, to be more competitive with resorts closer to the airport. The cost of transfers is generally included in the package price, but if there is the option of a boat transfer, the seaplane will be charged as an extra. Flights to Ari Atoll resorts take about 20 minutes and they're good fun.

Charter flights for sightseeing, photography and emergency evacuation can be arranged, for a price. Call all three companies for rates and availability.

**Helicopter** For some years, helicopter transfers were available to some resorts. Following several accidents, all helicopter operations were suspended in late 1999 and helicopter transfers will not be available until a complete review of safety standards is finished.

## SEA

You'll almost certainly spend some of your time in the Maldives on a boat. Dive trips and excursions are mostly within the sheltered waters of an atoll and will be very pleasant. If you're transferring from the airport to a resort outside North Male' Atoll, you'll be crossing much deeper, more open water and it might get a lot rougher.

The departure time and the duration of a trip depends on the weather and sea conditions. Skippers always allow lots of time for a trip and are very cautious. Boats that regularly carry passengers have life jackets, but radios, life rafts and rescue gear are only installed on fancier boats.

## Dhoni

The dhoni is the traditional all-purpose vessel of the Maldives. Dhonis come in various sizes with various superstructures, but the hull is always basically the same shape. Most are now powered by diesel engines, but they sometimes have a sail as a backup, or to save fuel when the winds oblige.

The basic fishing boat, the *mas dhoni*, has been modified for use as a short-distance ferry between Male' and the airport and to/from nearby resorts and islands. They have a diesel engine, a fabric roof to keep off the sun and the rain and a wooden bench running down each side. Passengers face each other and any luggage is stacked

down the middle. Most diving trips and island excursions are done on boats like this. If the weather is rough, passengers and luggage can both get wet.

**To/From Resorts** Dhonis move at the leisurely pace of around 10km/h, but they're fine for transfers to resorts close to the airport. Dhoni transfers will cost about US$30 to US$60 depending on distance, but they're usually included in the basic package price. If the resort is more than 20km away, then 2½ hours on a hard wooden seat may be a bit too much, especially after a long plane flight. For more distant resorts, there's usually a faster boat, which may be an option for an additional price, or it may be the only choice.

**Dhoni Charters** In Male', go along the waterfront at the eastern end of Marine Drive (Boduthakurufaanu Magu), and you'll find lots of dhonis waiting in the harbour. Most of these are available for charter to nearby islands. The price depends on where you want to go, for how long, and on your negotiating skills – somewhere between Rf 800 and Rf 1000 for a day is a typical rate, but if you want to start at 6 am and go non-stop for 12 hours, it could be quite a bit more. You can also charter a dhoni at most resorts, but it will cost more (maybe US$200 or US$250 per day) and only if they're not all being used for excursions or diving trips.

A chartered dhoni will only take you to places you're allowed to go, and the owner or the skipper will be responsible for you. If you want to visit a resort, for lunch or a day at the beach or whatever, you should call the resort first to let them know you're coming. The dhoni will drop you at the resort jetty and a security person will greet you. If you want the boat to wait, it will probably have to anchor away from the jetty.

From Male' you're allowed to go to Kudabandos and to inhabited islands in North and South Male' Atolls – strictly speaking, you should be accompanied by someone from your guesthouse or hotel when you visit inhabited islands, but in fact the dhoni

## The Dhoni

The truck and bus of the Maldives is the sturdy dhoni, a vessel so ubiquitous that the word dhoni will soon become part of your vocabulary. Built in numerous shapes and sizes, the dhoni has been adapted for use as an ocean freighter, inter-atoll cruiser, family fishing boat, local ferry, tourist excursion boat, dive boat, live-aboard safari yacht, delivery truck and mini-fuel tanker. The traditional dhoni is thought to derive from the Arab dhow, but the design has been used and refined for so long in the Maldives that it is truly a local product.

There is a natural conservatism among Maldivian seafarers, perhaps common to mariners the world over. It is evident when you ask how long a dhoni trip will take – the time is usually an over-estimate, allowing for bad weather and any other possible delay. No-one wants a tight schedule, which might lead them into adverse currents or leave them picking through treacherous reefs in the dark. No-one wants to push their boat anywhere near its limits.

Traditionally, dhonis have a tall, curved prow which stands up like a scimitar cutting through the sea breezes. Most Maldivians say this distinctive prow is purely decorative, but in shallow water a man will stand at the front, spotting the reefs and channels and signalling to the skipper while holding the prow for balance. With many boats now docking bow-first at crowded jetties, the prow can interfere with boarding or loading and it's often dispensed with on modern utility craft. Nevertheless, the attractiveness of the jutting prow, not least to tourists, is well recognised, so a common compromise is to have a removable prow-piece. This slots into the front of the boat for appearances, but lifts out for loading and unloading. If you want to stand at the front of a dhoni like a figurehead, be aware that a removable prow-piece can be a slightly wobbly balancing post!

The flat stern is purely functional – it's where the skipper stands and steers, casually holding the tiller with his foot or between his legs. The stern platform is also a place for fishing. Even if they're not on a fishing trip, most dhoni crews will throw a trolling line out the back as soon as they get beyond the shallow reefs, and they pause periodically to pull in lunch or dinner. Finally, when a small dhoni makes a long trip, the 'head' is at the back – if nature calls, go right to the stern of the boat, face forward or backwards as your need and gender dictate, and rely on the skipper, passengers and crew to keep facing the front.

skipper might be considered an adequate minder. If you want to charter a dhoni to another atoll, you'll have to be invited by someone from that atoll and have an Inter-Atoll Travel Permit (see the Facts for the Visitor chapter).

## Vedi

A *vedi* is a large dhoni with a big, square-shaped wooden superstructure used for trading between Male' and the outer atolls. Sail-powered vedis once made trading trips to Sri Lanka, India, Burma and Sumatra, but these days the vedis are diesel powered and used only for inter-atoll transport.

No vedi will take you as a passenger to an atoll unless you have a permit to go there. To get a permit, you must be sponsored by someone from that atoll, and it's best to have that person arrange transport on the vedi. The vedis use Inner Harbour in Male', west of the fishing harbour. You can tell which atoll a boat comes from by looking at the code letter, marked within a square on the bow, next to the registration number:

| | | | |
|---|---|---|---|
| Haa Alifu | (A) | Meemu | (K) |
| Haa Dhaal | (B) | Faafu | (L) |
| Shaviyani | (C) | Dhaalu | (M) |
| Noonu | (D) | Thaa | (N) |
| Raa | (E) | Laamu | (O) |
| Baa | (F) | Gaaf Alif | (P) |
| Lhaviyani | (G) | Gaaf Dhaal | (Q) |
| Kaafu | (H) | Gnaviyani | (R) |
| Alifu | (I) | Seenu | (S) |
| Vaavu | (J) | | |

Boats based in Male' itself have the letter T.

## The Dhoni

The details on a dhoni are a mix of modern and traditional. The rudder is attached with neat rope lashing, but nowadays the rope is always plastic. The top planks at the bow are usually secured with an X-shaped rope tie, perhaps a legacy of the time when the whole boat was held together with coir (coconut fibre) rope. The dhoni design required almost no adaptation to take a diesel engine – they just bolted an engine between the bulkheads, drilled a hole through the stern post, and put a propeller in front of the rudder and just above the line of the keel. A motorised *ingeenu dhoni* has the same shallow draft as a sail-powered *riyalu dhoni* and the protected propeller will not snag on mooring lines or get damaged on a shallow reef. Despite modern materials (cotton caulking instead of coir; red oxide paint as well as shark oil), a modern dhoni will still leak, just like a traditional one, so there is a bilge pump just forward of the skipper – it's a simple but effective gadget made from plastic plumbing pipes.

When the government wanted to know if the design could be improved further, they employed a well-qualified Danish naval architect. His new dhoni design actually retained many features of the original, especially the shallow draft and the flat stern. The new boats seemed to be better, but no-one wanted them and they had to be sold at a discount. It took several years for fishermen to accept the seaworthiness of the new design and to recognise its greater fuel economy. However, there is now a waiting list for the new boats from the Alifushi Boat Yard.

It's not that Maldivians are resistant to change, they are just cautious about discarding the old and adopting the new. They have sailed these waters for centuries, and the reckless genes foundered on reefs many generations ago.

Most inhabited islands usually have a dhoni or two under construction or repair and you may see them on an excursion from a resort (if you can get away from the souvenir shops). The best dhoni builders are said to come from Raa Atoll and teams of them can be contracted to come to an island to make a new boat. Twelve workers, six on each side of the boat, can make a 14m hull in about 45 days, if their hosts keep them well fed. The keel is made from imported hardwood, while the hull planks are sometimes from local coconut trees but these days are usually from imported timber. Some of the work is now done with power tools, but no plans are used.

Travel on a vedi is slow and offers basic food and no creature comforts. Your bunk is a mat on a shelf, the toilet is the sea and fellow passengers may include chickens. A trip down to Seenu (Addu Atoll), the most southerly and distant atoll, will take at least two days and cost around Rf 300.

### Fast Boat
Resorts more than 15km or 20km from the airport usually offer transfer by speedboat or launch, which costs from US$45 to US$105 depending on distance. This is generally included in the package price, unless there is the option of transfer by dhoni, in which case a speedboat is priced as an extra.

The boats range from a small runabout with outboard motor to a big launch with aircraft-type seats and a deafening engine.

International Sea Services Maldives (ISSM; ☎ 321198, ✆ issm@dhivehinet.net.mv), on Faamdheyri Magu, hires speedboats (for up to five passengers). These are expensive with rates from US$500 to US$700 a day depending on how far you want to travel and how many hours you mean by 'a day'. Resorts will also hire speedboats for similarly high prices.

### Private Yacht
Visiting yachts must go to Male' as soon as they can and clear customs there. If they want to cruise around the Maldives they must apply to Atolls Administration for a Cruising Permit, which is quite expensive, especially for more than one week. See the Getting There & Away chapter for information on 'clearing-in' and getting a permit.

You can arrange day visits to resorts, but you must sleep on board your yacht.

## YACHT CHARTER

A new possibility in the Maldives is a charter yacht you can sail yourself around North and South Male' Atolls. Based at Giraavaru Resort, not far from Male', is a branch of the well-established Sunsail charter company, with half a dozen modern sailing vessels. A seven-berth boat costs US$250 to US$310 per day, and a nine-berth boat is US$370 per day. You can order all the food and drink you'll need for your trip (which is not included in the charter rate), and if you're not a competent sailor, it can provide a skipper for an extra US$250 per day. The local operator is MV Kethi (☎ 312101, mobile 772172, fax 312037, ✆ kethi@dhivehinet.net.mv).

## SAFARI CRUISES

If you want to see more of the Maldives than a tourist resort, and particularly if you want to move around a number of different islands and have dive sites all to yourself, a safari cruise might be the best way to go. The number of companies offering safari trips has increased considerably in recent years and some are undoubtedly better than others.

The standard of boats varies widely, as does the cost of chartering them. The most basic ones are large dhonis with six berths in two or three cramped cabins and a small communal dining area. A small boat will have six passenger berths, a large one will have as many as 14. The biggest and best boats are like mini cruise ships with spacious cabins, a comfortable dining room, lounge bar, jacuzzi and on-board dive base. Costs vary from US$60 to US$200 per person per day (depending on the boat and the season), including a US$6 per day bed tax and all meals, plus US$50 per day for diving trips. It's cheaper per head if there are enough passengers to fill the boat. You may be charged extra for soft drinks, and for alcohol if it's one of the better boats, and you may have to pay extra for the occasional meal at a resort, but generally there are few extras to spend money on.

Accommodation on a safari boat is usually in very small cabins, with shower and toilet shared between a couple of cabins. The bigger, better boats have air-conditioning and slightly more spacious accommodation. On the more basic ones, the passengers often drag their mattresses out on deck for fresh air and a bit more elbow room. On some trips, there may be a campout on an uninhabited island. Food is prepared on board and varies from very ordinary to very good.

A potential problem, especially on longer sightseeing cruises, is the compatibility of the group. If you're confined to a small boat and you can't stand half the people on board, a 7-day trip could become a real ordeal. Operators try to match the passengers in terms of age, nationality and language, but this isn't always possible. It's best if you can arrange your own group of six or so people who get along well and share interests.

### Diving Safaris

On diving trips, compatibility is less of a problem as most of the passengers share a common interest in diving. Everyone on a diving safari should be a qualified diver. Dive clubs can often get together enough members to fill a safari boat and design an itinerary that suits their needs.

Diving safaris usually have a separate dhoni, which follows the main boat and has the compressor and most of the equipment on board. This means that compressor noise doesn't disturb passengers at night, and the smaller boat can be used for excursions in shallower water.

### Choosing a Safari Boat

It's hard to make firm recommendations because there are so many boats and they often change ownership, skipper and cook. When you're considering a safari boat trip, ask the operator about:

**Boat Size** Generally speaking, bigger boats will be more comfortable than small boats, and also more expensive. Boats with more than a dozen or so passengers may not have the camaraderie you'd get with a small group. Most boats have less than 12 berths; few have more than 20.

**Cabin Arrangements** Can you get a two-berth cabin (if that's what you want)? How many cabins/people are sharing a bathroom?

**Comforts** Does the boat have air-con, hot water and desalinated water available 24 hours?

**Companions** Who else will be on the trip, what language do they speak, have they done a safari trip before? What are their interests – diving, sightseeing, fishing?

**Diving** Does the price include unlimited diving? Ideally there should be a separate diving dhoni. What equipment is available on board? Is it equipped for night diving?

**Food & Drink** There's not much point asking if the food is good! Is there a bar serving alcohol, and if so, how much is a beer/wine/scotch etc?

**Recreation** Does the boat have a video player, CD player, fishing tackle or sun deck? Does the boat have sails or is it propelled by motor only?

## Itineraries & Permits

Most safari trips do a loop through the tourist atolls. The shorter, seven-day trips will take in North and South Male' Atolls and Ari Atoll, possibly including Rasdhoo. A 14-day trip may also go south to Felidhoo Atoll, or north to Baa and Lhaviyani Atolls. To make a safari trip outside the tourist zone, the tour operator is required to get Inter-Atoll Travel Permits for all the passengers. These have to be arranged in advance and cost extra.

If your group intends to dive in sites that may contain ancient artefacts, the trip may need permission from the relevant government authority, which can be difficult. The usual Inter-Atoll Travel Permit does not cover visits to uninhabited islands, so if you hope to look at any remote archaeological sites, you should make sure that the safari operator can get the necessary permission.

You may have to spend a night in Male' before or after your trip, which should be regarded as an interesting bonus.

## Operators & Bookings

Some of the big tour operators arrange packages with safari trips, and they have probably checked the boat and its standards. On the other hand, a safari trip is something you might want tailored to the needs of your group, in which case it may be better to make arrangements directly.

Some operators you could try include:

**Eslire Maldives** (☎ 327438, fax 313604, ✉ eslire@dhivehinet.net.mv) A quality dive safari operation.

**ISSM** (☎ 321198, fax 310270, ✉ issm@dhivehinet.net.mv)

**Jetwing Maldives** (☎ 314037, fax 314038, ✉ jetwing@dhivehinet.net.mv)

**Meerufenfushi** (☎ 313149, fax 314150, ✉ meeru@dhivehinet.net.mv) Several safari boats operate out of this North Male' Atoll resort.

**Panorama** (☎ 327066, fax 326542, ✉ panorama@dhivehinet.net.mv) Well-regarded operator with six sizable safari boats.

**Paradise Holidays** (☎ 312090, fax 312087, ✉ parahol@dhivehinet.net.mv) Books the 100-bed *Ocean Paradise*, among others.

**Sea Explorers** (☎ 316172, 316783, ✉ seaexplo@divehinet.net.mv) A reliable Male'-based safari-boat and dive operation.

**Universal Enterprises** (☎ 323080, fax 322678, ✉ sales@unisurf.com) Runs the recommended, 146-berth *Island Explorer* and the 40-berth *Atoll Explorer*.

**Voyages Maldives** (☎ 322019, fax 325336, ✉ voyages@dhivehinet.net.mv) Probably the biggest, most established, safari-boat operator.

## CAR & MOTORCYCLE

The only places where visitors will need to travel by road are Male' and the southernmost atoll, Addu. If you don't feel like walking around even small islands, taxis are available in both places.

# Male'

## Highlights

MALE'

**Administrative District:** Male'
**Code Letter:** T
**Inhabited Islands:** 2 (or 3)
**Uninhabited Islands:** 1 (or 2)
**Resorts:** 0
**Population:** 65,000

- Walking around the capital city in just over an hour
- Taking breaks in the numerous tea shops and eating *hedhikaa* (short eats) with your tea
- Seeing white coral stone mosques with intricate carvings inside

✼✼✼✼✼✼✼✼✼✼✼✼✼✼✼✼✼✼✼✼✼✼

Small, quaint and densely settled, Male' (pronounced 'Mar-lay') is not a spectacular capital city, but it's very clean and friendly, and has a certain charm all of its own. The island of Male' is about 2km long and 1km wide, and completely covered with roads, buildings and a few well-used open spaces. New building work is going on everywhere and the place feels like it will soon burst at the seams, though in some ways it's still like a sleepy country town.

Officially, the population is around 65,000, but with foreign workers and short-term visitors from other islands there may be as many as 100,000 people in town. The population includes some 18,000 expatriates, perhaps 15% of them European. The size of the island has been considerably increased through land reclamation projects. Look at a map of Male' and you will get an idea of the extent of the island early this century, when the population was around 5000: The streets laid out in rectangular blocks on the edges of the island are all on reclaimed land, which amounts to more than half the total area. Recent reclamation has provided an artificial beach and some sports fields at the eastern end of the island, while landfill is being dumped inside the breakwater along the south side. This will extend land reclamation to the outer edge of the surrounding reef; after this there will be no further possibility of enlarging the island. Further growth can only be accommodated by more high-rise buildings, or on neighbouring islands.

Nearby islands are already being used for the airport and other purposes, and the island of Viligili is being developed for housing. There's also an ambitious project to create a completely new island, north of the airport, to accommodate more housing and commercial activities (see the Around Male' section at the end of this chapter).

Obviously, the population density and the rate of growth are causing problems. Quaint old buildings are being demolished to make way for bigger, more modern ones, and the quality of ground water has declined severely. There are still some lovely streetscapes, overhung with shady trees, but the loveliness is imperilled by new construction, and the increasingly brackish water supply may not support trees much longer. The first five-storey building went up in 1987 and the maximum permitted height has since increased from five storeys, to eight, to 12 and is now 15. Tall buildings are erected on tiny blocks of land, and the land-tenure system and the division of land at inheritance into smaller and smaller lots makes urban planning difficult.

An interesting architectural feature is the rounded corners of walls and buildings, especially at street junctions. This makes it easier for vehicles to negotiate tight corners, but it also softens the appearance of many buildings that would otherwise be undistinguished boxes. Many new, multistorey buildings also have rounded edges and are reminiscent of the Bauhaus style, but might also be called Male' Modern.

Traffic has increased to unpleasant levels and it's estimated that there is about one car for every 16m of road in the capital. The island will have its first traffic lights installed in 2000. It's obvious that more vehicles will reduce, not improve, the general level of mobility, but cars and motorcycles are status symbols and, despite high import taxes, more and more people seem able to afford them. In fact, parking problems have made private cars almost unusable, and nearly all the cars you see on the road are taxis.

## HISTORY

Male' has been the seat of the Maldives' ruling dynasties since before the 12th century, though none left any grand old palaces. Some trading houses appeared in the 17th century, along with a ring of defensive bastions, but Male' did not acquire the trappings of a city and had only a very limited range of economic and cultural activities. Visitors in the 1920s estimated the population at only 5000.

Growth started with the modernisation of the country in the 1930s, and the first banks, hospitals, high schools and government offices appeared in the following decades. It is only since the 1970s, with wealth from tourism and an expanding formal economy, that the city has really burgeoned and growth emerged as a problem.

## ORIENTATION

Boats from the airport or from the resort islands pull into the congested inner harbour, along Marine Drive. This road is now officially named Boduthakurufaanu Magu, but is still known by its older, more manageable name – it now goes almost right around the island, wholly on reclaimed land. (A *magu* is a wide street, traditionally with a sandy surface, but now often paved with small concrete blocks. A *goalhi* is a narrow lane and a *higun* is a longer, wider goalhi.)

The main square, Jumhooree Maidan, is on Marine Drive, along with many of the government and office buildings. Just to the south is the big Islamic Centre and Grand Friday Mosque, with its golden dome and tall minaret. Chandanee Magu runs past the western side of the square and has quite a few shops and tourist-oriented businesses, as do Fareedhee Magu, Orchid Magu and some smaller back streets nearby. This area is sometimes called Singapore Bazaar, because of the many imported goods on sale.

The other principal street is Majeedi Magu, which crosses the island from east to west. It has lots of shops for local people and they throng here in the evenings.

The fishing and commercial harbours are west of the main square. The New Harbour, at the south-west corner of the island, is

### Definite Articles, Apostrophes & Accents

The full name of the country is Dhivehi Raajjeyge Jumhooriyyaa, or Dhivehi Raajje for short. In English it's officially 'Republic of Maldives', but almost universally it is called THE Maldives, pronounced *mawl-divs*. Why the definite article? No-one seems to know, but it is probably carried over from references to the Maldive Islands and the Maldives Archipelago. The article is omitted in many contexts, like 'Visit Maldives Year'.

The capital of the country, and the name of its most important atoll, is Male', also written as Malé or Male. It's pronounced Mah-Lay, which certainly suggests an acute accent. However, the most common local spelling is with an apostrophe, used because the name is a contraction – it comes from the Malei dynasty, which ruled for 160 years from the time of conversion to Islam.

It was often assumed that Maldivians adopted the apostrophe because they couldn't do an acute accent on an old English typewriter. Foreign publishers with fancy typesetting technology took the liberty of converting the apostrophe to an accent, which was soon accepted as correct. Modern Maldivian publishers, with the very latest in word processing and desktop publishing software, prefer the apostrophe ending. Unfortunately, the accent ending is catching on, not because it is more correct to Maldivians, but because it is seen as being better English.

MALE'

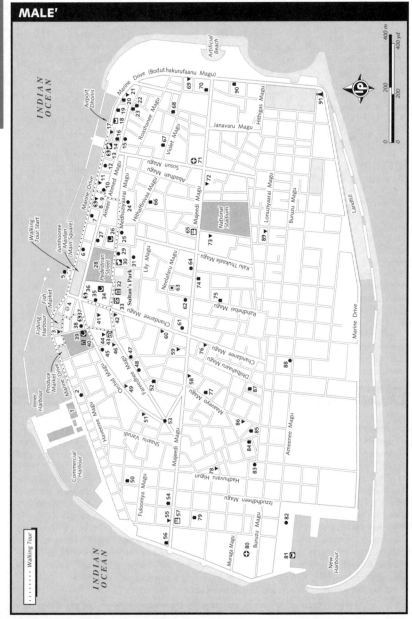

## PLACES TO STAY
16 Maadhhuni Inn
19 Nasandhura Palace Hotel
20 Maagiri Lodge
22 Kam Hotel
23 Relax Inn
50 Royal Inn
52 Maafaru Guesthouse
54 Male' Tour Inn
56 Villingili View Inn
66 Buruneege Residence
67 Kai Lodge
68 Extra Heaven Guesthouse
70 City Palace
74 Athamaa Palace Hotel
75 Central Hotel
77 Transit Inn
79 Classic Inn
84 Aquatic Residency
85 Onathoori Guesthouse
87 Blue Diamond Guesthouse
90 Holiday Lodge

## PLACES TO EAT
3 Dawn Cafe
9 Thai Wok
11 Beach Restaurant
17 Queen of the Night
21 Novanto Quatro
41 Nastha Tea Shop
42 Seagull Cafe
44 Slice Cafe
46 Food Bank
49 Twin Peaks Restaurant
51 Evening Cafe
55 Fini Tea Shop

58 Quench
59 Symphony Restaurant
60 Park View Restaurant
69 Haruge
72 Camy Cool Spot
73 Orange
76 Indian Restaurant
78 Symphonic
86 Kentucky
89 South Restaurant

## OTHER
1 Port Authority Building
2 People's Choice Supermarket
4 Public Toilet
5 President's Jetty
6 Ministry of Atolls Administration
7 Sun Travel & Tours
8 Bank of Maldives; Maldives Tourism Promotion Board
10 Indian High Commission
12 Airline Offices
13 State Bank of India
14 Danish, Finnish, Norwegian & Swedish Consulates
15 Inner Maldives
18 Post Office
24 Citizens' Majlis (Parliament Building)
25 Muleeaage
26 Hukuru Miskiiy (old mosque)
27 Immigration Department
28 NSS Headquarters
29 Esjehi Gallery
30 Sri Lankan High Commission

31 AMDC Clinic
32 National Museum
33 Dhiraagu (telephone office)
34 Islamic Centre & Grand Friday Mosque
35 Souvenir & Craft shops
36 Maldives Monetary Authority
37 Habib Bank
38 STO Trade Centre
39 Mosque
40 Theemuge (Presidential Palace)
43 Cyber Cafe
45 Universal Enterprises; American Express; German Consulate
47 Reethi Foto
48 Novelty Bookshop
53 Clock Tower
57 Star Cinema
61 Asrafee Bookshop
62 VSO Office
63 Tomb of Mohammed Thakurufaanu
64 National Library
65 Olympus Cinema
71 ADK Hospital
78 Novelty Bookshop
80 Indira Gandhi Memorial Hospital
81 Dhonis to Viligili
82 Outdoor Stage
83 Baansaree Laundry
88 SEA Dive School
91 Tetrapod Monument

used by safari boats and dhonis shuttling to the nearby island of Viligili. On the eastern side of the island, land reclamation has provided some much-needed space for recreation. There's not much grass as yet, but trees have been planted, and in the evenings it's an especially popular place for walking, socialising, kite flying, cricket and traditional Maldivian games like *bashi* (see Spectator Sports in the Facts for the Visitor chapter). The 'artificial beach' here offers an inviting semicircle of sea water, mainly for kids to splash in. A little farther south, a fair to middling right-hand wave attracts crowds of local surfers.

On the south side of the island, landfill is being dumped in the space between the breakwater and the waterfront road, which will extend the land area to the maximum possible extent.

For the purposes of street and postal addresses, the capital is divided into four districts, from west to east: Maafannu, which covers most of the western end of the island; Machangolhi, which runs north-south across the middle of the island; Galolhu, a crowded residential maze in the south-central part of Male'; and Henveiru, covering the east and north-east. These districts are not discernible to visitors, but the addresses are understood by taxi drivers (see also Post in the following Information section). Street numbers are rarely used – many premises are known by a building name.

MALE'

## Maps
The Maldives Tourism Promotion Board (MTPB) brochure has an adequate map; it's given out free at the airport and at their office in town.

## INFORMATION
As well as expanding, Male' is changing rapidly due to constant rebuilding. Government and commercial offices shift around and new developments spring up. As it only takes 30 minutes to walk from one end of the island to the other, the inconvenience is minimal and taxi drivers seem to know every business, office and household in town.

## Tourist Offices
The MTPB (☎ 323228) has an information counter on the 4th floor of the Bank of Maldives building on Marine Drive. It has some maps and other printed material and can answer specific inquiries. It's open from 7.30 am to 2.30 pm Sunday to Thursday. The information desk at the airport is run by Air Maldives, and is supposedly open when international flights arrive, but often isn't. Even when it's not staffed, look on the shelf out the front for some useful booklets.

Travel agents at the airport and in Male' may also supply information on resorts, safari trips and, to a lesser extent, the outer atolls. (See Independent Travel in the Facts for the Visitor chapter before you start dealing with local agents.) Sun Travel & Tours (☎ 325975), on Marine Drive, has the 'i' symbol outside and helpful staff inside. Also very helpful, and close to where the airport boats arrive, is Inner Maldives (☎ 326309), on Ameer Ahmed Magu.

## Money
Several banks are clustered near the harbour end of Chandanee Magu and east along Marine Drive, and will change travellers cheques. Most open from about 8 am to 1.30 pm Sunday to Thursday, maybe 9.30 am to 12.30 pm during Ramadan. The Maldives Monetary Authority, on Chandanee Magu, can be crowded and slow. For faster service, try Habib Bank, just around the corner next to the STO building, or the State Bank of India on Marine Drive. Some of the authorised moneychangers around town will give you US$ or Maldivian cash in exchange for US$ travellers cheques. Try some of the hardware shops, souvenir shops and guesthouses. Most tourist businesses will accept US$ cash at the standard rate, and the main European currencies at reasonable rates.

The Bank of Maldives has a few ATMs around town, but they can only access local accounts. The American Express agent is Universal Enterprises Ltd (☎ 322971, fax 322678), 39 Orchid Magu.

## Post
The post office is in new premises on Marine Drive, near the airport boat landing, and is open from 7.30 am to 6 pm, Sunday to Thursday. Postal addresses often consist simply of the name of a house or building preceded by an abbreviation for the district (see under Orientation earlier in this chapter): M for Maafannu, Ma for Machangolhi, G for Galolhu, H for Henveiru.

## Telephone & Fax
The Maldives telephone company, Dhiraagu, has an office on Medhuziyaarai Magu, near the intersection with Chandanee Magu. It's open Sunday to Thursday from 7.30 am to 10 pm, and on Friday and public holidays from 9 am to 6 pm. You can send telegrams and faxes, buy phonecards and make calls from the public phones outside. Operator-connected calls are also available, but more expensive than using a phonecard.

## Email & Internet Access
Dhiraagu operates Male's one and only cyber cafe, conveniently located a block west of the Chandanee Magu shopping strip. It's a small, comfortable facility with modern equipment and quite quick connections. It opens 9 am to 11 pm Saturday to Thursday, 2.30 to 11 pm on Fridays and religious holidays, but it's very popular and you may have to wait a while to get on a machine. There's an initial charge of Rf 15, plus Rf 20 for the first 15 minutes or Rf 30 for the first 30 minutes, and Rf 1 per minute after that. Printing and scanning is charged on a per-page basis.

## Travel Agencies

There's a plethora of travel agents in Male' – anyone with a table, chair and an Internet connection seems ready to call themselves an agent. Most of the smaller ones do nothing but try to sell an allocation of rooms at a resort or two. If you're an independent traveller looking for a resort or a safari tour, see Independent Travel in the Facts for the Visitor chapter, and be prepared to do some shopping around – ask in town, or call one or more of the following:

| | |
|---|---|
| AAA Travel & Tours | ☎ 325975 |
| Capital Travel & Tours | ☎ 315089 |
| Inner Maldives | ☎ 326309 |
| Island Holidays | ☎ 322719 |
| Ocean Travel & Tours | ☎ 320435 |
| Sun Travel & Tours | ☎ 325975 |
| Voyages Maldives | ☎ 325349 |

## Bookshops

Most bookshops deal mainly in school books, magazines and stationery. The Maldive's most avid readers must be teenagers, because the biggest stocks are of series like *Goosebumps*, *Sweet Valley High* and *Babysitters Club*, not to mention *Archie* comics. Asrafee Bookshop, on Chandanee Magu near the corner of Majeedi Magu, has a small selection of English paperbacks. Novelty Bookshop, on Fareedhee Magu, has a few very good books on the Maldives, some of which they publish themselves.

## Libraries

The National Library is in a big, newly renovated building on Majeedi Magu, and has quite a few English books, some from the library at the old RAF base which operated on the southern island of Gan from 1956 to 1976. Nonresidents can't borrow books, but are welcome to sit and read in the library which is open daily except Friday.

The British Voluntary Service Overseas (VSO) office (☎ 323167), has a book-exchange scheme, though this may not be permanent.

## Laundry

Any hotel will take care of your laundry for a few dollars per item. Guesthouses will do

it more cheaply, or arrange for someone to do it for you. Allow a couple of days if the weather is rainy. There are no laundromats (yet), and only a couple of dedicated laundry services – Baansaree Laundry, a few blocks from the New Harbour, charges Rf 3 for shirts, Rf 5 for jeans and Rf 10 for underpants!

## Toilets

The few public toilets are reasonably clean, provide toilet paper and cost Rf 2. One that's convenient to the shopping area is just west of the main square, on the street that goes behind the fish market.

## Medical Services

The government-run Indira Gandhi Memorial Hospital (☎ 316647) is a modern public facility, but visitors would probably be better off using either the European-run AMDC Clinic (☎ 325979) on Dharmavantha Magu, or the ADK Private Hospital (☎ 313553) on Sosun Magu, which has western-trained doctors and dentists. Neither is cheap, but both will make arrangements with travel-insurance companies. Both have doctors trained to do a diving medical check.

### Emergency

Hopefully you won't need to call the following numbers:

| | |
|---|---|
| Ambulance | ☎ 102 |
| Fire | ☎ 118 |
| Police | ☎ 119 |

## Dangers & Annoyances

It's hard to imagine a place less threatening, but there is a problem with theft and burglary. Locals are very careful about locking their houses, and unlocked bicycles tend to disappear quickly.

## WALKING TOUR

Start from the waterfront near **Jumhooree Maidan**, the main square, conspicuous for the huge Maldivian flag flying on its eastern side. The fountain here is illuminated in changing colours every evening. Tour boats from the resorts pull in here, near the carved

MALE'

wooden **president's jetty**. If you've come from the airport, your dhoni will pull in farther east, so just walk west towards the flag. Continue west along the waterfront and you'll pass the main fishing harbour – this is a great sight in the late afternoon when dozens of colourful dhonis are unloading fish by the hundreds, mostly large, silver tuna. On the left you'll find the **fish market**, with more fat fish than you've ever seen before. Farther on is the **produce market**, trading the limited range of fruit and vegetables grown in the Maldives. Coconuts and bananas are the most plentiful produce, but look inside for the stacks of betel leaf, for wrapping up a 'chew'. Continue for a few more blocks along the waterfront, a bustling area with hardware shops and hang-outs for sailors and fishermen. Fishing and marketing are men's work here, and though decent Maldivian women don't venture into these areas, they're perfectly safe – there's no alcohol sold in Male', so the waterfront 'bars' are actually tranquil tea shops.

Ahead you'll notice a big, modern white building, shaped like the bridge of a ship – this is the **Port Authority** headquarters. Retrace your steps, turn right after the produce market and turn down the street to your left one block inland. This passes behind the **Theemuge**, or Presidential Palace – notice the watchtowers on the corners with the narrow gun embrasures and remember that the last coup attempt was in 1988. Pass the back of the fish market, turn right at its south-east corner, walk one block, do a dogleg and walk another block. There are lots of shops and a few tea shops around here.

Turn right, on Orchid Magu, and continue on to the four-storey STO building, which houses a supermarket and various shops and offices. On the next corner is a charming, old-fashioned little **mosque**. Continue half a block to see the front of the presidential palace, then go back to the corner and turn south. Go down to the end of the block and turn left onto Fareedhee Magu, walk another block and you'll reach Chandanee Magu, one of the main commercial streets. The two irregular blocks between Chandanee Magu and the STO building have most of the sou-

## House Names

Although the street names in Male' will be strange to your ears, the house names are typically in picturesque English. Some Maldivians prefer rustic titles like Crabtree, Hillman, Forest and G Meadow (the G stands for Galolhu, which is the district that the house is in). Others are specifically floral, like Sweet Rose and Luxury Garden, or even vegetable, like Carrot, or the perplexing Leaf Mess. Marine titles and anything with blue in it are also popular, such as Sea Speed, Marine Dream, Dawn Dive, Blue Haven and Bright Blue. The tropical sun gives rise to the likes of Sun Dance, Radiant, Sunny Coast and Plain Heat.

There are also exotic names like Paris Villa and River Nile; more obscure choices like Remind House, Pardon Villa, Frenzy and Mary Lightning; or those that sound like toilet disinfectants – Ozone, Green Zest. For Anglophile ambiguity, it's hard to beat Aston Villa as a house name.

Shop names, on the other hand, often have an overt advertising message – People's Choice Supermarket, Fair Price, Goodwill and Neat Store. Premier Chambers is not a pretentious house name – it's where you'll find Male's first barrister.

venir shops and various eateries. This area was once known as 'Singapore Bazaar', because of the number of shops selling cheap electrical goods, but now it's the **tourist shopping area**, and you'll be met with numerous invitations to 'come and see my shop'. Go east on Medhuziyaarai Magu with the impressive **Grand Friday Mosque** on your left and the **National Museum** and **Sultan's Park** on your right (see separate entries later in this chapter).

Continue east on Medhuziyaarai Magu, with the wall of the NSS (National Security Service) headquarters on your left (no photos please), past the **Esjehi Gallery** (see the separate entry later). The ancient **Hukuru Miskiiy mosque**, with its carved tombstones and fat round minaret, is in the next block, and the **Muleeaage** is opposite (see the separate entry later in this chapter). Go another block to the new **Citizens' Majlis** (parliament), built with aid from Pakistan. Turn left and walk two blocks back to the waterfront, then turn right (east) to see a **dhoni jam** – the harbour here is crowded with boats, which go to the airport and anywhere else people charter them to. Turn around and go west along Marine Drive, past several banks and government buildings, and past the coastguard boats and you'll soon be back at the square where you started.

## WALKING AROUND THE ISLAND

If you have some spare time and energy, it is possible to walk right around Male' island. Allow at least an hour for this 4km clockwise trek; and don't try it in the heat of the day – there's very little shade. It's most pleasant in late afternoon, when lots of local people are out playing games or promenading.

Starting at the main square, walk east along Marine Drive past the busy harbour, and continue around to the east side of the island. The reclaimed land here looks pretty barren, but every evening you'll see people playing cricket, soccer, volleyball, basketball and that Maldivian speciality bashi. The **artificial beach** is actually a very attractive sheltered pool, and it will be even nicer when the palm trees grow to provide some shade and greenery. Continue south along the waterfront walking path and you'll have a good view of the Male' surf scene, at its best from March to November.

Near the south-east corner of Male' is the **tetrapod monument** to the construction of Male's sea defences. Tetrapods are cast concrete shapes with four fat legs, each maybe 1m long, sticking out like the four corners of a tetrahedron. Large numbers of blocks are placed in rows so they interlock together and form a breakwater that dissipates the force of the waves and protects the shoreline. A Japanese foreign-aid project provided the sea walls after severe flooding in a 1988 storm. Also nearby are some of the old **cannons** that were once part of Male's military defences.

The south side of the island can be quite unsightly (and sometimes smelly) as earthmoving machinery is dumping landfill in the space between the breakwater and the

waterfront road. Following Marine Drive (or Boduthakurufaanu Magu, if you can say it) to the west will eventually bring you past some more new sports grounds and then to the **New Harbour**, where many commercial boats are repaired and resupplied. A rectangular space by the harbour is the venue for an outdoor concert on Thursday evenings – traditional drum groups and popular rock bands belt it out over a powerful sound system, while lots of small shops provide refreshments and snacks at outdoor tables.

Marine Drive is interrupted by the harbour, but it resumes on the west side of the island, at the conspicuous Indira Gandhi Memorial Hospital. The west coast is also protected by a tetrapod wall, which offers good views west over the busy shipping channel to the neighbouring island of Viligili. It's a good place to watch the sun set, and local kids enjoy fishing and kite flying here. Continuing around to the north side of the island, Marine Drive passes the **commercial harbour**, where containers and freight are unloaded, and there are some associated workshops and warehouses. Then there's the fishing harbour and the fish market, and soon you're back on the main square.

## ISLAMIC CENTRE & GRAND FRIDAY MOSQUE

Opened in 1984, and built with help from the Gulf States, Pakistan, Brunei and Malaysia, this *miskiiy* (mosque) dominates the skyline in the middle of Male'. As your boat comes into the capital, you'll see the gold dome glinting in the sun. (The gold is actually anodised aluminium.) The *munnaaru*, or minaret, is supposed to be the tallest structure in Male', but some of the newer buildings may be higher.

Visits to the Grand Friday Mosque must be between 9 am and 5 pm, but not during prayer times. (It closes to non-Muslims 15 minutes before prayers and for the following hour.) Before noon and between 2 and 3 pm are the best times to visit. Invading bands of casual sightseers are not encouraged, but if you are genuinely interested and suitably dressed, you'll get in. Men must wear long pants and women a long skirt or dress.

The main prayer hall inside the mosque can accommodate up to 5000 worshippers and has beautifully carved wooden side panels and doors, a specially woven carpet and impressive chandeliers. The Islamic Centre also includes a conference hall, library and classrooms.

## HUKURU MISKIIY

Close by on Medhuziyaarai Magu, Hukuru Miskiiy is the oldest mosque in the country, dating from 1656. (The name means Friday mosque, but don't confuse it with the much bigger and newer Grand Friday Mosque.) The exterior is protected by a corrugated-iron covering, so it doesn't look much from the outside. The interior, however, is superb and famed for its intricate carvings. One long panel, carved in the 13th century, commemorates the introduction of Islam to the Maldives. Visitors wishing to see inside are supposed to get permission from an official of the Ministry of Justice & Islamic Affairs (☎ 322266). However, most of the staff are officials of the ministry and, if you're respectful and well dressed, they may well give you permission on the spot.

The mosque was built on the foundations of an old temple which faced west to the setting sun, not north-west towards Mecca. Consequently, the worshippers have to face the corner of the mosque when they pray.

Overlooking the mosque is the solid, round, blue and white tower of the munnaaru – at first you may think it's a water tank, but the doors in the side are a giveaway. Though it doesn't look that old, it dates from 1675. West of the mosque is a graveyard, with many elaborately carved tombstones. Those with rounded tops are for women, those with pointy tops are for men and those with gold-plated lettering are the graves of former sultans. The small buildings are family mausoleums and their stone walls are intricately carved. Respectful and respectably dressed tourists are welcome to walk around the graveyard.

## MULEEAAGE

Across the road from the Hukuru Miskiiy is a blue and white building with an elaborate gatehouse. This is the Muleeaage, built as a palace in the early 20th century. The sultan was deposed before he could move in and the building was used for government offices for about 40 years. It became the president's residence in 1953 when the first republic was proclaimed, but President Gayoom moved to a new official residence in 1994. At the eastern end of the building's compound, behind the gatehouse, is the **tomb of Abu Al Barakaath**, who brought Islam to Male' in 1153 AD.

## NATIONAL MUSEUM

Heading west from the Muleeaage on Medhuziyaarai Magu is the National Museum. Housed in a small, three-storey building, it is the only remaining part of the original sultan's palace, the rest was demolished in 1968 at the beginning of the second republic.

The museum has an ill-assorted collection that is not very well displayed, but it's worth a visit. Many of the exhibits are things once owned by the sultans – clothing, utensils, weapons and a throne. Some of the fabrics are beautiful, especially the rich brocades. Excellent, traditional lacquer work is displayed on large bowls and trays used to bring gifts to the sultan. Weapons include *bonthi* sticks, which were used in martial arts, and a *silvan bonthi*, used by a husband to punish an unfaithful wife.

Especially interesting are the pre-Islamic stone carvings collected by Thor Heyerdahl and others from sites all over the country. They include a fine Buddha's head, and various phallic images. Unfortunately they are poorly labelled and there's nothing to explain the significance or historical context of these fascinating finds.

Miscellaneous items include a WWI German torpedo (donated by a Royal Navy warship), a Maldivian flag taken into space by US astronauts, and two motorcycles with bullet holes from the 1988 coup attempt.

The museum is open from 8 am to noon and 3 to 6 pm Sunday to Thursday, 3 to 6 pm Friday and is closed on Saturday and government holidays. Entry is Rf 25 for foreigners, Rf 10 for Maldivians and Rf 5 for children under 12.

## SULTAN'S PARK

The park surrounding the museum was once part of the grounds of the sultan's palace. It is a small but pleasant retreat from the streets. Officially, it's only open on Friday from 4 to 6.30 pm, but the museum is inside the park gates, so you can get in any time the museum is open.

## ESJEHI GALLERY

On Medhuziyaarai Magu, just east of the Sultan's Park, one of Male's oldest buildings houses a small gallery and artists workshop dedicated to the preservation and promotion of traditional and contemporary Maldivian arts and crafts. The building dates from the 1870s and was originally the home of a nobleman. It's quite small, but has handsome rooms, beautifully preserved wooden panels and some fine carving. Occasional exhibitions feature, and sometimes sell, the work of local artists. The gallery is open from 8 am to 6.30 pm Saturday to Thursday and 2 to 7 pm Friday; entry to exhibitions costs Rf 20, and even if there's no exhibition, there's a good chance of meeting and talking with members of Male's arts community.

## GUEST SHOPPING AREA

This commercial zone, along and around Chandanee Magu, Fareedhee Magu and Orchid Magu, has lots of souvenir shops, a few cafes and a couple of hardware shops. It's convenient if you want to browse through a lot of shops in search of something special rather than a T-shirt or Balinese wood carving. (See the Shopping section in the Facts for the Visitor chapter for some suggestions.)

## TOMB OF MOHAMMED THAKURUFAANU

In the back streets in the middle of town, in the grounds of a small mosque, is the tomb of the Maldives' greatest hero, the man who liberated the country from Portuguese rule and was then the sultan from 1573 to 1585. He is also commemorated in the new name for Marine Drive – Boduthakurufaanu Magu (*bodu* means big or great).

## MOSQUES

There are more than 20 miskiiys in Male'; some are simple coral buildings with an iron roof and others are quite stylish with elegant minarets. Outside there is always a well or some sort of outdoor bathroom, because Muslims must always wash before they pray. Visitors usually can't go inside, but there's no need to – the doors are always wide open, and you can clearly see that the interior is nearly always devoid of furniture or decoration.

## CANNONS

An interesting diversion (or excuse for a walk around Male's coastline) is to go spotting ancient cannons. Most of Male's cannons are from the 10 old bastions built around the island in 1632 to deter any Portuguese attacks. The bastions were demolished in the 1960s and the cannons became landfill, but those recently uncovered by dredging have been cleaned up, decorated and proudly placed along the waterfront.

## PLACES TO STAY

Accommodation in Male' is quite expensive by Asian standards, with the most basic places starting at US$25 and quite ordinary air-con rooms costing around US$50. Foreigners, unless they have a resident permit, must pay a bed tax of US$6, which is always included in the price. A few guesthouses, used mainly by locals, quote their prices in Rufiya; others are priced in US$. Most places have only a few rooms, and the better ones fill up fast, so it's worth telephoning ahead.

## PLACES TO STAY – BUDGET

One of the best budget choices is the ***Blue Diamond Guesthouse*** (☎ 326125, ✉ *bdiamond@dhivehinet.net.mv*), on a small street called Badifasgandu Magu, south of Majeedi Magu. It's not a particularly interesting location, but the management is friendly, helpful and efficient, and the place is popular with VSO workers and various visitors on limited budgets. It costs US$25/35 for small, simple fan-cooled singles/doubles with private bathroom, cool showers, drinking water and breakfast.

Another good bet is **Holiday Lodge** (☎ 310279), on Marine Drive on the eastern side of the island, opposite the sea near the artificial beach. The rooftop terrace has a great outlook, but poor architectural design means that no rooms have views. Rooms are clean, but very plain, with a private bathroom, ceiling fan, firm bed (and not much else) for about US$25/35. The manager is a friendly guy, well informed about travel options.

In the back streets at the east end of town, the **Extra Heaven Guesthouse** (☎ 327453) is bigger than most. Its 18 rooms are small and nothing fancy, but they're clean and have bathrooms. Singles/doubles are US $25/35 with fan, or US$35/40 with air-con. There's satellite TV in the lounge and fresh water.

Some other cheapies are scattered in the blocks around the west side of town. **Maafaru Guesthouse** (☎ 313558), Champa Magu, has unattractive 1st-floor rooms from Rf 250, and might be tolerable if everything else is full. **Male' Tour Inn** (☎ 326220), Shaheed Ali Higun, is marginally more appealing, with small, basic rooms facing an open courtyard. It's cleanish, and costs US$25/30. **Classic Inn** (☎ 324311), on Iramaa Magu, has a few rooms at US$25/35. However, it's usually full with visiting Maldivians, as is the narrow-fronted, multistorey four-room **Onathoori Guesthouse** (☎ 320322), Alamaa Goalhi, which asks only Rf 260 for tourists.

## PLACES TO STAY – MID-RANGE

Mid-range accommodation in Male' starts at around US$35/45 for singles/doubles with breakfast, and offers considerably better standards. Most rooms will have air-con, a phone and hot water in the bathroom, and the better ones will have TV. You might get a discount at some of these places in low season or if you stay more than a few days.

The **Aquatic Residency** (☎ 316388), south-west of the centre on Javaahiru Hingun, has small but pleasant upstairs rooms from US$36/42. More central, slightly more expensive and often recommended is the **Transit Inn** (☎ 320420), Maaveyo Magu, which has 10 pleasant and spacious rooms

and a rooftop patio with a sea view. Air-con singles/doubles cost US$40/55 with breakfast, and the manager is a helpful gentleman.

Also on the west side of town, **Royal Inn** (☎ 320573), Izzudhdheen Magu, is a clean, friendly, well-run place with a variety of singles/doubles at US$45/55, and family rooms at US$60. **Villingili View Inn** (☎ 318696), at the west end of Majeedi Magu, has standard rooms at US$50/65, and slightly better deluxe rooms at US$60/75. However, only a couple have views over the water to Viligili Island, and none are very good value.

Two places handy to the airport boat harbour are **Maagiri Lodge** (☎ 322576), at the east end of Marine Drive, with smallish, fan-cooled single/double rooms with air-con, telephone, hot water and local TV for US$55/65; and **Maadhhuni Inn** (☎ 322824, 📧 maadhuni@dhivehinet.net.mv), a block inland on Ameer Ahmed Magu, with six small but well-furnished rooms for US $50/60.

A few blocks inland on Violet Magu, **Kai Lodge** (☎ 328742) has clean, comfortable rooms with bathroom, hot water, IDphone, satellite TV and air-con for US$50/60; US$5 more with breakfast. A couple of two-room apartments accommodate four people for US$100. Another nice, new place at the east end of Majeedi Magu, not far from the artificial beach, is **City Palace** (☎ 312152, 📧 citymale@dhivehinet.net.mv). It has comfortable, well-equipped rooms which cost US$55/66/77; US$5 more with breakfast.

**Athamaa Palace Hotel** (☎ 313118), near the middle of town on Majeedi Magu, has 15 rooms on various levels, all with air-con, satellite TV and bathrooms with hot water. Some of the rooms have a panoramic view of the town. Singles/doubles cost US$50/57 without breakfast.

The only place in an old-style building is the **Buruneege Residence** (☎ 330011), centrally located on Hithaffinivaa Magu. The rooms are set around an inner courtyard, and have private bathrooms and phones, but have no particular character. They cost US$40/50, or US$45/55 for an air conditioned room.

## PLACES TO STAY – TOP END

Three of Male's 'top-end' hotels are on the north-east corner of the island, handy to the airport dhonis, and a new fourth one is in the middle of town – all are comfortable, but none outstanding. If you have to spend a night in Male' awaiting a resort transfer, your tour operator will probably put you up in one of these. Note that alcohol is not served at any of these hotels. A new hotel will open on the airport island in 2000, which will be a more convenient but less interesting location than Male'.

*Nasandhura Palace Hotel* (☎ *323380, fax 320822, ℮ nasndhra@dhivehinet.net .mv)*, on Marine Drive, has a handsome lobby, but the rooms are just like an ordinary, comfortable mid-range motel, with air-con, IDD phone, minibar and satellite TV. Singles/doubles cost US$75/89, including breakfast. There is a business centre, conference facilities, 24-hour coffee shop and a good restaurant.

Just around the corner, side by side, are two good hotels, the *Kam Hotel* (☎ *320611, fax 320614, ℮ kamhotel@dhivehinet.net .mv)* and the *Relax Inn* (☎ *314531, fax 314533, ℮ relaxinn@dhivehinet.net.mv)*, both multistorey buildings on small allotments. They have smallish but comfortable rooms with all the usual facilities; some have great views over the town and out to sea. They both have restaurants on the top floor. The Relax is a little less expensive, at US$70/86 for bed and breakfast, and it may give a discount if it's quiet. The Kam is slightly classier and has a swimming pool, albeit tiny. It costs around US$80/96 for bed and breakfast.

The new *Central Hotel* (☎ *317766, fax 315383, ℮ central@dhivehinet.net.mv)* is in a high-rise building on Rahdhebai Magu, just south of Majeedi Magu – the big neon sign is easy to spot. The standard and deluxe rooms are a bit small, but are comfortable and well furnished and have all the mod-cons. Prices start at US$66/77. The junior suites are more spacious and cost US$90/101. All rooms on the upper floors offer good views over the town. It's some distance from the airport harbour, but they provide free transfers.

On Hulhule, the airport island, *Hulhule Island Hotel* (☎ *330888, ℮ sales@hih.com .mv)* plans to open in 2000, and will be mainly used by transit passengers and air crews. It will have 88 rooms, a swimming pool, restaurant, coffee shop and a bar serving alcohol (this may become an attraction for foreigners living in Male'). Rates will be around US$118/128 for singles/doubles.

## PLACES TO EAT

Basically, there are two sorts of places to eat in Male': tea shops, serving Maldivian food, and modern restaurants, serving a range of European and Asian dishes. The distinction is becoming a little blurred as some traditional tea shops have broadened their menus, installed air-conditioning and improved their service. The big hotels have their own restaurants, and during the fasting month of Ramadan these are the only places serving meals between sunrise and sunset.

### Tea Shops

Tea shops are frequented by Maldivian men – it's not the done thing for a Maldivian women to be in one, but there's no law against it. Foreign women use them sometimes, generally with a male companion, and there's no problem. They're a great place to meet the locals, and they are very cheap.

Tea shops will always have 'short eats' – a selection of small items called *hedhikaa*, which include little bowls of rice pudding; tiny bananas; wobbly, gelatinous colourful morsels made from an indeterminate substance; curried fish cakes; and frittered dough balls, which are sometimes empty, sometimes filled, usually fishy and mostly spicy. The goodies are displayed at a counter behind a glass screen, and customers line up and choose, cafeteria style. This can be a little difficult if you don't know what the things are called, but it's easy enough to point, and you have a chance to ask about the items on display. Tea costs Rf 2 and the hedhikaa are Rf 1 to Rf 3. You can fill yourself for under Rf 10.

At meal times they also serve 'long eats', such as omelettes, soups, curried fish, *roshi* (unleavened bread) and sauce. At breakfast or lunch, Maldivians tear up roshi and mix it in a bowl with soup or curry. A cup of *sai* (tea) accompanies the food and is usually drunk black and sweet. (See the Food section in the Facts for the Visitor chapter.) A good meal costs from Rf 12 to Rf 25.

A bigger and slightly better tea shop might be called a cafe or 'hotel'. Often you can phone the local tea shop and it will deliver short eats.

Tea shops open as early as 5 am and close as late as 1 am, particularly around the port area where they cater to fishermen. During Ramadan they're open till 2 am or even later, but closed during the day. They close their doors for 15 minutes at prayer times, but if you're already inside, you won't have to stop talking or eating, and they certainly won't throw you out.

There are dozens and dozens of tea shops in Male', mostly low-key, inconspicuous establishments without a big sign out the front. You'll find them on almost every street. They're all have quite similar decor, menus, service and prices. The following suggestions are a sample, and include places with good atmosphere in different parts of town.

There are quite a few tea shops along the waterfront. Near the east end of Marine Drive, the very popular **Queen of the Night** has tables next to the street where men play *carrom* and chess till all hours. The tables in the back and upstairs are always busy with guys grabbing some short eats. Further west is the **Beach Restaurant**, one of the newer, more elegant tea shops. It has a selection of curries (Rf 10), noodles (Rf 32), steaks (Rf 65), and snacks on its 'Menu of Most Satisfaction', as well as the usual short eats which are not on the menu. It's air-conditioned, and for young local guys it has the great attraction of young women waiting on tables. Everyone is very well behaved, but this passes for wild nightlife in Male'.

In the Guest Shopping Area, on a side street west of Chandanee Magu, *Nastha* has an air-conditioned section upstairs, with comfortable seating and a good selection of short and long eats. The downstairs section is not air-conditioned and is thick with cigarette smoke.

In the area around the fish market there are quite a few standard tea shops. One of the bigger ones is the **Dawn Cafe**, where you can get a brilliant meal – try it on Friday afternoon when people come in after going to the mosque.

At the west end of Majeedi Magu, across the road from the Star Cinema, the **Fini** tea shop is a cool place for a breakfast of roshi and *mas huni* (flat bread and shredded tuna with spices).

There are quite a few tea shops around the stadium. Near the entrance is **Orange**, with excellent, take-away hedhikaa. **Camy Cool Spot**, on Majeedi Magu, has some of the spiciest snacks. **South Restaurant**, behind the National Stadium, has a consistently good selection of short eats.

## Restaurants

Most of the Male' restaurants are distinguished by their fancier appearance, higher prices and the fact that there are women inside. They serve a range of international, usually palatable but rarely outstanding, dishes. Remember that nearly everything is

Hookahs can be seen and heard all over the Maldives.

imported, including the prawns and the lobsters, which will be the most expensive items if they're available. The customers are mostly business people, young Maldivian couples, sundry expats and day-trippers from nearby resorts. None of these restaurants serve alcohol, but some serve nonalcoholic beer for about Rf 15 per can.

One of the most pleasant and popular places is the *Seagull Cafe*, at the corner of Chandanee Magu and Fareedhee Magu, with its delightfully shaded outdoor eating area. It serves sandwiches and snacks from Rf 25 to Rf 50, delicious juices (Rf 25), full meals from Rf 90, and a genuine cappuccino for Rf 25. The specialty is the range of ice creams and sundaes starting at Rf 35. Nearby, on Faamudheyri Magu, *Slice Cafe* is good for breakfast and snacks, including burgers (Rf 12 to Rf 15), juice (Rf 10) and cappuccino (Rf 12).

The well-established *Twin Peaks* is an Italian restaurant on Orchid Magu. It has pretty good pizzas for Rf 100 to Rf 140, pastas for around Rf 100, fish from Rf 100, as well as ice cream and real coffee. The atmosphere is pleasant and the service is good. It's quite a smart place and popular with business people and expats. Another good Italian place is *Novanto Quatro*, at the north-east corner of the island, which incorporates the Manik's Pizza delivery service (☎ 320012), said to produce the best pizzas in town.

Another interesting option is the *Thai Wok*, on Marine Drive. The Thai curries and the rice dishes are very good and not too expensive at Rf 25 to Rf 35.

For something different, try *Haruge*, which faces the artificial beach on the east side of the island. At street level there's a snack bar with burgers from Rf 10 to Rf 20, while upstairs is a delightful, open-sided eating area decorated with Maldivian antiques and marine artefacts. The food is well prepared and reasonably priced, but it's the friendly management, the interesting Maldivian and international clientele, and the sea views that make this a really fun place to eat.

The *Park View* is an Indian restaurant on Chandanee Magu, with thick table cloths,

tasteful furniture and the highest prices in town. A very good curry will cost from Rf 90 to Rf 160, plus a 10% service charge. The restaurant at *Athamaa Palace Hotel*, on Majeedi Magu, also serves fine Indian food, as does the less expensive *Evening Cafe*, on Orchid Magu, and the extremely cheap *Indian Restaurant*, on Chandanee Magu.

At *Quench*, in the middle of Majeedi Magu, you can eat indoors in chilly air-con or outdoors under a thatched roof. The menu includes hamburgers, egg and chips, spaghetti, sandwiches and Chinese dishes. Main courses cost from Rf 15 to Rf 50, salads are around Rf 15 and juices about Rf 15. Other, similar restaurants worth a try include the *Symphony*, *Symphonic*, *Food Bank* and *Kentucky* – most main courses will cost around Rf 40 at all these places.

The hotel restaurants include those on the top floors of the *Relax Inn* and the *Kam Hotel*, with both offering good views and OK food, though the service may be variable. Most main courses will cost from around Rf 50. The restaurant at the *Central Hotel* has no view, slow service and average food. At the Nasandhura Palace Hotel, *Trends* is a pleasant outdoor restaurant, popular with expats, offering a varied menu including Trendy Special Rice for US$4 – it's pretty tasty.

At the airport there's an expensive snack bar, with lots of white plastic tables, where you can get a Rf 40 salad roll or a Rf 30 Coke. Outside the terminal building, facing the dhoni dock, is the *Satellite Restaurant* with US$7 fish and chips, US$9 burgers and fries, and US$4.50 fruit juices. This is more expensive than food in many resorts, and the quality is nothing special.

## Supermarkets

People's Choice, and the supermarket in the STO building offer a good selection of packaged food and some fresh fruit and vegetables. These stores are handy for self-catering, which is another option during Ramadan.

## ENTERTAINMENT

There may be no bars, nightclubs, dance halls or discos in town, but Male' is a surprisingly lively place from about 8 pm to late in the evening. Majeedi Magu bustles with late-night shoppers and cafes full of people. Visitors and expats dine out or drink in (if they have a liquor permit).

Two cinemas do good business, though both have suffered from the increasing popularity of VCRs – numerous video outlets rent tapes for Rf 15 a night with any sexy scenes censored. The *Star*, at the west end of Majeedi Magu, is the place to see an American action movie or a Hindi epic (about Rf 25). The *Olympus*, on Majeedi Magu across from the stadium, now specialises in Maldivian movies, made for TV, shown on video and usually imitative of Hindi love stories. Neither of these theatres is air-conditioned.

The weekend begins on Thursday night, often with an outdoor concert for young people on the outdoor stage down by the New Harbour. Some performances may be less than totally professional, but the audience is enthusiastic and it can be a wild night – Maldivians get unbelievably excited dancing and singing, without any help from alcohol or ecstasy.

On Thursday night and Friday, some expats head out to one of the nearby resorts for a fancy dinner, a drink or some socialising, but there is no regular venue. One resort used to provide a free boat for this purpose, but after some excessive behaviour upset their regular guests the resort stopped doing so. Another resort might take up the challenge, or the new hotel on the airport island may offer an alternative for the alcoholically inclined.

## SPECTATOR SPORTS
Except during holidays and festivals, the only daytime diversions are football and cricket matches at the National Stadium. Tickets cost Rf 15 or Rf 20 for centre seats. More casual games of football, volleyball, basketball and *bashi*, the girls' game, can be seen any evening in the parks at the east end of the island. For more details, see Spectator Sports in the Facts for the Visitor chapter.

## SHOPPING
Most of the shops selling imported and locally made souvenirs are on and around Chandanee Magu. (See the Facts for the Visitor chapter for some information on possible purchases.) Many of them have a very similar range of stock, but it's worth browsing in quite a few if you're looking for a particular item. For more interesting antiques and Maldivian craft items, look carefully in Antique & Style and Gloria Maris, both upstairs on the east side of Chandanee Magu. Sifani, on the west side of Chandanee Magu, has a good selection of quality jewellery, including sapphires and rubies from Sri Lanka.

For less conventional souvenirs, look in the local hardware, chandlery and general stores along the waterfront west of the fish market and down Fareedhee Magu.

Reethi Foto, on Fareedhee Magu, does E6 slide processing and has a range of camera equipment and accessories.

## GETTING THERE & AWAY
### Air
All international flights to the Maldives use Male' International Airport, which is on a separate island, Huhule, about 2km east of Male' Island. Domestic flights and seaplane transfers to resorts also use Huhule.

Most visitors won't need to contact their airline because their tour operator will reconfirm outward flights. However, most airline offices are in a new building on Marine Drive, including:

| | |
|---|---|
| Air Maldives | ☎ 318758 |
| Emirates Airlines | ☎ 314805 |
| Indian Airlines | ☎ 314806 |
| Malaysia Airlines | ☎ 316375 |
| PIA | ☎ 314809 |
| Singapore Airlines | ☎ 314803 |
| SriLankan Airlines | ☎ 328456 |

Air Maldives handles bookings and reconfirmation for several airlines: ☎ 318459 for Aeroflot, Air Europe, Austrian Airlines, Balair, Balkan Airlines, Condor, Equatorial International, Lauda Air, LTU International Airways and Tamair.

### Boat
Boats on excursions from the resorts will dock on Marine Drive near the main square, but if you want to get out to a resort, it may

MALE'

be better to go to the airport and take a transfer boat with a new arrivals. Dhonis to/from the airport dock at the east end of Marine Drive, also the best place to charter a dhoni for a short trip or for a day. To charter, ask at the small ticket booth facing the harbour.

Dhonis to nearby Viligili use the New Harbour on the south-west corner of Male'.

Safari boats are usually moored in the lagoon west of the new island, north of the airport – the operator will normally pick up arriving passengers and ferry them directly to the boat. Private yachts usually moor in the same place (see the Getting There & Away chapter for details).

## GETTING AROUND
### To/From the Airport
Regular dhonis shuttle between the airport and the harbour, usually docking towards the east end of Marine Drive. They leave when they're full and charge Rf 10, but if it's late and you're the only passenger it will cost Rf 70.

### Taxi
There are plenty of taxis, but the main reason for using them is that the drivers can find any address, or perhaps because you need a few minutes of cool, air-conditioned comfort. Many streets are one way and others may be blocked by construction work or stationary vehicles, so taxis will often take roundabout routes. Fares are the same for any distance. Most taxis are white Toyota sedans, distinguished by yellow licence plates. They cost Rf 10 if you phone them first and they pick you up, or (officially) Rf 15 if you hail one on the street (in practice, many charge only Rf 10 even from the street). After midnight they cost Rf 20. They may charge extra for luggage, but you don't have to tip. There are quite a few taxi companies, including:

| Express | ☎ 323132 |
| Mobile | ☎ 316727 |
| New | ☎ 325757 |
| Regular | ☎ 322454 |

If these numbers are busy, try ☎ 325656 or ☎ 329292 for other taxi operators.

### Bicycle
The best way to get around is definitely by bicycle, but there's no place to rent one. Your guesthouse might be able to arrange something. Be sure to lock it up and always use a light at night or you'll be fined. You can also be fined for riding (or even pushing) a bike the wrong way on a one-way street. It's fashionable to have a 21-speed mountain bike but a big black Anglo-Indian bicycle (a Raleigh or a BSA) would be both much more suitable and less attractive to thieves.

## AROUND MALE'
### Diving Sites
While the waters around Male' are said to be thick with rubbish and wrecked bicycles, there is some excellent diving within easy reach. The SEA dive school (☎ 316172, @ seaexplo@divehinet.net.mv), Thuniveli, 2nd floor, Ameenee Magu, does dive courses and dive trips for locals and the expat community. It charges US$35 for a single dive with full equipment, US$30 with tank and weights only (including the boat trip). If you do nine dives, the tenth dive is free. A PADI open-water course is US$420, including dives, equipment and certification.

Some of the best dives are along the edges of the Vaadhoo Kandu (the channel between North and South Male' atolls), which has two Protected Marine Areas. There is also a well-known wreck.

**Kikki Reef** Also called Hans Hass Place, this is a demanding wall dive beside the Vaadhoo Channel in a Protected Marine Area. There is a lot to see at 4m or 5m, so it is good for snorkellers and less experienced divers if the current is not too strong. There's a wide variety of marine life, including many tiny reef fish and larger species in the channel. Further down are caves and overhangs with sea fans and other soft corals, where divers must take care to avoid damaging the reef.

**Lion's Head** This Protected Marine Area was once a popular place for shark feeding, and though this practice is now strongly discouraged, grey reef sharks and the occasional turtle are still common here. The reef edge is thick with fish, sponges and soft corals; although it drops steeply, with numerous overhangs, to over 40m, there is much to see at snorkelling depth.

**Wreck of the *Maldive Victory*** This is an impressive and challenging dive because of the potential for strong currents. This cargo ship hit a reef and sank on Friday 13 February 1981 and now sits with the wheelhouse at around 15m, and the propeller at 35m. The ship has been stripped of anything movable, but the structure is almost intact and provides a home for a rich growth of new coral and large schools of fish.

## Viligili

Just a couple kilometres to the west of Male' is the island of Viligili (also spelled Villingili), a one-time resort closed down to make room for a telecommunications station. It's now being developed as a residential satellite of Male' to relieve the pressure of growth in the capital, and the plan is for as many as 9000 people to settle here. Though it's close to Male' and much more spacious, people are not keen to come here as it's still seen as a separate island, without the cachet of the capital.

Potentially it's a very attractive place, with lots of greenery and some nice beaches on the north-east shore – there's an interesting view of Male' and the many ships at their moorings. The initial development was very untidy with some very makeshift dwellings, but it has been considerably cleaned up and there are now several quite palatial houses and a very modern-looking apartment block. It's an interesting place to visit if you've been stuck in Male' for too long, and many Male' residents come here on holidays. There's a tea shop or two if you're hungry.

Viligili is easy to get to. Just catch one of the dhoni ferries from the New Harbour on the south-west corner of Male' (15 minutes, Rf 5).

## Funadhoo

The oil tanks you can see from Male' are on Funadhoo Island.

## Huhule

This island was once densely wooded, with a sinister reputation and a few inhabitants, including a beautiful female *jinni* (witch). The first airstrip was built in 1960, but it was extended greatly in 1968, incorporating a second small island, to become Male's international airport. It's a remarkable piece of land reclamation. The island has a sizable airport building, workshops and administrative buildings, a 3000m runway and a new

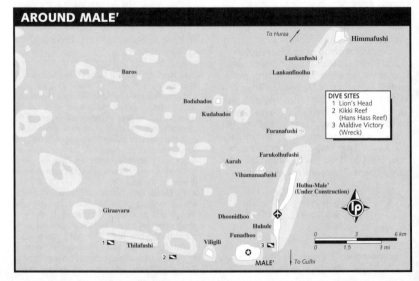

AROUND MALE'

To Huraa
Himmafushi
Lankanfushi
Baros
Lankanfinolhu

Bodubados
Kudabados

DIVE SITES
1 Lion's Head
2 Kikki Reef
  (Hans Hass Reef)
3 Maldive Victory
  (Wreck)

Furanafushi

Farukolhufushi
Aarah
Vihamanaafushi

Hulhu-Male'
(Under Construction)

Giraavaru

Dhoonidhoo
Huhule
Funadhoo

Thilafushi
Viligili

MALE'    To Gulhi

0    3    6 km
0    1.5    3 mi

hotel (see Male' Places to Stay). Seaplanes 'land' in the lagoon on the east side of the island.

## Hulhu-Male'

Between the airport and the island of Farukolhufushi, about 3km of reef is being built up to create a new island to relieve the pressure of growth on Male'. Sand and coral is being dredged from the lagoon and pumped onto the reef to raise it a metre or so above sea level; palm trees have been planted, street lights installed and the construction of a number of 10-storey apartment blocks has been planned. A strip of dry land some 3km long will be created, which will eventually join up to the island of Farukolhufushi, which was home to the Club Med resort (Club Med is to move farther north to the island of Kanifinolhu). From the air, you can see that quite a large area has already been created, along with a safe anchorage for yachts, but the whole project remains controversial (see the boxed text 'A New Island?').

## Thilafushi

Although it's common for Maldivian islands to decrease or increase in size through erosion, deposition and land reclamation, Thilafushi is one of the fastest growing islands in the country. It's where the garbage from the capital is dumped, and it's also known as 'Trash Island'. The land is earmarked for industrial development, and its three conspicuous round towers are part of a new cement factory.

## Dhoonidhoo

This island, just north of Male', was the British governor's residence until 1964. The house is now used for detaining people who may disrupt Maldivian society (officially, there are no political prisoners in the Maldives).

### A New Island?

Anyone who has been on the island of Male' will have no doubt that it's full to capacity. At the same time, the pressure for further growth seems inevitable, as educational and employment opportunities in the outer atolls are so limited. In this light, one might think that the prospect of a new island, as big as Male' and just a few kilometres across the water, would be a welcome development. But many Maldivians have misgivings about the Hulhu-Male' project.

At a strategic level, some people feel that it would be better to invest resources in decentralising economic and social infrastructure, rather than facilitating more growth in and around the capital. Others are concerned about environmental damage, such as interference with the movement of sea water in and around the atoll, and silt covering the coral reefs.

But at least some of the concern seems to be at a very philosophical level. People don't talk about it as a 'new island', perhaps because the whole thing is seen as being so unnatural. It's as if they find it hard to accept that this artificial creation can ever be a real, habitable island.

## Aarah

A little further north again, this island is a holiday retreat for the president.

## Kudabados

This island was saved from resort development and became the **Kuda Bandos Reserve**, to be preserved in its natural state for the people's enjoyment. It has a few facilities for day trippers, but is otherwise undeveloped and very picturesque. Maldivians come here on weekends and holidays, and it's also visited by island-hopping trips from nearby resorts. You do not need a permit to visit.

# North & South Male' Atolls

## Highlights

**Administrative District:** Kaafu
**Code Letter:** H
**Inhabited Islands:** 11
**Uninhabited Islands:** 63
**Resorts:** 43
**Population:** 10,133

- Surfing on the Maldives' best surf breaks
- Exploring the many diveable ship wrecks
- Island hopping on day excursions
- Excellent diving sites for coral, fish, sharks and rays

The administrative atoll of Kaafu comprises South Male' Atoll, North Male' Atoll, the small atoll of Gaafaru Falhu to the north of that, and the island of Kaashidhoo, which is even farther north. The district extends for over 100km from north to south and has dozens of sandbanks and islands, of which only 11 are inhabited. The capital of Kaafu is the island of Thulusdhoo in North Male' Atoll.

Male', the capital of the Maldives (see the previous chapter), is in the south of North Male' Atoll, but is not part of the Kaafu Atoll administration.

Because of their proximity to the capital and, more importantly, to the international airport, the islands of North and South Male' atolls were the first to be developed for tourism – there are more than a dozen resorts within 15km of the airport. Some of these resorts are excellent, having undergone at least one major upgrade since they were first established. The advantages of a resort close to Male' include the saving of time, trouble and expense in transferring from the airport, and the ease with which you can make an excursion to the capital. Surprisingly, the number of resorts does not really affect the appeal of the area – you will see lights across the water at night, passing boats all day and planes flying overhead, but most of these inner resorts still feel isolated and relaxed.

Some excellent dive sites are found on these atolls, though all the shallower corals have been affected by coral bleaching. Sites close to Male' have been heavily used, but generally they are in very good condition. Some of the most interesting sites are on either side of Vaadhoo Kandu, the channel that runs between North and South Male' atolls. At the outer edge of the atolls, the dive sites are accessible from only a few resorts or by safari boat, and you'll probably have them all to yourself. Gaafaru Falhu Atoll, north of North Male' Atoll, has at least three diveable shipwrecks.

The Maldives' best and most accessible surf breaks are in North Male' Atoll, all of which can be reached by boat from the nearby resorts. There are also some smaller breaks in South Male' Atoll that are easily reached by boat from some resorts in that atoll. (See Surfing in the Facts for the Visitor chapter for more details.)

Expatriates living in Male' make short visits to the nearby resorts for some R and R and a taste of the alcoholic delights prohibited in the capital. Some resorts make their beaches and facilities available for day use, at a price, or host a party in the evening, providing boat transfers from Male'. Currently no resorts are arranging any expat social functions on a regular basis, but if you're in Male' for more than a week or so get the low-down on what's happening from the grapevine.

## KAASHIDHOO

Though in the Kaafu administrative district, the island of Kaashidhoo is way out by itself, in a channel between much larger atolls. It's inhabited with over 1000 people, which makes it one of the biggest villages in Kaafu. Few tourists visit, but boats going to or from the northern atolls sometimes stop here to shelter in the lagoon. The islanders are known as 'big toddy tappers' – people who extract *raa* (toddy, the sap of a palm tree, to drink fresh or slightly fermented – which may be another reason to stop.

## GAAFARU FALHU

This isolated atoll has just one island, also called Gaafaru, with a population just over 1000, more than one third of them students at the island's school. The channel to the north of the atoll, Kaashidhoo Kuda Kandu, has long been a shipping lane, and several vessels have veered too far south and finished on the hidden reefs of Gaafaru Falhu. There are three diveable wrecks but none is anywhere near intact.

## NORTH MALE' ATOLL

Kaafu's capital island is **Thulusdhoo**, on the south-eastern edge of North Male' Atoll, with a population of about 700. It's an industrious island, known for *bodu beru* drums and traditional dancing. Contemporary products include Coca-Cola and modern fibreglass dhonies.

The island of **Huraa** (population 600) is visited by tourists on island-hopping trips, but it's not yet as touristy as other North Male' islands. The people are hoping to get more tourist dollars from the newly-opened Four Seasons Resort on the next island, Kudahuraa. Huraa's dynasty of sultans, founded in 1759 by Sultan Al-Ghaazi Hassan Izzaddeen, built a mosque on the island.

Many tourists visit **Himmafushi** on excursions arranged from nearby resorts. Unfortunately the experience is dominated by souvenir selling, just as the main street in this otherwise attractive village is dominated by souvenir shops. The good news is that the population, some 760 people, derive a substantial income from this, and the crafts and souvenirs sold here are about the least expensive in the country. They are not all imported either – carved rosewood manta rays, sharks and dolphins are made locally.

### An Early Aficionado

There's an interesting footnote to the wreck of the SS *Seagull*, which went down on Gaafaru Falhu in 1879. A British civil servant from Ceylon was sent to investigate the wreck and he was immediately fascinated by the Maldives. The man was HCP Bell and he returned in 1920 and 1922 to lead archaeological expeditions to all corners of the country. His main work, *The Maldive Islands: Monograph on the History, Archaeology & Epigraphy* was published in 1940, three years after his death, and is still regarded as the definitive book on the early history and culture of the Maldives.

A sand spit has joined Himmafushi to the once separate island of **Gaamaadhoo**, which has a prison on it. The surf break here, aptly called **Jailbreaks**, is a great right-hander (see the Surf Breaks map under Activities in the Facts for the Visitor chapter) but you need a special permit to surf here (see Surfing under Activities in the Facts for the Visitor chapter).

The island of Girifushi, which has a military training camp, is off limits.

Farther north, **Dhiffushi** is one of the most appealing local islands, with about 930 people, three mosques, and two schools. Mainly a fishing island, it has lots of greenery and grows several types of tropical fruit.

### Diving

North Male' Atoll has been well explored by divers and has many named sites. Some are heavily dived, especially in peak seasons. Consult with the resort dive operator to pick the most suitable dives for a given day, with regard to your abilities and interests. The following is just a sample of the best-known sites, listed from north to south:

**Shark Point** Also called Saddle, or Kuda Faru, this dive is in a Protected Marine Area and is subject to strong currents. Lots of white-tip and grey reef sharks can be seen in the channel between a thilla and the reef, along with fusiliers, jackfish, stringrays and some impressive caves.

NORTH & SOUTH MALE' ATOLLS

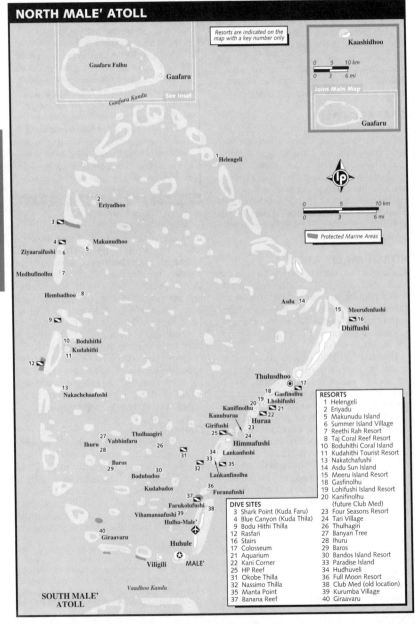

# NORTH MALE' ATOLL

Resorts are indicated on the map with a key number only

Kaashidhoo

| | | |
| --- | --- | --- |
| 0 | 5 | 10 km |
| 0 | 3 | 6 mi |

Joins Main Map

Gaafaru

Gaafaru Falhu

Gaafaru

Gaafaru Kandu

See Inset

1 Helengeli

2 Eriyadhoo

3

4    5
Makunudhoo

Ziyaaraifushi  6

Medhufinolhu  7

Hembadhoo  8

Asdu  14

15    Meerufenfushi
16
Dhiffushi

9

10  Boduhithi
Kudahithi
11

12

13
Nakachchaafushi

Thulusdhoo  17

18  Gasfinolhu
20  19  Lhohifushi
Kanifinolhu    21
Kanuhuraa    22
Girifushi    23
25    24
Himmafushi

27    Thulhaagiri
Vabbinfaru  26
Ihuru
28

Baros
29    30
Bodubados

Kudabados

34  Lankanfushi
33
31    35
32
Lankanfinolhu

36  Furanafushi
37
Farukolufushi  38
Vihamanaafushi  39
Hulhu-Male'

40
Giraavaru

Huhule

Viligili

MALE'

Vaadhoo Kandu

SOUTH MALE'
ATOLL

Protected Marine Areas

## RESORTS
1 Helengeli
2 Eriyadu
5 Makunudu Island
6 Summer Island Village
7 Reethi Rah Resort
8 Taj Coral Reef Resort
10 Boduhithi Coral Island
11 Kudahithi Tourist Resort
13 Nakatchafushi
14 Asdu Sun Island
15 Meeru Island Resort
18 Gasfinolhu
19 Lohifushi Island Resort
20 Kanifinolhu
   (future Club Med)
23 Four Seasons Resort
24 Tari Village
26 Thulhagiri
27 Banyan Tree
28 Ihuru
29 Baros
30 Bandos Island Resort
33 Paradise Island
34 Hudhuveli
36 Full Moon Resort
38 Club Med (old location)
39 Kurumba Village
40 Giraavaru

## DIVE SITES
3 Shark Point (Kuda Faru)
4 Blue Canyon (Kuda Thila)
9 Bodu Hithi Thilla
12 Rasfari
16 Stairs
17 Colosseum
21 Aquarium
22 Kani Corner
25 HP Reef
31 Okobe Thilla
32 Nassimo Thilla
35 Manta Point
37 Banana Reef

**Blue Canyon** The alternative, less picturesque name is Kuda Thila, which means small thila. A canyon, 25m to 30m deep and lined with soft, blue corals, runs beside the thila. The numerous overhangs make for an exciting dive, but require good buoyancy control. It's recommended for experienced divers.

**Rasfari** The outer reef slope here drops down to well over 40m, but a couple of thillas rise up with their tops at about 25m. Grey reef sharks love it around these thillås – you might see 20 or 30 of them, as well as white-tip sharks, barracuda, eagle rays, and trevally. It's a Protected Marine Area.

**Bodu Hithi Thila & the Peak** Bodu Hithi is a prime manta spotting site from December to March, with a good number of sharks and many reef fish. The soft corals on the sides of the thila are in excellent condition. If currents are moderate, this site is suitable for intermediate divers. Nearby, the Peak is another great place to see mantas in season, and has some very big napoleon fish.

**Stairs** A series of regular coral ledges on the outer reef slope form a set of stairs descending to 30m. The upper steps are rich with reef fish, while large grouper, sharks and turtles live around the bottom step.

**Colosseum** A curving cliff near a channel entrance forms the Colosseum, where pelagics perform – shark and barracuda are often seen here. Experienced divers do this as a drift dive, going right into the channel past ledges and caves, with soft corals and the occasional turtle. Even beginners can do this one in good conditions.

**Aquarium** As the name suggests, this site (a coral rock formation about 15m down) features a large variety of reef fish. A sandy bottom at 25m can have small sharks and rays, and you might also see giant wrasse and schools of snapper. It's an easy dive.

**Kani Corner** Across the kandu from the Aquarium, this corner is the start of a long drift dive through a narrow channel with steep sides, caves and overhangs decorated with soft corals. Lots of large marine life can be seen, including sharks, barracuda, napoleon wrasse and tuna. Beware of fast currents.

**HP Reef** This thila, also called Rainbow Reef or Himmafushi Block, sits beside a narrow channel where currents provide much nourishment for incredibly rich growths of soft, blue coral and support a large variety of reef fish and pelagics. The formations include spectacular caves and a vertical swim-through. It is a Protected Marine Area.

**Okobe Thilla** Also called Barracuda Thilla, the attraction here is the variety of spectacular reef fish that inhabit the shallow caves and crannies, including lionfish, scorpionfish, batfish, sweetlips, moray eels, sharks and big napoleons.

**Nassimo Thilla** This demanding dive follows the north side of a fine thilla, also known as Paradise Rock, which has superb gorgonians and sea fans on coral blocks, cliffs and overhangs. Numerous large fish frequent this site.

**Manta Point & Lankan Caves** May to November are the best months to see the mantas for which Manta Point is famous. Coral outcrops at about eight metres are a 'cleaning station', where cleaner wrasse feed on parasites from the mantas' wings. Cliffs, coral tables, turtles, sharks and numerous reef fish are other attractions, as are the nearby Lankan Caves.

**Banana Reef** This Protected Marine Area has a bit of everything: dramatic cliffs, caves and overhangs; brilliant coral growths; big predators such as sharks, barracuda, and grouper; and prolific reef fish including jackfish, morays, napoleons and bluestripe snapper. It was one of the first dive sites in the country to become internationally known.

## Resorts

*Helengeli* (☎ *444615*), Helengeli Island, is the most northerly resort in North Male' Atoll and was extensively renovated in 1996. It's on a fair-sized island with fine beaches and dense vegetation. The 50 modern rooms have air-con, hot water and are pleasantly decorated. Prices are reasonable, at around US$140/170 for single/double with full board in low season. It's popular with keen divers, many from Switzerland, but it's not known for its nightlife. The 2km-long house reef is excellent, so you need not venture far for snorkelling. Unguided scuba dives can be done from the shore.

Dive costs are not cheap, at around US$45 for a boat dive with equipment, but service is good; open-water courses are US$480. There are dozens of other recognised dive sites accessible by a short boat ride, with very few divers visiting them. About 43km from Male' International Airport, most transfers are done by speedboat (one hour, US$110), though seaplane transfers are possible. The resort's Male' office (☎ 328544, fax 325150, ✆ engeli88@dhivehinet.net .mv) is on Boduthakurufaanu Magu.

***Eriyadu*** (☎ *444487)*, Eriyadhoo Island, like several resorts in the north-west part of North Male' Atoll, has access to a good number of uncrowded dive sites. The 46 rooms have polished timber floors and furniture, TV, minibar and other mod cons. The food, on the other hand, is disappointing. Most of the guests are German and Swiss, with a few Brits and Scandinavians, and the resort usually has a friendly, fun atmosphere. The house reef is accessible and good for snorkelling, with lots of reef fish and larger marine life commonly seen. Dive costs are low if you take a multidive package. It's an inexpensive resort with single/double rooms from around US$44/80 half board in low season. Transfers from the airport are usually by speedboat (42km, one hour, US$80). The resort's Male' office (☎ 324933, fax 324943, *e* eriyadu@aaa.com.mv) is AAA Hotels & Resorts on the 3rd floor of the STO Trade Centre.

***Makunudu Island*** (☎ *446464)*, Makunudhoo Island, is a very tasteful, top-end, luxury resort with just 36 individual thatched-roof bungalows, all spacious and well furnished. The service is of a high standard and the food is excellent (there's some French influence in the management). It's a small island with lots of trees, white beaches and a blue lagoon – it's picture perfect. Guests are mainly British and French couples who come to relax, or have a honeymoon. The single-dive rates are quite high, but the PADI open-water course is very reasonable at US$450. Dive groups tend to be small and friendly. The mid-season full-board rate of around US$360/390 includes extras like a fishing trip, inter-island excursion, introductory scuba dive, and snorkelling equipment. The resort is 37km from the airport and transfers are usually by speedboat (one hour, US$168). If you've come in your own yacht, you'll find a safe anchorage here. The local operator in Male' is Sunland Hotels (☎ 324658, fax 325543, *e* sunland@ dhivehinet.net.mv) in the STO Trade Centre.

***Summer Island Village*** (☎ *443088, e siv @dhivehinet.net.mv)*, Ziyaaraifushi Island, is a budget resort with 92 rooms and a few over-water bungalows. Despite recent landscaping efforts it's a sparsely vegetated island, and has unattractive breakwaters protecting the narrow beaches. The lagoon is wide and shallow, so the resort is more suited to windsurfing than to snorkelling or swimming, but there are some great dive sites within about 5km. Rooms are clean and functional, and have air-con – the single-storey ones have the more pleasant outlook. Most guests are British and German staying on a rate that includes some activities, all meals, and house wine, spirits and beer – guests seem to have a good time here. High-season room prices are US$170/190, but most packages will be much cheaper than this. FIT visitors might get a good discount deal. The resort is 35km from the airport and transfers are usually by speedboat (one hour, US$80). The Male' operator (☎ 322212, fax 318057) is at H Roanuge, Male'.

***Reethi Rah Resort*** (☎ *441905, e rrresort@ dhivehinet.net.mv)*, Medhufinolhu Island, was one of the first resorts in the country. It's an excellent example of traditional, laid-back Maldivian hospitality. Reethi Rah means beautiful island, and the thick tropical vegetation justifies the name. The 50 individual bungalows have palm-thatch roofs, wood panelling, louvre shutters and privacy – they *don't* have TV or air-con. The ten new over-water rooms have none of this natural charm. The main restaurant and reception area, at one end of the island, is delightfully casual. An open-sided bar/coffee shop stands over the water on stilts, while the bungalows are scattered among trees off a shady path that runs the length of the island.

The wide, shallow lagoon is not ideal for swimming or snorkelling, but it's perfect for windsurfing, and the Club Mistral windsurfing school operating here has the latest in equipment and instructional techniques. Board rental is US$15 an hour, US$170 for a week, A 10-hour course runs to about US$235, including the equipment. There are good dive sites nearby: on the outer reef facing the ocean, at several thillas within the atoll and around the channels where water funnels in and out of the atoll. The dive base is run by Eurodivers, a very efficient opera-

ALL PHOTOGRAPHS BY JAMES LYON

Traditional crafts, either lacquered and decorated boxes **(middle left & middle right)**, mats woven from reeds, screwpine and other vegetable fibres **(top left)** or embroidered collars of traditional dresses **(bottom right)**, are beautifully made and finely detailed.

Mosques are some of the Maldives' most interesting coral stone buildings. Theemuge (the President's Palace, **bottom left**) has the distinctive rounded edges of local buildings, built in Bauhaus, or 'Male' Modern' style.

tion with moderate charges for dive trips and courses – a PADI open-water course is US$345.

A room with half board will cost US $109/158 in low season, US$112/164 in high season and US$179/255 around Christmas (the Christmas lights here are a sight to behold). Over-water rooms are about US$30 more expensive. The food is excellent, and the atmosphere is very relaxed and friendly, making this resort good value – it's popular with British, German and Swiss guests, many of whom are repeat visitors. It's about 35km from the airport, and transfers are usually by speedboat (US$60). The local operator in Male' (☎ 323758, fax 328842) is at Ma Sheerazeege, Sheeraazee Goalhi.

**Taj Coral Reef Resort** *(☎ 441948, ☻ tajcr@ dhivehinet.net.mv)*, Hembadhoo Island, has been virtually rebuilt in the last few years, and is now a very modern and efficiently run resort, with swimming pool, gym, spa and massage centre, and very good food. The 30 beachfront rooms are big, comfortable and fully furnished with TV, in-house movies, minibar and the works. The 36 over-water bungalows are even bigger. It all looks very new and neat, the restaurant is enclosed and air-conditioned, and the bar opens onto a deck rather the beach – no sand floors here. Landscaping work should soon soften the look of the island a little. The Blue In dive centre is on the expensive side, but equipment is first class. Full-board rates are from about US$210/230 in low season (US$40 more for over-water bungalows), putting this in the top-end price bracket. Transfers by very flash speedboats cost US$100. It's run for the Indian Taj Group by Taj Maldives (☎ 313530, fax 314059) at 10 Medhuziyaaiy, Male'.

**Asdu Sun Island** *(☎ 445051, ☻ info@ asdu.com.mv)*, Asdhoo Island, is one of the original Maldives resorts, small, natural, and very easy-going (don't confuse it with the new Sun Island resort on Ari Atoll, which is just the opposite). The 30 rooms are characterised by what they *don't* have – there's no TV, air-con, nor hot water, just louvre windows, ceiling fans and refreshing showers. It's an inexpensive resort, and the

diving and drinks are reasonably priced. Many guests are on packages from Italy, and there's a sprinkling of fully independent travellers (FITs) who sometimes get very cheap rates here (US$70/100 with full board in the off season). Asdu is 32km from the airport, with transfer by speedboat (1½ hours, US$80). It's run by a friendly Maldivian family, but there is a Male' office (☎ 322149, fax 324300) on Kurangi Goalhi. Check the resort's Web site (www.asdu.com) for more details.

**Meeru Island Resort** *(☎ 443157, ☻ meeru@ dhivehinet.net.mv)*, Meerufenfushi Island, is at the eastern corner of North Male' Atoll. It's one of the largest resorts, with 227 rooms, and it was totally redeveloped in the late 90s. Meerufenfushi means 'sweet water island', and its wells were often used to replenish passing boats. The ground water sustained a quite dense, lush, natural vegetation, but much of the 28-hectare island was cleared in the renovation work, and some parts are now decidedly sparse. Some fruits and vegetables are cultivated for use in the resort. The guests are from Britain, Scandinavia and other parts of Europe, many of them young (mostly couples), and quite a few families – there might be 50 or more kids on the island over Christmas and in August. The resort is not big on organised entertainment, but the bars are cheerfully busy most evenings.

The new standard rooms are prefabricated pine boxes from New Zealand, uninspiring but comfortable, with air-con and good bathrooms. The new prefabricated pine villas from Finland have a more interesting pentagonal design and better finish – some are built with balconies over the water. The two honeymoon suites are large and well furnished, and stand on stilts over the lagoon 60m from shore – a small boat is provided for access.

Facilities include a huge round restaurant with sand floors and a soaring thatched roof. The buffet meals are served here, and considering the size of the place, they're very good. There are also three bars (beer is US$2.50 a can), two coffee shops serving a la carte snacks (pizzas are US$8 to US$9), a swimming pool, tennis courts, gym and a spa offering massage and beauty treatments. Snorkelling near the island is not good, but boats go to the edge of the house reef every two hours (US$4). All the usual water sports are offered, as well as inexpensive excursions to the fishing village on neighbouring Dhiffushi Island. Those interested in Maldivian history and culture will also appreciate the small **museum** at Meeru – a commendable feature.

Up to a third of the visitors here are scuba divers, and the Ocean-Pro dive school is a large and efficient operation. A single dive is US$29 with tank and weights only, or US$39 including full equipment rental, plus US$10 per dive for the boat trip. A 10% discount applies after seven dives. A PADI open-water course will cost about US$460, including equipment, boat trips and nine dives. There's a whole slew of great dive sites in the channels within 5km of Meeru.

In low season, Meeru's standard rooms are among the least expensive around, from US$80/100 with full board, while the better land villas cost US$100/120, and water villas are US$145/180. Add about US$20 to these prices in high season, or nearly double them for Christmas. Packages and last-minute deals may be even less. The resort is about

## Maldivian Multinationalism

As an island nation, the Maldives is almost exclusively a producer of fish and coconut products; everything else is imported. Thus the tourism industry must ship in everything needed for a resort except the sunshine, the sea and the island itself, which always remains Maldivian property. The diversity of imports can be surprising. A Maldivian island can be leased to a Sri Lankan company to develop a resort for the Italian market, with pasta imported from Australia, wine from South Africa, fruit from New Zealand, beer from Singapore, plumbing from Germany, air-conditioners from Japan, hairdryers from Canada, labourers from Bangladesh, dive instructors from Austria, and prices in US dollars. When it comes to doing business, Maldivians are anything but insular.

40km from the airport and transfers are by speedboat (one hour, US$80). The local operator is Champa Trade & Travels (☎ 314149, fax 314150), Champa Building, Male', or check its Web site (www.meeru.com) for more details.

***Boduhithi Coral Island*** *(☎ 443981),* Boduhithi Island, is a mid-range resort with 87 rooms and virtually 100% Italian clientele. All the booking is done through the Italian agent, Club Vacanzi, though independent agents in Male' may have the occasional cheap room here in the low season. It's very much a club-style resort, with lots of activities and fine Italian food. It's 29km from the airport and transfers are by speedboat (45 minutes, US$60). The local operator in Male' is Holiday Club Maldives (☎ 313938, fax 313939, ✉ hcmmale@clubvacanze.com .mv), 4th Alia Building.

***Kudahithi Tourist Resort*** *(☎ 444613),* Kudahithi Island, is one of the smallest, most exclusive and most expensive resorts in the country. The tiny island's resort has just six rooms, each one decorated with a theme – for example, there's a Sheik's Room, Maharani Room, Safari Lodge and Captain's Cabin. It's the only resort that doesn't have its own scuba-diving operation, but guests can use the facilities at nearby Boduhithi – the resorts are related and share the same local operator, Holiday Club Maldives; see the Boduhithi Coral Island entry earlier for contact details.

***Nakatchafushi*** *(☎ 443847),* Nakachchaafushi Island, is a mid-range resort with 51 attractive, round, thatched, air-con rooms, a swimming pool and a number of eating options. The main restaurant, a coffee and snack shop, Asian restaurant and a beach grill and barbecue are all packed onto this small island. To sample these alternatives, take a bed & breakfast or half-board plan. There's a big lagoon on the north side that is good for swimming and windsurfing, while the house reef is near the southern shore and easily accessible for snorkelling. The island has stylish thatched buildings in a tropical garden setting, shaded by palm trees and dripping with bougainvillea. The guests are mostly from Britain, Germany and elsewhere in Europe. The price of a single/double room with half board ranges from US$165/185 in low season to US$170/195 in high season, and US$230/255 over Christmas. The resort is 24km from the airport and transfers are by dhoni (1½ hours, US$55). It's one of the resorts operated by the well-established Universal Enterprises Ltd (☎ 322971, fax 322678), 39 Orchid Magu, Male'. Check the resort's Web site (www.unisurf.com) for further details.

***Thulhagiri Island Resort*** (☎ 445930, ✉ reserve@thulhaagiri.com.mv), Thalhaagiri Island, is also on a small island and is a very pleasant mid-range resort with 58 aircon bungalows, a swimming pool and very good food. The buildings have some style and rustic charm while the island itself is pleasantly green and lush. It was once a Club Med resort, but is now independently managed and attracts guests mainly from Britain, France and Germany. Diving is reasonably priced, and there's a learn to windsurf package with eight hours of instruction and unlimited use of a windsurfer. Single/double rooms with full board cost from US$157/198 in low season and up to US$173/221 in high season. Packages with room only and half board are also available. Transfers to the airport are by speedboat (13km, half hour, US$60). The local agent (☎ 322844, fax 321026) is at H Jazeera, Boduthakurufaanu Magu, Male'.

***Banyan Tree*** (☎ 443147, ✉ maldives@banyantree.com), Vabbinfaru Island, is a very classy luxury resort operated by the international Banyan Tree group. Accommodation is in superbly finished beach-front or garden villas with conical roofs and elegant, spiral-shaped floor plans inspired by the shape of a sea shell. Each villa has a king-sized four-poster bed, ceiling fans, marble bathroom, tastefully carved wooden furniture, and a private sun deck overlooking beach or garden. Villas are not air-conditioned, but the design is intended to provide natural cooling.

This was one of the first resorts to offer massage, spa facilities and a range of health and beauty treatments – it can't promise complete renewal, but does its best. Cuisine is superb. Activities such as night fishing, windsurfing and snorkelling are included in the package, while the cost of excursions and diving is no more expensive than at many mid-range resorts. A single/double garden villa with full board costs around US$491/557 in high season; it might be less as part of a package in low season, but this is not a resort for the price-conscious. It's 16km from the airport, and transfers are by speedboat (20 minutes, US$90). The local operator in Male' is Dhirham Travels & Chandling (☎ 323369, fax 324752), Faamudheyri Magu. Check the resort's Web site (www.banyantree.com) for details.

***Ihuru Tourist Resort*** (☎ 443502, ✉ ihuru@dhivehinet.net.mv), Ihuru Island, is a mid-range 45-room resort on a picture-perfect little island. With its canopy of palm trees and surrounding white beach, it conforms exactly to the tropical island stereotype and it often features in photographs publicising the Maldives. The house reef, known as the 'Wall', is handy for snorkelling and accessible from the shore. The Swiss-run Sea Explorer Diving School charges about US$50 for a single dive, including the boat and all equipment; and US$500 for a PADI open-water course. It's a friendly, Maldivian-run resort with fan-cooled, thatch-roofed bungalows at US$165/220 for singles/doubles in high season. The local operator (☎ 326720, fax 326700) is at H Bodukosheege, Ameer Ahmed Magu, Male'.

***Baros Resort*** (☎ 442672), Baros Island, was one of the first islands to open as a resort, and it's a longstanding favourite with many British and German guests. It's an attractive island, small but well vegetated, with good beaches. The food and the service are very good, in keeping with the mid-range to top-end bracket. The standard rooms are smallish thatched cottages by the beach, with natural finishes and air-con, but no TV. They cost about US$175/200 in low season, US$190/215 in high season and US$250/275 over Christmas (all with half board). The 12 octagonal over-water bungalows have wide balconies and lovely furnishings, and cost US$100 extra. The resort is 15km from the airport and transfers are by speedboat (20 minutes, US$60) or dhoni (one hour, US $50). The resort operator is the efficient Universal Enterprises Ltd (☎ 323080, fax 322678, ✉ sales@unisurf.com), 39 Orchid Magu, Male'.

***Bandos Island Resort*** *(☎ 440088, ✉ info@ bandos.com.mv),* Bodubados Island, with 225 rooms, is one of the biggest resorts in the country. It opened in 1972, has expanded several times since and has an extensive range of facilities. There's a 500-seat conference centre, coffee shop, several restaurants, disco/bar, tennis courts, billiard room, sauna, gym, two swimming pools, beauty salon and spa-massage service. The childcare centre is free during the day, and only about US$5 per hour in the evening. With all these facilities, the island is quite intensely developed, and resembles a well-manicured town centre more than a typical tropical island. All the recreation facilities are available to day visitors with a 50% surcharge on the usual prices. At the dive centre, a single dive costs US$57, including equipment, boat and service charges; a PADI open-water course will run to about US$500. There's a fully equipped and staffed diving health clinic here, with a recompression chamber – see Health in the Facts for the Visitor chapter.

Bandos caters for day-trippers (or evening visitors) from Male', but currently does not provide a regular boat – call the resort if you want to arrange something. Airline crews and travel agents often use Bandos for short-term stays, as well as guests from Europe and Japan, so there can be a very mixed group here. The nearby uninhabited island of Kudabados has been turned into a public reserve and is a popular day trip from Bandos and Male'.

The rooms are modern, with red-tiled roofs, white-tiled floors, air-con, hot water, hairdryer, minibar, and IDD phone. With half board, a standard single/double will cost around US$141/172 in low season, up to US$231/262 at Christmas; for full board add US$13 per person. A 'junior suite' will cost about US$66 more per night. The resort is about 8km from the airport and transfers are by speedboat (20 minutes, US$45). The resort's Male' office (☎ 327450, fax

321026) is at 15 Boduthakurufaanu Magu. It's Web site, (www.bandos.com) has a ton of information.

***Gasfinolhu*** *(☎ 442078),* Gasfinolhu Island, a small, natural-looking island resort with 40 rooms, caters exclusively to the Italian market. Rooms are all air-con, and have no TV, and no keys. The atmosphere is animated, and the pasta is *al dente*. Bookings are through Valtur (☎ 39-6-47061, fax 39-6-4706334) in Rome, which has packages from around US$110 per person per day with full board. The local operator is Imad's Agency (☎ 323441, fax 322964), Chandanee Magu, Male'.

***Lohifushi Island Resort*** *(☎ 443451, ✉ lohifushi@dhivehinet.net.mv),* Lhohifushi Island, is quite a big resort on a long, narrow island and has 130 budget to mid-range rooms, most with air-con, hot water, open-air bathroom, and IDD phone. There are tennis and squash courts (US$10 per hour), a football field, a volleyball court, a small swimming pool, children's play area and a new holistic health centre with treatments from US$25 to US$98. For entertainment there is a disco, the occasional live band, cultural performances and 'animators' to help people enjoy themselves. The guests are generally a good international mix, from Germany, Japan, Switzerland, France, Australia and the UK.

As well as the usual sailing, windsurfing and water-skiing, there's a surfable left-hand wave off the south-east corner of the island, about 300m east of the rooms, overlooked by a rustic surfers bar. Other breaks are accessible by boat (US$7 per person for three hours, minimum four persons) – boats should be booked at least a day ahead, and aren't always punctual. The dive base charges US$35 for a single dive or US$310 for a 10-dive package with equipment provided, plus US$10 for each boat trip. A PADI open-water course will cost about US$460.

Lohifushi has three classes of room; a choice of bed & breakfast, half board or full board; and different prices for low, high and peak season. A standard, single/double room with half board (no air-con) is about US$109/128 in low season or US$125/155 in high season; a standard room with air-con will be slightly more, and probably the best value. A deluxe room is around US$159/189, or US$185/215 in high season, and may not be worth the extra money. The resort is about 20km from the airport, a comfortable trip by dhoni (1½ hours, US$30) or speedboat (½ an hour, US$60). It's operated by Altaf Enterprises (☎ 323378, fax 324783, **@** altaf@dhivehinet.net.mv), STO Trade Centre, Male'.

***Kanifinolhu*** *(☎ 443152, **@** kanifin@ dhivehinet.net.mv),* Kanifinolhu Island, is a medium-sized, mid-range resort about 20km from the airport. The 145 rooms are comfortably furnished and feature lots of natural timber. There's a full range of recreational facilities and excursions, and a nicely equipped kindergarten/childcare centre (US$10 per day). The lagoon is good for sailing, but the reef slopes are not very accessible for snorkellers. The surf break on the east side of the island is an undemanding right-hander, or surfers can paddle over to the break off Lhohifushi (beware of currents).

It's expected that by September 2000, Kanifinolhu will be a Club Med resort, with the same style and standards as Club Med's resort on the island of Farukolufushi (see later in this chapter). Club Med must move from Farukolufushi to make way for the Hulhu-Male' development (see the Male' chapter). Kanifinolhu's current operator is Cyprea Ltd (☎ 322451, fax 323523), 25 Boduthakurufaanu Magu, Male'. Check Club Med's Web site (www.clubmed.com) for more details.

***Four Seasons Resort*** *(☎ 444888, **@** info@ kudahuraa.com),* Kudahuraa Island, is one of the finest luxury resorts in the country. The island itself is quite small and not especially lush, but the beaches have all been artificially widened, there are plenty of palm trees, and landscaping work will continue. It has been beautifully developed with public areas that are expansive but not pretentious, appealing Bali-style beach villas and a gorgeous horizon pool. A spine-like jetty at the south end of the island gives access to the 36 over-water bungalows. A less obvious feature is the innovative waste-water treatment plant, which provides both irrigation water and dry fertiliser.

One restaurant is for breakfasts and buffet nights, and caters for Japanese guests; another serves South Asian cuisine including gourmet vegetarian and Maldivian specialities; and a beachside grill does Mediterranean dishes and fine seafood. Other facilities include a couple of bars, a gym and a spa offering massage, relaxation and beauty treatments.

The well-equipped dive base offers a single dive, including all equipment, guide and boat, for about US$60; a 10-dive package is US$540 and a PADI open-water course is US$540. Nitrox is available for about US$5 more per tank. The wide, shallow lagoon is not very interesting for snorkelling.

Room rates start with single or double beach villas from US$295 in low season, US$350 in high season (even more over Christmas). Villas with outdoor showers or private pools will cost more. Water bungalows are around US$570 in low season, US$625 in high season. These prices include breakfast only; for half board add US$50 per person per day, and expect to pay at least that much for dinners. Kudahuraa is 16km from the airport and transfers are by speedboat (30 minutes, US$60). The resort's Male' office (☎ 325529, fax 318992) is at 15 Boduthakurufaanu Magu, or check its Web site (www .fourseasons.com) for details.

***Tari Village*** *(☎ 440013),* Kanuhuraa Island, is a small, casual, budget to mid-range resort with a mixed clientele of young Europeans and a contingent of surfers, from Australia and elsewhere, between March and November. The island has some scrubby vegetation with a few big shade trees, and looks more natural than pretty. You can choose between a sandy beach with a safe, shallow lagoon; or Tari's private surf break on the south side of the island – it's a consistent left-hander called Pasta Point. Surf packages to Tari, operated exclusively by Atoll Adventures (see Surfing in the Facts for the Visitor chapter), include boat trips to other breaks nearby, permits for Jailbreaks, and local guides who really know the local conditions. The Blue One dive school offers friendly and personal attention at quite low rates.

Rooms are spacious, recently renovated, double-storey air-con cottages, ideal for families. Cheap rates are sometimes available to FITs (but not for surfing), but all-inclusive packages, with three meals and alcoholic drinks included, can be a good deal, US$140/170 in low season, US$160/190 in high season. The resort is 13km from the airport and transfers are usually by dhoni (one hour, US$45) or speedboat (25 minutes, US$55). The resort's Male' office (☎ 322165, fax 324776) is at 8 Boduthakurufaanu Magu.

*Hudhuveli* (☎ 443982, @ hudhuveli@ flashmail.com), Lankanfushi Island, is a small, very laid-back place, with 44 rooms around the edges of a narrow, scrubby island. It used to be an Italian resort, but now attracts mainly German and a few British guests. The restaurant and bar areas are friendly enough, but are due for a renovation. The lagoon here is very wide – good for windsurfing at high tide, but not great for snorkelling. There are great dive sites in the area, and the diving centre is inexpensive. Most rooms are cute little round bungalows, nice and natural, but with minimal facilities; there's a block of ten with air-con. The best feature of this resort is its low rates. They are US$85/121 with half board, and US$10 more for rooms with air-con. Hudhuveli is about 13km from the airport by dhoni (45 minutes, US$30) or speedboat (20 minutes, US$45). The resort's Male' office (☎ 325529, fax 321026) is at H Jazeera, Boduthakurufaanu Magu.

*Paradise Island* (☎ 440011, @ paradise@ dhivehinet.net.mv), Lankanfinolhu Island, is one of the biggest and most modern resorts around, with 260 rooms and lots of facilities, but still in the mid-range price bracket. It's nicely landscaped with good beaches and a swimming pool. The guests are from all over, including Europe, Japan, Taiwan and quite a few from Russia. Activities include gym, spa, squash, badminton, tennis, billiards etc – everything costs extra except darts and table tennis. Snorkelling is not good in the shallow lagoon and a snorkelling trip by boat

will cost US$10 per person. The diving operation is expensive, too – a PADI open-water course here will cost over US$600.

The food in the main restaurant is good, but not outstanding so get a half-board package and try the Sunrise (seafood) Restaurant, Sunset (Italian) Restaurant, Japanese Restaurant, or the big coffee shop. There are several bars, and a pretty full program of evening events.

The rooms are very clean and modern, with every comfort including air-con, bidet and satellite TV. Prices, with half board, run from US$162/172 in low season to US $252/262 at Christmas. An over-water bungalow is US$40 to US$115 more expensive. Full board, bed & breakfast and room-only deals are also available. If you want a tranquil holiday, make sure all the construction work is finished before you stay here. The resort is 10km from the airport, with transfers by speedboat (20 minutes, US$40). The Male' operator is Villa Hotels (☎ 324478, fax 327845, @ vilahtls@ dhivehinet.net.mv), STO Trade Centre, or check its Web site (www.villahotels-maldives.com) for details.

*Full Moon Resort* (☎ 442010, @ fullmoon@ dhivehinet.net.mv), Furanafushi Island, is another big, new resort, with 154 mid-range to top-end rooms and a full range of facilities squeezed onto a small island. Rooms are in white-concrete, motel-style two-storey blocks with blue-tiled roofs – no attempt at the rustic look here, but every square centimetre is meticulously cultivated with tropical plants. The business centre caters to those who need it, and the recreational facilities include tennis courts, gym and health club. The Eurodivers base is well run and reasonably priced. Most guests are here for a short, relaxing holiday, and the delightful swimming pool is a big attraction, as are the Thai and Mediterranean restaurants, the grill/pizza place, coffee shop, bars and disco. Big-game fishing trips are available on request, for US$350 to US$500.

Only the main restaurant is included in full-board packages, so take a bed and breakfast package and bring lots of money to spend in the specialty restaurants. For bed & breakfast, prices start at around US$140/155 for a standard room in low season, US$175/185 in high season; US$80 extra for an over-water bungalow. It's only 8km from the airport and transfer is by dhoni (45 minutes, US$30). The resort operator is Universal Enterprises Ltd (☎ 323080, fax 322678), 39 Orchid Magu, Male', or check its Web site (www.unisurf.com) for details.

***Club Med*** *(☎ 443021)*, Farukolufushi Island, is a very pleasant resort with 152 rooms and prices which are mid-range at the most when you allow for the extras. The Club Med style works well in the Maldives – all its resorts here are isolated from the local community and self-contained. Club Med is particularly good value because a holiday package includes all meals (with wine, beer, water or juice), sailing, windsurfing, canoeing and one scuba dive per day. If you're not an experienced diver, a PADI open-water course will cost only US$290 extra. Snorkelling near the island is not great, but there are two free snorkelling trips every day. Club organisers (called 'GOs') promote all sorts of games and activities (in French, English, Japanese, Chinese and Korean) to keep guests happy. The meals are of the all-you-can-eat-buffet type with a huge variety of excellent food.

Club Med must move from Farukolufushi to make way for the Hulhu-Male' development (see the Male' chapter), and it's expected that by September 2000, Club Med will reopen on the island of Kanifinolhu, about 17km farther north. Rates will probably remain around US$100 to US$120 per person per day, depending on the season, exchange rates, and how good a package you get. Currently Club Med's Male' office (☎ 322976, fax 322850) is at No 1 Ibrahim Hassan Didi Magu, or check its Web site (www.clubmed.com) for more details.

***Kurumba Village*** *(☎ 442324,* ✉ *kurumba@ dhivehinet.net.mv)*, Vihamanaafushi Island, was established in 1972 – the first resort in the Maldives. After several upgrades, it's now a comfortable resort serving the needs of business people and day visitors from Male'. It's quite a big island which, despite the development, retains lots of palm trees and natural vegetation. The resort has 180 rooms and a full range of recreational and conference facilities, but. As well as the main restaurant and the coffee shop, there's also a barbecue/grill, an Indian restaurant, and a French-Japanese style restaurant (full meals cost at least US$30). Visitors from Male' can use the swimming pools and public facilities for US$10 per day, but should make a reservation with the resort first. Tennis, billiards and the gym cost a little extra. The new 'Harmony Centre' offers massages, aromatherapy, reflexology, Shiatsu and so on, for US$25 to US$50 a session. Several computers are available, and you can access the net for US$0.50 per minute.

The diving operation is run by Eurodivers for very reasonable prices – a single dive is US$31 or US$36 with all equipment provided, a 10-dive package is US$245/306, it's US$14 for each boat trip and a PADI open-water course costs around US$450. A good range of excursions is offered to Male' and other islands, and big-game fishing can be arranged for US$350 to US$500.

Accommodation on a bed & breakfast basis lets you take advantage of the various eating options, and costs from US$140/155 in low season to US$190/205 at Christmas. It's close to the airport and transfers by dhoni take only 30 minutes, while a speedboat (US$30) is even quicker. If you're sensitive to aircraft noise, you may find it a little too close the airport. The local operator is Universal Enterprises Ltd (☎ 323080, fax 320274), 38 Orchid Magu, Male', or check its Web site (www.unisusrf.com) for more details.

***Giraavaru*** *(☎ 440440,* ✉ *giravaru@ dhivehinet.net.mv)*, Giraavaru Island, is a mid-range resort on a tiny island. The Giraavaru people, believed to be descended from the earliest inhabitants of the Maldives, were moved to Male' a few years ago when the population on the island no longer included the 40 adult males required to support a mosque. The resort is small, with nice beaches, palm-thatched buildings, plenty of vegetation and a natural feel. It's looking a little worn, but that seems to go with the very casual atmosphere. A very friendly place, it attracts guests from Britain, Italy and Germany, as well as visiting yachties and expatriates enjoying a break from Male'. There are some excellent dive sites nearby, along the edges of the Vaadhoo channel, and the diving is reasonably priced at US$50 for a single dive including boat and all equipment.

The 64 rooms are all comfortable, with air-con, phone, fridge and TV. Singles/doubles are around US$145/185 with full board, but you may get a better rate in a package, or as an FIT. The resort is 11km from the airport and can be reached by dhoni (45 minutes, US$40) or speedboat (15 minutes, US$80). The resort's Male' office (☎ 318422, fax 318505) is in the old Alia building, Handuvaree Higun.

## SOUTH MALE' ATOLL

There are only three inhabited islands in this atoll, but they have all been inhabited for a long time. The most populous is **Guraidhoo** with around 550 people. Sultans from Male' sought refuge here during rebellions from as early as the 17th century. Its lagoon has a good anchorage, which is used by fishing dhonies and safari boats. It also has a couple of dozen souvenir shops catering to island-hopping visitors from the resorts.

The biggest island is **Maafushi** which has a big reformatory, providing skill training and rehabilitation for wayward youth. An STO warehouse here buys salted fish from the local fishing villages and packs it for export.

The island of **Gulhi** is not large, but is inhabited by around 630 people. Fishing is the main activity, and there's also a small shipyard and recently upgraded school.

## Diving

The best dive sites are beside the **Vaadhoo Kandu**, which funnels a huge volume of water between North and South Male' Atolls. Various smaller kandus channel water between the atoll and the surrounding sea, and also provide great diving. Some typical, well-known sites include:

**Velassaru Caves** These rugged caves and overhangs, on the steep wall of the Vaadhoo Kandu, have very attractive coral growth. You may see sharks, turtles and rays on the bottom at around 30m. This dive's not for beginners.

**Vaadhoo Caves** There is a row of small caves here, and a bigger one with a swim-through tunnel, as well as excellent soft coral, gorgonians, jackfish and the odd eagle ray.

**Embudhoo Express** This is a 2km drift dive through the Embudhoo Kandu, which is a Protected Marine Area. With the current running in, rays, napoleons and sharks often congregate round the entrance. The current carries divers along a wall with overhangs and a big cave. The fast current makes for a demanding dive, but also provides the ideal environment for soft corals and a large variety of fish.

**Dhigu Thilla** This thilla sits in a channel and creates strong and potentially difficult currents. Its southern side has caves and overhangs with abundant soft corals and large numbers of snapper and bannerfish. From May to November, plankton-laden water runs out through the kandu, attracting magnificent manta rays.

**Vaagali Caves** This is an exciting dive and not especially demanding. It's in a less exposed location and has many caves at around 15m filled with sponges and soft coral. There is excellent hard coral and lots of fish on the top of the reef.

**Guraidhoo Kandu** A central reef splits this kandu into two channels, with many possibilities for divers, even those with less experience. There are lots of reef fish, larger pelagics near the entrance and mantas when the current is running out. The kandu is a Protected Marine Area.

## Resorts

*Laguna Beach Resort (☎ 445906, ✉ lgr@ dhivehinet.net.mv),* Velassaru Island, is a sizable, modern mid-range to top-end resort with 115 rooms and a full range of facilities. The five restaurants include Italian, Chinese and an outdoor barbecue/grill, as well as a bar with regular entertainment. Despite the development, the island is very attractive with lots of trees and gardens and very pretty beaches. The rooms are new, clean and comfortable, with a split-level design. Guests are mostly from Europe and the resort has a very high occupancy rate. It's quite good for families, and offers childcare and a children's swimming pool.

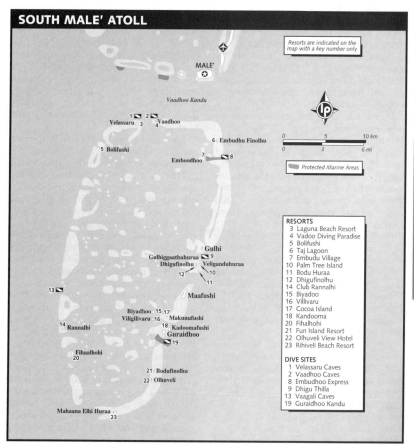

SOUTH MALE' ATOLL

Resorts are indicated on the map with a key number only

MALE'

Vaadhoo Kandu

1 2
Velassaru 3
4 Vaadhoo

5 Bolifushi

6 Embudhu Finolhu

7
Emboodhoo 8

0    5    10 km
0    3    6 mi

Protected Marine Areas

Gulhi

Gulhiggaathuhuraa 9
Dhigufinolhu   Veliganduhuraa
12        10
11

13

Maafushi

Biyadhoo 15 17
Viligilivaru 16 Makunufushi
14 Rannalhi    18 Kadoomafushi
Guraidhoo
19

Fihaalhohi
20

21 Bodufinolhu
22 Olhuveli

Mahaana Elhi Huraa
23

RESORTS
3 Laguna Beach Resort
4 Vadoo Diving Paradise
5 Bolifushi
6 Taj Lagoon
7 Embudu Village
10 Palm Tree Island
11 Bodu Huraa
12 Dhigufinolhu
14 Club Rannalhi
15 Biyadoo
16 Villivaru
17 Cocoa Island
18 Kandooma
20 Fihalhohi
21 Fun Island Resort
22 Olhuveli View Hotel
23 Rihiveli Beach Resort

DIVE SITES
1 Velassaru Caves
2 Vaadhoo Caves
8 Embudhoo Express
9 Dhigu Thila
13 Vaagali Caves
19 Guraidhoo Kandu

The dive centre has PADI, CMAS and SSI instructors, and charges reasonable rates, but the boat trips are expensive and add to the cost of diving. A single/double room with half board will cost about US$155/185 in low season or US$205/235 in high season, and there's a US$150 supplement for the new over-water suites. The resort is 10km from the airport, and transfers are by dhoni (55 minutes, US$25) or speedboat (20 minutes, US$50). The operator is Universal Enterprises (☎ 322971, fax 322678), 39 Orchid Magu, Male', or check its Web site (www .unisurf.com) for more details.

***Vadoo Diving Paradise*** (☎ 443976, *e vadoo@dhivehinet.net.mv*), Vaadhoo Island, is small resort appealing mainly to divers, many of them Japanese. The place has an interesting combination of lovely, luxury over-water bungalows and some charmingly time-worn buildings for the restaurant, office and dive centre. The house reef is great for snorkelling and diving, and there are excellent dive sites in the area, many along the edges of the Vaadhoo channel. Most dives will be in areas with medium to strong currents and are perhaps not ideal for beginners. A single dive is

US$32 with tank and weights only, or US$41 with all equipment *except* a wetsuit (bring your own). Six days' unlimited diving is US$292/371 respectively, and a PADI open-water course is US$468. Apart from occasional excursions and fishing trips, there are few other activities – this really is a divers' resort.

Meals are OK, and usually include Japanese dishes, which can be very good. The rooms are recently built and well finished (no TV or minibar) – the cheapest ones are called 'deluxe'. The over-water bungalows are delightful, with the most interesting feature being a glass coffee table through which you can look down onto your own miniature coral garden. Rates, with full board, are from US$140/180 to US$180/220 for deluxe rooms (depending on the season), US$330/370 to US$370/410 for over-water bungalows, and even more for over-water suites. It's 10km from the airport, and transfers are by dhoni (one hour, US$40) or speedboat (20 minutes, US$80). The resort's Male' office (☎ 325844, fax 325846) is at H Maarandhooge Irumathee Bai, Filigas Magu.

***Taj Lagoon*** *(☎ 444451, @ tajlr@ dhivehinet.net.mv),* Embudhu Finolhu Island, is a mid-range resort with 16 standard beach cottages and 48 over-water rooms. The island is long and narrow with scrubby vegetation and few swaying palm trees – it's not the prettiest island around, but it does have nice beaches on the lagoon side, secured by a set of groynes. The lagoon is wide and shallow – good for sailing and boating, but it's a long way out to the reef edge for snorkelling. The resort is close to the Vaadhoo channel and the Embudhoo channel, which offer excellent diving. Single dives are moderately priced, at US$35 with tank and weights or US$43 with all equipment, and boat usage is US$8; the 10-dive packages are better value at US$270/ 350 respectively. PADI open-water courses are expensive at US$520 plus boat charges.

The less active can enjoy the massage centre or the pleasant bar. The air-con restaurant is interesting for its variety of Asian and European dishes, catering for the British, German and Japanese guests. Standard air-con beach rooms cost from US$110/130 in low season, US$140/160 in high season, and more over Christmas. Over-water rooms cost about US$40 more. The resort is only 8km from the airport, with transfers by very smart speedboat (US$60). It's run for the Indian Taj Group by Taj Maldives (☎ 313530, fax 314059) at 10 Medhuziyaaiy, Male'.

***Embudu Village*** *(☎ 444776, @ embvil@ dhivehinet.net.mv),* Emboodhoo Island, with 124 rooms, is one of the bigger budget to mid-range resorts with a friendly, informal atmosphere and predominantly young, European guests. It's a good-sized island with lots of shady trees, nice beaches and a very accessible house reef. The restaurant is a spacious, sand-floored, open-sided pavilion with lots of potted plants, and you can sit inside or outside at the casual beach bar. There's great diving in the area and the dive school is reasonably priced, with an all-inclusive open-water course for US$455. A single dive with all equipment is US$40 and a 12-dive package is US$420, or 10% less if you have your own regulator and BCD; boat trips are about US$10 each. Windsurfing is also popular, and there's a good range of excursions to Male' and various other islands.

All accommodation is on a full-board basis with very pleasant, fan-cooled standard rooms from US$66/98 in low season to US$86/132 in high season. Superior rooms, with air-con, hot water, fridge and phone, cost about US$22 more per person. There are also 16 deluxe over-water bungalows at about US$200. The resort is about 8km from the airport, and transfers are by 'fast dhoni' (40 minutes, US$38). The local operator is Kaimoo Hotels & Travel Services Pty Ltd (☎ 322212, fax 320614, @ kaimoo@ dhivehinet.net.mv), H Roanuge, Meheli Goalhi, Male'.

***Bolifushi*** *(☎ 443517),* Bolifushi Island, is a mid-range resort with 55 rooms, appealing especially to divers because of the excellent dive sites in the area. Dives are reasonably priced if you have your own equipment (US$35 for one dive, US$250 for a 10-dive package), but quite expensive if you need to rent a BCD and regulator (US$46 and US$400 respectively), and the US$15 boat charge is quite steep. The island is very small and quite cute, with lots of palm trees, nice beaches and a good house reef close to shore. Most guests are from Europe and Japan. Standard rooms with full board cost around US$145/185; the 15 new and well-finished over-water bungalows cost a lot more. Bolifushi is 12km from the airport, with transfers by dhoni (40 minutes, US$40) or speedboat (20 minutes, US$55). It's operated by Gateway Maldives (☎ 317526, fax 317529, ✆ gateway@dhivehinet.net.mv), Alia Building, Male'.

**Dhigufinolhu** (☎ 443599, ✆ dhigu@dhigufinolhu.com), Dhigufinolhu Island, is a mid-range resort of 97 rooms on a narrow island only a few hundred metres long. The name means 'long sand bank' and the island has sandy beaches and a wide lagoon, which is good for windsurfing. It has the unusual feature of being linked by long wooden walkways to the resorts of Palm Tree Island and Bodu Huraa, and the service island of Bushi, which has the dive base, staff quarters, workshops, generator and desalination plants for all three resorts. This means an 800m walk to and from the dive base, but this has the advantages of access to the other resorts and an absence of machinery noise. There's a bar in the middle where the walkway branches off to the three islands.

It's a well-run resort, the meals are very good and a 'soft animation' policy provides for a little entertainment and plenty of relaxation. The Scuba Sub dive base is also well run – a single dive is US$65 including boat and full equipment rental, but costs are a lot less for frequent divers. The comfortable, air-con rooms cost US$140/187 with full board in low season or US$168/224 in high season (US$20 more for deluxe bungalows). About 21km from the airport with transfers by dhoni (90 minutes, US$50) or speedboat (45 minutes, US$160). The Male' office (☎ 314009, fax 327058) is at H Athireege Aage, Lotus Goalhi. Check its web site (www.dhigufinolhu.com) for details.

**Palm Tree Island** (☎ 443882, ✆ veli@veliganduhuraa.com), Veliganduhuraa Is-

land, is much smaller and more expensive than Dhigufinolhu, but guests are welcome to cross the walkway and use facilities on the bigger island. Another walkway connects to the resort on Boduhuraa (see the following entry). The very pleasant open-air restaurant is surrounded by palm trees in the middle of the island, and the thatched rooms all have a beach frontage. Rates are US$176/222 in low season or US$206/263 in high season, with full board. Transfers and Male' agent are the same as for Dhigufinolhu .

**Bodu Huraa,** (☎ 440172, ✆ boduhuraa@palmtree.com.mv), Boduhuraa Island, is a very new resort with 38 over-water bungalows, all booked by the Italian Hotelplan group. It wouldn't be much fun staying here unless you speak Italian, but from other resorts you can go over to this little Italy for an evening of pasta, pizza and pizzazz.

**Biyadoo** (☎ 447171, ✆ admin@biyadoo.com.mv), Biyadhoo Island, is a good-value, mid-range resort with 96 rooms on a spacious, attractive and well-manicured island. The atmosphere is a little more formal than some resorts, but it's exceptionally well run, the food is delicious and, with the nearby sister island of Villivaru (see the following entry), which you can visit using free dhoni transfers, you get access to two resorts for the price of one. The house reef is easily accessible around the whole island and offers superb snorkelling. Diving is also excellent and reasonably priced with the PADI five-star dive base, and you can do interesting dives from the beach.

The rooms, with air-con, hot water, and minibar, are modern, spacious and comfortable, in solid two-storey blocks with a nice outlook over beach and water. Singles/doubles with full board cost from US$145/155 in low season to US$165/175 in high season. The resort's Male' office (☎ 314009, fax 327058) is at H Athireege Aage, Lotus Goalhi, or check its Web site season, special deals may even make a stay even cheaper.

**Villivaru** (☎ 447070), Viligilivaru Island, the sister resort of Biyadoo, has 60 rooms, all at ground level. The island is smaller, and not quite so well vegetated, the rooms aren't as well finished, and the bar and restaurant are pretty charmless. The resorts use the same dive centre and the prices are the same. You're welcome to use the facilities on Biyadoo and charge them to your Villivaru account, or vice versa. Room rates and special offers are exactly the same. Both resorts are popular with British guests and many of them are repeat visitors (who are eligible for a 10% discount if they book directly with the resort). The islands are very close to each other, about 340m from the airport, and transfers are by speedboat (one hour, US$85). The local operator for both resorts is Prabalaji Enterprises (☎ 324699, fax 327014), H Maarandhooge, Meheli Goalhi, Male'.

**Cocoa Island** (☎ 443713), Makunufushi Island, was formerly a tiny, natural, exclusive, expensive and simply delightful resort 30km from the airport. It has closed for redevelopment, and the plan is for 30 overwater bungalows designed in the style of traditional dhonis.

**Kandooma** (☎ 444452, **@** kandooma@ dhivehinet.net.mv), Kadoomafushi Island, has some 124 rooms and is one of the least expensive resorts in the country. It's not the prettiest island, and the only beach is artificially pumped up from the lagoon. It attracts mostly German couples and dive groups on bargain-priced packages – nearly half the guests are divers. There's no handy house reef for snorkelling, but there are three free boat trips a day to good snorkelling sites not far away. Some nearby channels, including the Guraidhoo Kandu Protected Marine Area, offer excellent diving. A single dive, including tank, weights and the boat, is US$48, or US$54 with full equipment provided. After six dives, the prices drop to US$40 and US$45. A PADI open-water course is US$419.

The bars are very informal, drinks are reasonably priced (beer is about US$2.50 a can) and there are disco nights twice a week. The big, cafeteria-like restaurant gets mixed reports. Clean rooms are basic with cold freshwater showers, but no telephone or TV. High season rates are US$65/90 for a single/double with half board, US$10 more with air-con; low season rates are about US$10 cheaper, and FITs sometimes

get a very cheap rate. The resort is 35km from the airport and most transfers are by dhoni (2½ hours, US$50) or speedboat (40 minutes, US$70). The resort's Male' office (☎ 323360, fax 326880) is at 46 Orchid Magu.

**Fun Island Resort** (☎ 444558, **@** fun@ dhivehinet.net.mv), Bodufinolhu Island, is a mid-range resort with 100 rooms in modern motel-like blocks. The rooms are fully equipped with air-con, hot water, phone and minibar, and there are two restaurants and three bars, including a nice wooden terrace over the lagoon. It's a long, narrow island, 800m by 30m, but if it feels a little crowded there are two smaller, uninhabited islands nearby that you can wade to at low tide. The lagoon is very wide and not great for snorkelling, but there are good dive sites in the area. The dive school is good, but a little pricey – single dives cost US$35 plus US$13 for the boat and US$19 for full equipment rental; a 10-dive package is US$270 with tank and weights only; and a PADI open-water course is US$540, plus boat trips.

Singles/doubles with full board cost about US$133/148 – more at Christmas, less in low season. It's 38km from the airport, and transfers are usually by speedboat (55 minutes, US$80). The operator is Villa Hotels (☎ 316161, fax 314565, **@** villahtls@ dhivehinet.net.mv), STO Trade Centre, Male', or check its Web site (www.villahotels-maldives.com) for more details.

**Olhuveli View Hotel** (☎ 441957, **@** olhuveli@ dhivehinet.net.mv), Olhuveli Island, is a mid-range to top-end resort with 112 rooms and 13 over-water bungalows, mostly used by Japanese guests, many of them divers. There are three restaurants (one Japanese), and the activities include tennis, sauna, a disco and karaoke. The big saltwater swimming pool is an attraction, and landscaping, with lots of imported palm trees, has improved the appearance of this resort. Nevertheless, it has a very modern, almost sterile appearance, notably in the big, stark, white rooms. Standard singles/doubles with full board cost around US$160/194 in high season, but most packages and FITs should get lower rates than this. The resort is 39km from the airport and transfers are usually by speedboat (50 minutes). Olhuveli doesn't list a Male' address, so contact the resort directly, or try a Male' tour operator like Paradise Tours (☎ 312090, fax 312087, @ parahol@dhivehinet.net.mv).

***Club Rannalhi*** *(☎ 442688, @ rnl4628@ dhivehinet.net.mv)*, Rannalhi Island, on the western edge of the atoll, is an Italian club-style resort with 116 rooms and 16 over-water bungalows. It's an attractive island with tall palm trees, fine beaches and good snorkelling on the house reef, but it's so built up that there's hardly any open space left on the island. The diving is good here, and reasonably priced, but the main attraction is the program of activities, which start with morning aerobics, continue with volleyball and dance competitions, and finish late at night with amateur theatrics and karaoke. The food is very good, and the rooms are comfortable and well finished. Nearly all the guests come through the Italian agent Viaggi del Ventaglio, better known as Club Venta. However, keen Italophiles can book a room through Male' operators from around US$130/180 with full board in low season to around US$160/210 in high season. It's about 34km from the airport, and transfers are by speedboat (35 minutes, US$100). The resort's Male' office is Jetan Travel Services (☎ 323323, fax 317993), STO Aifaanu Building, Boduthakurufaanu Magu.

***Fihalhohi Resort*** *(☎ 442903, @ fiha@ dhivehinet.net.mv)*, Fihaalhohi Island, is a great choice for families – an unpretentious, budget to mid-range Maldivian-run resort. The island is attractive with waving palm trees and beautiful beaches, and the buildings are modest with a natural look. Guests are a mix of Swiss, German and British; most are couples and quite a few bring children in August and over Christmas. The dive operation is very professional, with a variety of courses and dives at reasonable prices. Nitrox diving and instruction is available. The house reef is very good for snorkelling, and is also used for night dives and individual dives.

Meals are good and mostly buffet with plenty of variety. In low season, a room with full board will cost around US$74/86 for a standard single/double; US$84/96 for superior (with hot water), US$96/108 for deluxe (larger, with air-con). High-season rates are about US$25 more. Half board is US$8 less per person. Children under 12 are charged at US$22 for full board. The resort is about 35km from the airport, on the south-western edge of the atoll, and transfers are by speedboat (one hour, US$60). The local operator is Dhirham Travels (☎ 323369, fax 322678), Faamudheyri Magu, Male'.

***Rihiveli Beach Resort*** *(☎ 443731)*, Mahaana Elhi Huraa Island, is a small, high-quality resort that is very much the personal creation of a French owner who has lived in the Maldives since 1977. The 48 rusticated rooms are made of coral stone and have thatched roofs, hot water and natural ventilation – there's no air-con, fridge, phone or TV. The open-air bar has a sand floor and shady trees overhead, while the restaurant is built over the lagoon and has a lovely outlook and truly mouth-watering cuisine. The Eurodivers dive base has very reasonable prices – US$45 for a single dive, including the boat and all equipment.

The usual water sports (windsurfing, sailing, canoeing, even water-skiing) plus tennis are all included in the room price. You can wade across to two other, uninhabited islands where the resort organises regular barbecue lunches. Guests are mostly from France, Italy, Switzerland and Australia – the atmosphere is informal, with mixing gently encouraged, and shoes politely discouraged. Prices run from US$163/261 to US$204/333, depending on the season, with all meals. The resort is 40km from the airport, and transfers are by speedboat (one hour, US$135). The resort's Male' office (☎ 322421, fax 320976) is on Ahmadhee Bazaar.

# Ari Atoll

## Highlights

**Administrative District:** Alifu
**Code Letter:** I
**Inhabited Islands:** 17
**Uninhabited Islands:** 46
**Resorts:** 29
**Population:** 9793

• Experiencing traditional life at the South Ari Cultural Centre
• Exploring the underwater wonders of protected marine areas
• Staying out in the lagoon in an over-water bungalow
• Taking a cruise or diving safari through the atoll

Ari Atoll and, to the north, Rasdhoo Atoll and Thoddoo Island, make up the administrative district called Alifu Atoll. Some maps show an earlier administrative division between North Ari Atoll and South Ari Atoll, but the whole area is commonly called Ari. It's west of South Male' Atoll, across a 40km-wide channel.

Ari Atoll is about 80km from north to south and 30km wide with 16 inhabited islands, 46 uninhabited islands and 29 resorts. Rasdhoo Atoll is less than 10km across and has one inhabited island and two resort islands, one of which is unusual in that it has three resorts – usually there is only one resort per island. Thoddoo is a single-island atoll, inhabited and by itself to the north of Rasdhoo.

The capital of Alifu is **Mahibadhoo**, with a population of around 1500, mostly employed in the fishing industry, but **Rasdhoo** serves as a capital for North Ari. Other inhabited islands include **Maamigili** in the south of the atoll, with over 1300 people, many of whom work in nearby resorts. The

island of **Fenfushi**, on the south-west corner of the atoll, supplies sand and coral-stone for buildings in Male' and elsewhere, and is noted for coral carving.

Ari was opened up for resort leases later than the Male' atolls and is popular for its many excellent dive sites.

Access to Ari's resorts from the airport is usually by speedboat or seaplane (or helicopter, if services have resumed; see the Getting Around chapter). By speedboat, most resorts can be reached within a few hours, but it's too far for resorts to offer excursions to the capital – if you want to see Male', arrange for a day there at the start or the end of your trip. This may be unavoidable if your flights cannot connect directly with a transfer to your resort – seaplanes and fast boats don't operate at night.

Most cruises and diving safaris include Ari Atoll on their itinerary. A typical trip might start from Male', go south through South Male' Atoll, west across the channel, north through Ari Atoll, east across to North Male' Atoll and back to the capital (this can be done in either direction).

## THODDOO ISLAND

All by itself about 11km north of Rasdhoo Atoll, Thoddoo is a single oval island about 2km across. It's known for its market-garden produce – watermelons and betel leaf especially. There is evidence of the island being occupied from ancient times – a Buddhist temple here contained a Roman coin minted in 90 BC, as well as a silver bowl and a fine stone carving of a Buddha head, which is now in the Male' museum. The old Friday Mosque, **Hukuru Miskiiy**, was built in the late 17th century during the reign of Sultan Mohammed Ibn al-Haj Ali. It may be possible to do a day-trip here from one of the Rasdhoo Atoll resorts.

## RASDHOO ATOLL

The small atoll of Rasdhoo lies off the north-eastern corner of Ari Atoll. The main island of the atoll, also called Rasdhoo, has a population of about 780 and is the administrative capital of North Ari Atoll. Facilities include a junior secondary school, a health centre and four mosques. The island has been settled for many centuries and there are traces here of a Buddhist society predating the arrival of Islam. Rasdhoo Island is neat, clean and quite attractive and often visited as a day trip from the nearby resorts.

All the Rasdhoo resorts have a sheltered lagoon on one side, which is good for windsurfing, and deep water on the other side beyond a narrow outside reef, where there is excellent snorkelling.

## Diving

Two boats have been sunk off the island to provide an attraction for divers. A decompression chamber was due to be installed on Kuramathi in 2000, with trained hyperbaric specialists.

**Kuramathi House Reef** Accessible from the shore, this reef is good for beginners. The wrecks of a small dhoni and a 30m freighter make for an interesting dive, and there are many fish.

**Rasdhoo Madivaru** This is a more demanding dive on an outer reef where hammerhead sharks, mantas and other large pelagics are frequently seen. Outside this reef the depth drops rapidly to over 200m and the water is exceptionally clear. Caves on the reef edge at about 25m have batfish and black coral.

## Resorts

*Veligandu* (☎ 450594, ✉ veli@dhivehinet.net .mv), Veligadu Island, on the east side of the atoll, is a medium-sized, mid-range resort with 63 air-con rooms. The main attraction is the natural ambience and rustic simplicity – the reception area and restaurant have sand floors. Guests are mainly German, Austrian and Italian. 'Superior rooms' (the least expensive ones) are around US$115/140 for singles/doubles with full board – less in low season and more over Christmas. Deluxe rooms, slightly bigger and closer to the water, cost US$40 more, and the nicely decorated over-water bungalows cost at least

US$40 more than that. The resort is 51km from the airport and transfer is usually by seaplane (US$135 per person return). The resort's Male' office (☎ 322432, fax 324009) is at H Sea Coast, Marine Dr.

The island of Kuramathi used to be inhabited, but the population was in decline, so in 1970 the 120 remaining residents relocated to Rasdhoo, leaving Kuramathi available for resort development. Kuramathi island is about 1½km long by 500m wide and has three related resorts, Kuramathi Village, Kuramathi Cottage Club and Blue Lagoon. In all, there are 274 bungalows and rooms. Guests can use the facilities and restaurants at all the resorts, and a minibus, running the length of the island, shuttles between them. The large swimming pool and well-equipped gym are near the centre of the island.

Rasdhoo Atoll Divers serves all three resorts and is quite inexpensive – a single dive is US$37 including all equipment; a 10-dive package is US$270, or US$320 with all equipment. For boat dives add US$12 each. A PADI open-water course is US$420. Sometimes there is a resident marine biologist, who gives lectures and accompanies dives. The lagoon is perfect for windsurfing, and the water sports centre has boards from US$18 per hour to US$180 per week, as well as a range of courses – a five-lesson beginners' diving course will have you diving well for US$210. Canoes, catamarans and water skiing are also available.

*Kuramathi Village* (☎ 450527), Kuramathi Island, is the largest resort, with 144 rooms. It's also the least expensive, with budget to mid-range accommodation. Rooms are mostly pleasant, thatched cottages set among luxuriant vegetation; they're priced around US$128/161 with full board, or US$150/205 all-inclusive (the latter includes transfers, a couple of excursions, use of a windsurfer and snorkelling gear, and basic beer, wine and spirits – this could be good value if you like windsurfing and/or drinking). Low-season prices may be less; high season will definitely cost more. This end of the island has younger patrons, many of them Brits and Germans on all-inclusive deals and ready to party.

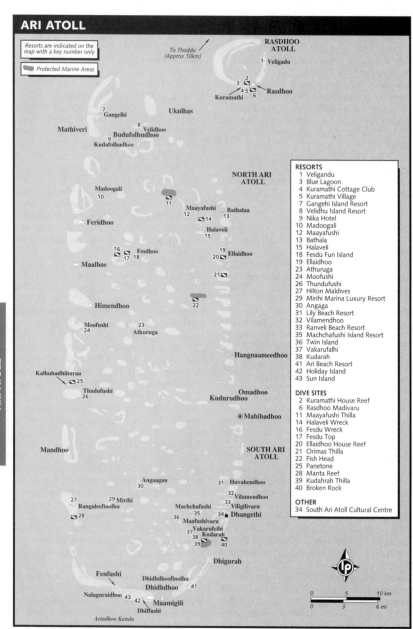

# ARI ATOLL

Resorts are indicated on the map with a key number only

Protected Marine Areas

RASDHOO ATOLL

To Thoddu (Approx 10km)

1  Veligandu

2
3
4 5
6  Rasdhoo
Kuramathi

Gangehi 7
Ukulhas

Mathiveri

8  Velidhoo
Budufolhudhoo
9
Kudafolhudhoo

NORTH ARI ATOLL

Madoogali
10

11

Maayafushi
12        14    Bathalaa
              13

Feridhoo                Halaveli
                        15

16      Fesdhoo            19    Ellaidhoo
17  18                  20

Maalhos

21

22

Himendhoo

Moofushi    23
24      Athuruga

Hangnaameedhoo

Kalhuhadhihuraa
25

Thudufushi
26

Omadhoo
Kudurudhoo

Mahibadhoo

SOUTH ARI ATOLL

Mandhoo

Angaagau                31    Huvahendhoo
30
                    32  Vilamendhoo
27      29  Mirihi      33  Viligilivaru
Rangaleefinolhu    Machchafushi  34  Dhangethi
28              36  35
            Maafushivaru
                37  Vakarufelhi
                38  Kudarah
                39  40

Dhigurah

Fenfushi
        Dhidhdhoofinolhu
        Dhidhdhoo  41
Nalaguraidhoo  43  42  Maamigili
            Dhiffushi
Ariadhoo Kandu

### RESORTS
1  Veligandu
3  Blue Lagoon
4  Kuramathi Cottage Club
5  Kuramathi Village
7  Gangehi Island Resort
8  Velidhu Island Resort
9  Nika Hotel
10  Madoogali
12  Maayafushi
13  Bathala
15  Halaveli
18  Fesdu Fun Island
19  Ellaidhoo
23  Athuruga
24  Moofushi
26  Thundufushi
27  Hilton Maldives
29  Mirihi Marina Luxury Resort
30  Angaga
31  Lily Beach Resort
32  Vilamendhoo
33  Ranveli Beach Resort
35  Machchafushi Island Resort
36  Twin Island
37  Vakarufalhi
38  Kudarah
41  Ari Beach Resort
42  Holiday Island
43  Sun Island

### DIVE SITES
2  Kuramathi House Reef
6  Rasdhoo Madivaru
11  Maayafushi Thilla
14  Halaveli Wreck
16  Fesdu Wreck
17  Fesdu Top
20  Ellaidhoo House Reef
21  Orimas Thilla
22  Fish Head
25  Panetone
28  Manta Reef
39  Kudahrah Thilla
40  Broken Rock

### OTHER
34  South Ari Atoll Cultural Centre

0        5        10 km
0      3      6 mi

ARI ATOLL

It's never that busy in the Maldives – no crowds, no queues.

Older buildings and walls are constructed with dead coral stones but you can still find wood and thatch on village islands.

The **Blue Lagoon** (☎ 450579), Kuramathi Island, is at the quiet end of the island and is the honeymooners choice. It's a mid-range to top-end resort with 30 rooms at around US$145/180 for full board, and 20 over-water bungalows costing US$70 more.

The **Kuramathi Cottage Club** (☎ 450532), Kuramathi Island, is in the middle of the island, and the guests tend to be older, and intent on relaxation. Prices are the same as for the Blue Lagoon.

The specialty Thai restaurant, Indian restaurant, Grill, and coffee shop are excellent, but not included in full-board packages (though a nominal discount is offered). If you want to eat around, or you're not a big eater, a half-board package may suit you better. Regular disco nights and special shows are held at the Cottage Club, where drinks aren't covered by all-inclusive packages. Access is usually by fast boat (1¾ hours, US$85), though some transfers are by seaplane. All three resorts share the same email address (✆ kuramathi@dhivehinet.net.mv) and all are operated by Universal Enterprises (☎ 323080, fax 320274, ✆ sales@unisurf .com), 39 Orchid Magu, Male'. Check its Web site (www.unisurf.com) for details.

## ARI ATOLL
## Diving

All of the resorts have diving operations and a number are significant destinations for serious divers. During peak season some sites may have several groups diving on them at one time, but good dive operators will know when to avoid the crowds and where to find equally attractive but less visited sites. The following is a brief description of some well-known sites (from north to south) to give an idea of the possibilities.

**Maayafushi Thilla** This is a classic round thilla known for the white-tip reef sharks that circle it. Caves and overhangs around the thilla have lots of gorgonians, soft corals and schools of reef fish. It's a Protected Marine Area.

**Halaveli Wreck** This well-known site was created when a 38m cargo ship was deliberately sunk in 1991. It's famous for the friendly stingrays enticed here by regular feeding – keep your fingers away from their mouths.

**Fesdu Top** This interesting reef dive is suitable for beginners. There are lionfish, schools of bluestripe snapper, the occasional turtle and caves with sunlit cracks. It makes a good night dive.

**Fesdu Wreck** This 30m trawler has a good covering of coral at a depth of 18m to 30m. Moray eels and grouper live inside the hull, which is easily entered and has good growths of soft coral and sponges. Divers can also check the adjacent thilla, which has hard and soft coral and lots of fish.

**Ellaidhoo House Reef** Only accessible to Ellaidhoo's guests, this excellent house reef has a long wall just 25m from the beach. It has a row of caves with seafans, whip coral, schools of bannerfish, Napoleons, stingrays and morays, and even a small wreck. This reef is popular with night divers.

**Orimas Thilla** Overhangs, caves, crevices, canyons and coral heads make this Protected Marine Area an exciting dive. Marine life includes good growths of soft coral, seafans, anemones and clownfish. The top of the thilla is only 3m down, and can be easily enjoyed by snorkellers if the conditions are calm.

**Fish Head** Also called Mushimasmingali Thilla, this Protected Marine Area is one of the world's most famous dive sites. Its steep sides are spectacular, with multi-level ledges, overhangs and caves supporting many seafans and black coral; its top is heavily encrusted with anemones. Beware of stonefish. The prolific fish life includes fusiliers, large Napoleons, trevally and schools of hungry barracuda. The main attraction, however, is the numerous grey reef sharks, which can be seen close-up. Strong currents can make this a demanding dive, and extreme care should be taken not to damage this superb but heavily used site.

**Panetone** The north side of Kalhuhadhihuraa Faru is subject to strong currents, so the caves and overhangs are thick with soft coral growth. As well as the many reef fish there are giant trevally, sharks, barracuda and turtles. From December to April mantas feed around the outside of the channel; March to November are the best months to see sharks.

**Manta Reef** Also called Madivaru, this dive is at the end of a channel where powerful currents carry plankton out of the atoll during the northeast monsoon (December to April) – fast food for manta rays. Mantas also come to be cleaned. Reef fish include Napoleon wrasse, snapper and parrotfish, while pelagics such as turtles, tuna and sharks visit the outer reef slope. For advanced divers only.

**Kudahrah Thilla** This Protected Marine Area is a very demanding but exciting dive – if there is a current running, this is strictly for experienced divers. There are gorgonians, whip coral, black coral and a whole field of seafans swaying in the current, surrounded by sharks and trevally from the open sea. In the gaps between large coral blocks, bluestripe snapper, tallfin, batfish, goby and other unusual small fish can be seen.

**Broken Rock** This thilla, in the mouth of the Dhigurashu Kandu, is bisected by a canyon up to 10m deep and only 1m to 3m wide. Swimming through the 50m canyon is unforgettable, but extreme care is needed not to damage the coral formations on either side. Rock formations around the thilla are decorated with seafans and superb coral, and inhabited by abundant marine life.

## Resorts

Ari has a variety of resorts, from exclusive rustic hideaways for rich Robinson Crusoes to slick new places with every modern convenience. They are listed here from north to south.

*Gangehi Island Resort (☎ 450505), Gangelhi Island*, is a small, high-price resort with just 25 beautifully furnished rooms, all filled by guests from Italy. It is operated by Holiday Club Maldives (☎ 313938, fax 313939,❷ hcmmale@club-vacanze.com.mv), 4th floor, Alia Building, Male', and marketed exclusively by the Italian group Club Vacanzi.

*Velidhu Island Resort (☎ 450018, ❷ velidhu@dhivehinet.net.mv)*, Velidhoo Island, is a budget to mid-range resort with 87 rooms on a sizeable island with great beaches and a good house reef. It has improved greatly in the last few years, and offers fine food, good service, and some super new overwater bungalows. The Blue Ocean dive centre is very professional, and reasonably priced. The standard rooms are interesting round buildings with thatched roofs, and are very good value at US$95/130 with full board in low season; not quite so good in high season at US$165/190. The over-water bungalows cost US$185/220 in low season, US$255/280 in high season. It's some 85km from the airport, with transfers usually by seaplane (25 minutes, US$180). The resort's Male' office is Travel Club (☎ 313738, fax 326246), Roashanee Magu.

*Nika Hotel (☎ 450516, ❷ nika-htl@ dhivehinet.net.mv)*, Kudafolhudhoo Island, is often cited as the finest resort in the country. It has just 24 individual villas, each one spacious and imaginatively designed in a seashell shape. Tastefully decorated with thatched roofs and handcrafted timber furniture, the villas have private gardens and preserve a rustic image – cooling is by natural ventilation through wooden louvre windows. The only air-con here is in the wine cellar! The whole island is beautifully landscaped with soil imported from Sri Lanka. It even has a lawn tennis court and jetties where you can park your own yacht. Nika was developed by an Italian architect who has designed several other Maldivian resorts, but this is his masterpiece. The excellent food is Italian and international. The guests are mostly European or Japanese, and rich. Expect to pay US$300 to US$450 for a double, depending on the room and the season. Seaplane transfer from the airport costs US$200. The Male' office (☎ 325091, fax 325097) is at 117 Majeedi Magu, PO Box 2076.

*Madoogali (☎ 450581, ❷ madugali@ dhivehinet.net.mv)*, Madoogali Island, is another small, mid-range resort, on a lush little island circled by perfect beaches. The 50 air-con rooms have coral walls, steep pitched thatched roofs and natural style. The landscaping is a feature of the island. The cuisine is Italian, as are most of the guests, many of whom are repeat visitors. It's booked through agents in Italy, as well as its own Male' office (☎ 317975, fax 317974) on Medhuziyaarai Magu. The island was home to 43 Maldivians until 1943, when they were transferred to Mandhoo Island.

*Maayafushi (☎ 450588, ❷ maaya@ dhivehinet.net.mv)*, Mayafushi Island, predominantly a divers' island, offers very good value for an unpretentious island holiday. The island is small and quite intensively developed, but it has good beaches and a wonderful house reef. Most of the guests are divers from Germany, Switzerland or Austria, but there's a few families with young children who get on well here. The dive school offers a wide range of courses, night dives and trips to the famous dive sites nearby. A single dive with a boat and all equipment will run to about US$58, and an open-water course is US$450. The 60 rooms all have basic furnishings, air-con, hot water, and beach frontage. Rates are around US$104/122 with full board in shoulder season, but for much of the year a good package or a good FIT rate might be a lot less. Transfers are by seaplane (25 minutes, US$195). The resort's Male' office (☎ 320097, fax 326658) is at H Luxwood 1, Boduthakurufaanu Magu.

**Bathala** (☎ 450587, @ bir0587@dhivehinet .net.mv), Bathalaa Island, a small, lower mid-range resort, is ideally located for divers. It would also appeal to those looking for a very low-key tropical hideaway, with its 37 circular thatched cottages and reliably good meals. There are excellent beaches and the house reef is great for snorkelling. Guests are mostly German and British, and the atmosphere is informal, with very little organised entertainment. The dive school is reasonably priced, but bring your own wet suit. Standard single/double rooms, without hot water or air-con, cost from US$95/150 with full board in low season to US$115/190 in peak season (superior rooms cost US$30 per night more). The resort is about 56km from the airport and most transfers are by seaplane (US$180 return). The resort's Male' office (☎ 315236, fax 315237) is in the STO Alfaanu Building, Boduthakurufaanu Magu.

**Halaveli** (☎ 450559, @ halaveli@dhive hinet.net.mv), Halaveli Island, a pretty island with very nice beaches, is a lively lower mid-range resort with excellent food. Virtually all the guests are Italians (half are honeymooners) brought in by Grande Viaggi of Rome. The dive school is operated by a group with the unusual name of Tropical Gangsters Incorporated, but the instructors are PADI-qualified and give an open-water course for about US$420. The 56 air-con rooms are all tastefully furnished, comfortable and well priced at around US$100 a double with full board in low season. Independent travellers can often get even cheaper prices from May to July (as low as US$75 a double). The

Male' agent is Eastinvest Ltd (☎ 322719, fax 323463), Akiri, Boduthakurufaanu Magu.

**Ellaidhoo** (☎ 450514), Ellaidhoo Island, is a budget to mid-range resort with a reputation as the most hard-core diving destination in the Maldives. Over 100 dive sites are accessible within a half-day trip. Around 90% of the guests here are divers, mostly German, but with a good selection of other nationalities. Apart from the dive sites accessible by boat, the Ellaidhoo house reef is only a few metres offshore and offers some great diving with a 750m wall, lots of caves, coral, rich marine life (turtles, sharks, mantas and eagle rays) and even a small wreck. Qualified, experienced divers can dive independently on the house reef at any time.

The dive school is run by Sub-Aqua of Munich. A diving course with certification by PADI, NAUI or CMAS takes from four to six days and costs about US$500, all-inclusive. A single dive with a guide and all equipment supplied is US$50, but if you have your own equipment the cost with tank and weights only is US$44. A six-dive package with a guide, tank and weights is US$240. Add US$10 for every boat dive. Sub-Aqua also runs courses in marine biology.

The 50 rooms are rustic in style, but they have air-con and cost around US$137/156 for singles/doubles with full board in high season, quite a bit less in low season and almost twice as much at Christmas. If you're a hungry diver, you'll find the food OK. Ellaidhoo is 57km from the airport, and transfers are usually by seaplane (20 minutes, US$175). The resort's Male' agent is Travelin Maldives (☎ 317717, fax 314977, @ mail@travelin-maldives.com), STO Alfaanu Building, Boduthakurufaanu Magu.

**Fesdu Fun Island** (☎ 450541), Fesdhoo Island, is a mid-range resort with 55 rooms in thatched bungalows. It is a pretty island with good beaches and house reef. A double room is about US$120 in the low season and US$160 in the high season. It is 72km from the airport; transfers are by speedboat (2½ hours, US$105) or seaplane (20 minutes, US$155). It is one of nine resorts operated by Universal Enterprises Ltd (☎ 322971, fax 322678), 38 Orchid Magu, Male'.

ARI ATOLL

***Moofushi*** *(☎ 450598, @ moofushi@ dhivehinet.net.mv)*, Moofushi Island, has 60 attractive, natural style, thatched rooms, all of them filled by Italians. It's a pretty island, but the beach is suffering from erosion and some of the breakwaters are unsightly. Generally it's a mid-range resort, but prices rise very steeply over Christmas. Transfers from the airport are by seaplane (25 minutes, US$180). The resort's Male' office (☎ 326141, fax 313237) is at H Sun Night.

***Athuruga*** *(☎ 450508, @ athadmin@ dhivehinet.net.mv)*, Athuruga Island, on a small island, is now marketed on an all-inclusive basis, so it's better value than the high-mid-range price tag might suggest. The 42 air-con rooms are spacious and comfortable and all face onto the nice but narrow beach. Guests are mostly from Italy, Germany and the UK, in that order, and the atmosphere is casual. The food is consistently very good. The Crab dive base is only a little more expensive than most – there are some good dive sites nearby, but it's an hour by boat to the exciting dives on the western rim of the atoll. Rates are around US$205/310 in shoulder season, US$285/330 in high season, and US$655/660 over Christmas – this includes full board, most drinks, snorkelling equipment, excursions, and laundry. Transfers are by seaplane (25 minutes, US$210). The Male' office (☎ 310489, fax 310390) is on Dhambu Goalhi.

***Thundufushi*** *(☎ 450597, @ thuadmin@ dhivehinet.net.mv)*, Thudufushi Island, is a sister resort to Athuruga with the same management and similar standards of food and service. The buildings and the style may be a little more formal (no sand floor in the bar), but the island itself is just beautiful. In high season the majority of its guests are Italian, booked through Francorosso, but at other times there are more Germans and Brits. It's better placed for dives on the atoll edge and the house reef is excellent. Also spelled Thudufushi, it has the same rates and inclusions for its 47 rooms as Athuruga, the same transfer arrangements and the same dive-school operator (The Crab) and dive prices.

***Angaga*** *(☎ 450510)*, Angaagau Island, is a budget to mid-range resort, which attracts a good international mix – it's popular with Germans, Italians, Brits and Australians, as well as the occasional Japanese. The island has wide beaches all round, an accessible house reef, and a spacious sand-floored bar and restaurant. The 51 thatch-roofed bungalows, with a traditional *undholi* (swing seat; see the boxed text 'Sitting in the Maldives' in the Facts about the Maldives chapter) in front of each one, have a little more character than many of the mid-range resorts. There's a good, German-run dive operation here, giving a full range of PADI and CMAS courses and running trips to the many well-known dive sites in the area.

Rooms all have air-con and full board costs from around US$115/130 in low season to US$135/150 in high season. The resort is 90km from the airport and transfer is by speedboat (around 2½ hours, US$100) or by seaplane (US$190). The resort's Male' office (☎ 313636, fax 323115) is at STO Koshi 9, Ameenee Magu.

***Mirihi Island Resort*** *(☎ 450500, @ mirhi@ dhivehinet.net.mv)*, Mirihi Island, is a comfortable, mid-range resort, on a tiny island, with 34 rooms, most of them built over the water on one side of the island. A first-class beach and house reef are easily reached on the other side. Room rates are inexpensive, but the diving and the extras are a little on the expensive side. All the guests are on packages from Germany and Austria. The resort's Male' office (☎/fax 325448) is at H Silver Star, 3 Haveeree Hingun, Male'.

***Hilton Maldives*** *(☎ 450629, @ hilton@ dhivehinet.net.mv)*, Rangali Island, actually occupies two islands – the main part of the hotel, with reception, the main restaurant, bar and 100 beach villas is on Rangali Finolhu; 30 over-water villas are at one end of a second island, which also has a bar for breakfast, snacks and quiet drinks. The two are connected by a walkway bridge. One of the most luxurious resorts in the country, it has tennis courts, a swimming pool, spa/health club, excellent beaches and a good house reef, which is easily accessible for snorkelling. There are good dive sites nearby and the Subaqua dive base is not exceptionally expensive. Despite the first-class facilities, it presents a natural appearance with lots of wood and cane finishes, fine fabrics and a sand floor in the bar and reception area. A single/double room with full board costs from around US$290/355 to more than US$500 at Christmas, and an over-water bungalow will be around US$453/505. The resort is about 96km from the airport and transfers are by seaplane (35 minutes, US$205). The local operator is Crown Company Pty Ltd (☎ 324232, fax 324009), Marine Dr, Male'. Check the resort's Web site (www.hilton.com) for further details.

*Twin Island* (☎ 450596), Maafushivaru Island, has a modern, 38-room resort crowded onto a rather small island. The beaches are attractive, but the circle of sea walls, which protect them, are not. The rooms are boxy and modern, with distinctive blue tiled roofs, but comfortable and well furnished. The main attraction is the sociable atmosphere and the lively Italian crowd. It's a mid-range place, with all the rooms booked through the Italian company, Turisanda. The airport is 80km away, and transfers are by speedboat (2½ hours). The resort's Male' operator is Universal Enterprises (☎ 322596), 39 Orchid Magu, but it won't take local bookings.

*Machchafushi Island Resort* (☎ 454545), Machchafushi Island, one of the newer resorts, is on a small island with fine beaches and a good house reef, suitable for diving as well as snorkelling. In fact, this is pretty much a divers' island, with an almost entirely German clientele (it may be trying for the Japanese market, too). Diving is well priced here, with a single dive at US$37, or US$40 with all equipment provided. Boat charges are US$10 per dive. There's a swimming pool and tennis court too, but they seem to be little used. The 48 air-con rooms are nicely furnished, and their metal roofs have a thin covering of palm thatch to give the place a rustic look. It's an inexpensive resort, with a standard double room at US$135 in shoulder season, including all meals. The ten over-water bungalows cost US$30 or so more. The resort is 87km from the airport and transfers are by seaplane (30 minutes, US$180). The resort's Male' office (☎ 327849, fax 327277) is at Ocean View No 2, Boduthakurufaanu Magu.

*Lily Beach Resort* (☎ 450013, ✆ lilybech@ dhivehinet.net.mv), Huvahendhoo Island, is a neat, modern, mid-range resort, with 84 air-con rooms, tennis court, gym, a good swimming pool, and sand floors in the bar and restaurant. The vegetation is a bit sparse, but the beaches are superb and the house reef is easily accessible – the main drawback is the circle of ugly breakwaters. The atmosphere is friendly and informal, with mostly European guests, including a strong British contingent, and quite often families with children (a children's play

ARI ATOLL

MARTIN HARRIS

**Over-water bungalows provide simplicity, comfort and privacy.**

area is a new feature). The dive centre is reasonably priced – US$44 for a single dive with everything supplied, plus US$9 for a half-day boat trip. An open-water course costs US$490.

Everyone is on an 'all-inclusive' price plan, which includes all meals, snacks, coffee, beer, wine, whisky, gin, vodka rum, water sports (except diving), tennis and one island-hopping excursion. If you're keen on windsurfing or drinking, these extras could save you US$10 or US$20 per day compared with other resorts. A standard room is US $135/190 in high season, but most packages will give a better rate than this. The deluxe over-water villas cost about US$30 more, but the standard rooms actually have a nicer outlook. Lily Beach is 80km from the airport and transfers by seaplane cost US$170 return. The local operator is Lily Hotels (☎ 317464, fax 317466), Orchid Magu, Male'.

***Vilamendhoo*** (☎ 450637, **✆** vilamndu@ aaa.com.mv), Vilamendhoo Island, is on a very lush, well-vegetated island with plenty of space to accommodate this modern, mid-range 100-room resort. The rooms are all air conditioned, spacious, clean and comfortable – no rustic island style here. The beaches are beautiful and the house reef is particularly good for snorkelling. The resort is efficiently managed, but friendly and informal, and it attracts a good mix of visitors, mostly from the UK and Germany. The food is good here too – it even has real coffee (most resorts offer instant coffee).

Plenty of top dive sites are in this corner of the atoll; dives here are cheap if you have your own equipment (US$36), but expensive if you don't (US$57). The boat charge is US$8 per trip, and a PADI open-water course is US$504.

It's a very reasonably priced resort in the low season, from as low as US$40/70 with full board; but a lot more in higher seasons, from US$114/140. Superior rooms are bigger, closer to the beach and better furnished, but cost US$20 more. It is 82km from the airport, transfers are by seaplane (30 minutes, US$205). The resort's Male' agent is AAA Hotels & Resorts (☎ 324933, fax 324943), 3rd floor, STO Trade Centre, Orchid Magu.

The ***Ranveli Beach Resort*** (☎ 450570), Viligilivaru Island, is a mid-range resort with 100% Italian guests (many of whom are divers) who book through Club Vacanza. With 77 rooms in two-storey blocks, this small island seems distinctly overbuilt. The main restaurant is offshore, in an elegant pavilion on a pier over the lagoon. The house reef is good for snorkelling and the diving is very good. It's 77km from the airport with transfers by seaplane (25 minutes). The resort's Male' office (☎ 316921, fax 316922) is at M Velidhooge, Dhambu Goalhi. Check its Web site (www.ranveli-maldives.com) for details.

***Vakarufalhi*** (☎ 450004, **✆** vakaru@ dhivehinet.net.mv), Vakarufelhi Island, is a mid-range to top-end resort with 50 rooms on an attractive little island. The individual bungalows are clean and modern inside with tiled floors, air-con, hot water and open-air bathrooms; on the outside, they are surrounded by shady trees and have thatched roofs to give them a more natural appearance. Guests are mostly German, Swiss and British. The sand-floored, spiral-shaped restaurant is impressive, and it serves very good food.

The dive operation, Pro-Divers, is in fact very professional, and very reasonably priced. A single dive with all equipment provided is US$39, and a 10-dive package is US$348. Boat trips are US$10 and an all-inclusive open-water course is US$548. The published room rate with full board is US$230/250 in high season, but package deal prices are much cheaper than this. The resort is 90km from the airport and transfers are by seaplane (35 minutes, US$205). The local operator is Champa Trade & Travel (☎ 314149, fax 314150), Ahmadhee Bazaar, Male'.

***Kudarah*** (☎ 450610), Kudarah Island, is a small luxury resort with 30 rooms, a tennis court and swimming pool. It's a Club Vacanza resort, catering to the Italian market. With white walls, columns, arches and tiles, even the buildings look Italian. The local operator is Holiday Club Maldives (☎ 313938, fax 313939, **✆** hcmmale@ clubvacanze.com.mv), 4th floor, Alia Building, Male'.

## South Ari Atoll Cultural Centre

On the island of Dhangethi, on the lower eastern side of Ari Atoll, is one of the few attempts to depict and display the traditional Maldivian way of life. The centre comprises three dwellings and several other structures typical of those in which the various activities of an island community were carried out. The buildings are all reproductions, but they have been made using traditional construction techniques and local materials, and they are furnished with authentic artefacts and tools.

The finest house is of a type that might have been occupied by an island headman and his family, and is partly designed to formally entertain guests. It features carved wooden decorations, large lacquerware bowls for serving food and raised platforms for guests of the highest status. Specific areas of the house are reserved for men and women, whose roles were largely segregated in traditional Maldivian communities.

The house of a fishing family is similar in its basic layout, though smaller and less well finished. The verandah has an assortment of nets, fish hooks and other tools for fishing in the traditional way.

The smallest house comprises a single room, with an outside bathing area and a separate kitchen. The kitchen is made from loosely woven palm fronds, to allow smoke from the cooking fires to clear. It displays the utensils and ingredients which were used to smoke or dry fish, the dietary staple and an important trading commodity.

The largest building is the *haruge*, the boatbuilding shed, where you can see the tools and techniques of dhoni construction, and also an ingenious machine used to make coconut fibre rope. Another working building is the weaving shed, where screwpine leaves are woven into mats, and coconut fibre is turned into coir products like nets and bags.

Dhangethi is handy to at least seven resorts in South Ari Atoll, and accessible on longer island-hopping trips from several others – if you don't see a trip advertised, ask your resort if they can arrange one. The Cultural Centre conducts demonstrations of traditional industries and crafts, and ideally your visit should coincide with these. At other times you get a guided tour of the exhibits. The entry cost is usually included in the cost of the excursion – it's only a couple of dollars, plus a couple of dollars more if there are demonstrations being conducted during your visit. Additional donations are appreciated.

*Ari Beach Resort* (☎ 450513, ✆ aribeach@ dhivehinet.net.mv), Dhidhdhoofinolhu Island, has 121 rooms of various standards scattered among scrubby vegetation, but generally it's a very casual, inexpensive resort. It's popular with singles, young people and independent travellers, and it has something of a reputation as a party island. The coffee shop and bar are inexpensive by Maldives standards (a beer is US$2.75) and the meals are all buffet style and not bad. Though there are miles of lovely beach, the fringing reef is quite wide and it's a long way to the best snorkelling areas. However, boats go out for free snorkelling trips twice a day. The dive school is reasonably priced – a single dive is US$40 with all equipment supplied and boat trips are US$10.

Standard rooms are basic boxes and somewhat worn, but they do have air-con and phone, and they're pretty cheap at US$88/100 with half board; from April to October they're even cheaper than that but over Christmas they're more. Superior rooms are bigger, with cathedral-like ceilings, hot water and minibar, and cost around US$114/130. The new, deluxe over-water bungalows are around US$149/170. Add US$10 per person per day extra to these prices for full board – it's probably worth it. The resort is 91km from the airport and transfers are available by speedboat (2½ to three hours, US$90) or seaplane (35 minutes, US$220). The Male' office (☎ 321930, fax 327355) is at 35 Boduthakurufaanu Magu (www.aribeach.com doesn't get updated very often).

*Holiday Island* (☎ 450011, ✆ holiday@ dhivehinet.net.mv), Dhiffushi Island, was regarded as a big, new, modern resort until its new neighbour, Sun Island, opened. No longer the newest and fanciest, Holiday Island is still a comfortable mid-range resort with 142 beach-front rooms surrounded by attractive landscaping and facing sandy beaches. The rooms are fitted out with everything from satellite TV to hot water in the bidet. The food and the service are good, entertainment such as disco nights or karaoke is offered most evenings and recreational facilities include tennis and badminton courts, a billiard room and gymnasium.

There's a typical island fishing village close by on the neighbouring island of Maamigili. Snorkelling is not good near the beaches, but there are frequent free boat trips out to the reef edge. The dive school here is quite pricey – a single dive with rental equipment is US$58. In fact, most of the extras here are expensive – a beer or a bottle of mineral water is over US$4.

Rooms cost around US$167/187 in high season with full board, more at Christmas and less from May to November; half board is available for about US$10-less per person, per day. The resort is 97km from the airport and transfers are by speedboat (three hours, US$105 return) or seaplane (35 minutes, US$165 return). It's one of three resorts operated by the Villa Group (☎ 316161, fax 314565, ✉ vilahtls@dhivehinet.net.mv), STO Trade Centre, Male'. See its Web site (www.villahotels-maldives.com) for more details.

**Sun Island** (☎ 450088, ✉ sun@dhivehinet .net.mv), Nalaguraidhoo Island, is the Maldives' biggest and most modern resort, with 350 rooms. The island is about 1.6km long and 380m wide; three years ago it was covered in coconut palms and native plants. The sandy beaches and many of the trees have been retained, but the development has been so total that the island is manicured from end to end, circled and crossed with paved paths. Riding round it on a bicycle is particularly enjoyable (US$3 per day). Opinions are divided about this resort – many feel that it's not in keeping with the Maldives 'natural' image.

The huge swimming pool features fake waterfalls and a horizon edge, which makes it seem part of the lagoon. The reception area is cavernous and the main dining room is vast. In addition there are four specialty restaurants, a coffee shop, four bars and 24-hour room service. Water is US$3.50 a bottle, beer US$4 a can, house wine US$5 a glass, but there's a 10% service charge on top of these prices. Separate shops sell jewellery, cosmetics, electronics and souvenirs. For amusement there's a video arcade (at US$1 a game), billiards (US$10 per hour) or darts (US$3 per hour). Squash, badminton, aerobics, gym and tennis are all available at a price (and there's a scale of charges if you damage the equipment – a dart is US$20). For relaxation try a shiatsu-anma massage treatment (US$35 per hour). Diving costs are moderate – a single dive is US$52 with all equipment, boat trips are US$12 each, and an open-water course is US$420.

The rooms themselves are large and have super quality indoor-outdoor bathrooms, bidets, minibars, mini-safes, and TVs that can show in-house movies (US$10 per day) or access the Internet (US$6.80 per half hour). The room-key tag is used to activate the room's electrical appliances – it's an energy conservation measure, so when you go out with your key, everything is turned off (US$75 charge for lost keys).

Low-season rates with half board are US$85/95, single/double deluxe, US$98/108 for super deluxe, and US$186/196 for an over-water bungalow. In high season these rise to US$159/169, US$179/189, and US $307/317. Full board is US$15 extra per person, per day. For a resort that bills itself as 'five-star plus', these rates are surprisingly low (maybe they'll make their profit from the extras). Sun Island is 100km from the airport and transfers are by speedboat (three hours, US$105 return) or seaplane (35 minutes, US$165 return). It's operated by the Villa Group (☎ 316161, fax 314565, ✉ vilahtls@dhivehinet.net.mv), STO Trade Centre, Male'. For further details, see its Web site at www.villahotels-maldives.com.

# Northern Atolls

## Highlights

- Seeing the restored wooden palace of Maldivian hero Mohammed Thakurufaanu on Utheemu
- Eating the best cuisine in the Maldives at Sonevafushi resort
- Picnicking on picturesque isolated islands
- Pampering yourself with massages and spa treatments at Raison d'Etre
- Climbing the Maldives' highest natural point, on Faridhoo Island

Most of the northern atolls are outside the tourist zone, except for Lhaviyani, Baa and part of Raa Atolls which are the closest to Male' and on which there is one resort each. The northern atolls are infrequently visited, even by safari boats, and there are few recognised dive sites, though the potential must be as great as anywhere in the Maldives.

About 200km to the north on the submerged Lacadive-Chagos ridge, the Lakshadweep Islands (formerly known as the Lacadives) are Indian territory, though they have a long association with the Maldives. On Minicoy, the largest island of the group, people speak a language very similar to Divehi.

## IHAVANDHIPPOLHU & NORTH THILADHUNMATHEE ATOLLS

**Administrative District:** Haa Alifu
**Code Letter:** A
**Inhabited Islands:** 16
**Uninhabited Islands:** 23
**Resorts:** 0
**Population:** 12,031

Haa Alifu includes both Ihavandhippolhu Atoll, the northernmost in the country, and the northern section of Thiladhunmathee Atoll. Almost 2000 people live on Dhidhdhoo, the capital island, which offers good anchorage for passing yachts, but Uligamu, the second northernmost island, is the 'clear-in' port for private yachts – you get a security clearance here but there are no immigration officers, so you'll be told to go to Male' to complete the process. Following a feasibility study, the government has decided to establish a yacht marina in the northern atolls, but Uligamu has been ruled out for financial and environmental reasons. Huvarafushi, the next largest island, is noted for its music, dancing and sporting activities, and it also has a fish-freezing plant.

The island of **Utheemu** is the birthplace of Sultan Mohammed Thakurufaanu who, with his brothers, overthrew Portuguese rule in 1573. A memorial to this Maldivian hero, with a small museum and library, was opened in 1986. Thakurufaanu's wooden palace has been restored and Maldivians come to pay homage to the great man (see the boxed text 'The Legend of Thakurufaanu' in the Facts about the Maldives chapter).

**Kelaa** was the northern British base during WWII, mirroring Gan at the other end of the archipelago. The mosque here dates from the end of the 17th century. Yams and *cadjan* (mats made of coconut palm leaves) are the island's products.

## SOUTH THILADHUNMATHEE & MAAMAKUNUDHOO ATOLLS

**Administrative District:** Haa Dhaal
**Code Letter:** B
**Inhabited Islands:** 17
**Uninhabited Islands:** 16
**Resorts:** 0
**Population:** 12,890

Haa Dhaal includes South Thiladhunmathee Atoll (which actually seems more like a central section of a longer, single atoll), and the

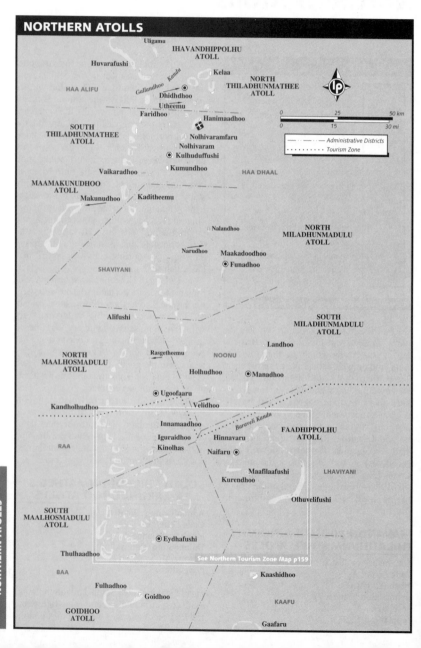

smaller Maamakunudhoo Atoll, which is separate and about 20km west of the main atoll. **Kulhuduffushi** is the capital island, and also the most populous, with more than 3500 people, electricity, a community school and a hospital. The islanders have a reputation throughout the country for hard work. They specialise in rope making and shark fishing.

There is an airport on **Hanimaadhoo** (airport code HAQ) and Air Maldives has flights from Male' and back, but check their frequency. Nearby **Nolhivaramfaru** is another important island, and has been recommended as the most suitable site for a private yacht marina in the northern atolls.

**Faridhoo** has the highest natural point in the Maldives, at the heady elevation of 3m above sea level. On **Kumundhoo** there are ruins, in the form of a stone circle, which suggest the remains of a Buddhist stupa. The ruins of a *hawitta* (artificial mound) can still be seen on **Vaikaradhoo**.

The area around Haa Dhaal suffers severe storms and quite a few vessels have gone down in these waters. Maamakunudhoo Atoll is the graveyard of several ships, particularly around the northern tip of the island of **Makunudhoo**. The English ship *Persia Merchant* was wrecked here in 1658 and another English vessel, the *Hayston*, ran onto a reef in 1819. In each case, survivors were treated with kindness by the local people.

## NORTH MILADHUNMADULU ATOLL

**Administrative District:** Shaviyani
**Code Letter:** C
**Inhabited Islands:** 15
**Uninhabited Islands:** 26
**Resorts:** 0
**Population:** 9022

The ruins of an ancient mosque and 13th-century tombstones lie on the pretty capital island of **Funadhoo**. The most populous island, with almost 1000 inhabitants, is **Maakadoodhoo**, which specialises in the production of jaggery, a coarse brown sugar made from palm sap. This island has been ravaged by storms and diseases throughout its history.

The main mosque on the island of **Kaditheemu** incorporates the oldest-known example of the Thaana script – it's an inscription on a door frame, which notes that the roof was constructed in 1588. Another famous island is **Nalandhoo**, where the Thakurufaanu brothers hid their boat between guerilla battles with the Portuguese. **Narudhoo**, with its freshwater lakes, is said to be the most beautiful island in the atoll.

## SOUTH MILADHUNMADULU ATOLL

**Administrative District:** Noonu
**Code Letter:** D
**Inhabited Islands:** 14
**Uninhabited Islands:** 57
**Resorts:** 0
**Population:** 8437

**Manadhoo** is the capital island, with about 1000 people. **Holhudhoo** has about 800 people, while **Velidhoo** has about 2100. On the island of **Landhoo** are the remnants of a hawitta supposedly left by the fabled Redin, a people who figure in Maldivian folklore. It is a 15m-high mound known locally as *maa badhige*, or 'great cooking pot'. Thor Heyerdahl writes extensively about the tall, fair-haired Redin in his book *The Maldive Mystery*. He believes them to have been the first inhabitants of the Maldives, as long ago as 2000 BC.

## NORTH MAALHOSMADULU ATOLL

**Administrative District:** Raa
**Code Letter:** E
**Inhabited Islands:** 16
**Uninhabited Islands:** 65
**Resorts:** 1
**Population:** 11,303

**Ugoofaaru** is the capital of this atoll and has one of the largest fishing fleets in the country. **Kandholhudhoo** (also spelt Kandoludhu) is the most populous island with almost 2000 people crowded onto it. The island's importance derives from its proximity to the rich western waters – one of the best fishing areas in a country that depends on fish.

The island of **Alifushi**, which is actually in a small, separate atoll to the north of Raa proper, is reputedly the home of the finest dhoni builders in the country. The government-owned Alifushi Boat Yard continues the tradition, producing a modern version of the dhoni. **Iguraidhoo** and **Innamaadhoo** are also boat-building and carpentry centres.

According to local legend, the now uninhabited island of **Rasgetheemu** is where Koimala Kaloa and his princess wife landed after being exiled from Sri Lanka and before moving to Male' to found a ruling dynasty. Another important visitor to the atoll was the Arab seafarer Ibn Battuta, who landed at **Kinolhas** in 1343 and then moved on to Male'.

The channel between Baa and Raa, locally known as Hani Kandu, is also named Moresby Channel, after the Royal Navy officer Robert Moresby who was responsible for the original marine survey of the Maldives made from 1834 to 1836 (see the boxed text 'Mapping the Maldives' in this chapter).

### Resorts

The southern part of this atoll was included in the tourism zone in the late 1990s, but so far only one new resort is a definite starter.

*Pearl Island Resort (☎ 230116, @ admin@ pearlresort.com)*, Meedhupparu Island, a big new resort with 215 rooms, is due to open in mid-2000. It will be an upmarket place, with a swimming pool, tennis courts and so on, but it may give heavily discounted rates in its first year or so of operation. It will certainly offer access to a whole range of currently undocumented dive sites. Being 130km from the airport, transfers will probably be by seaplane.

### SOUTH MAALHOSMADULU ATOLL

**Administrative District:** Baa
**Code Letter:** F
**Inhabited Islands:** 13
**Uninhabited Islands:** 51
**Resorts:** 5
**Population:** 7716

Baa includes South Maalhosmadulu Atoll and the small Goidhoo Atoll, 10km farther south. Fishing is the most important activity here, but Baa is also famous for its lacquer work and fine woven cotton *feylis* (traditional sarong). **Eydhafushi**, the capital and principal island, is also the feylis centre. **Thulhaadhoo** is the second largest island and the main centre for the production of lacquered boxes and jars.

Because of its isolation, **Goidhoo** has been a place for castaways and exiles. In 1602 François Pyrard, the French explorer, found himself on the island of **Fulhadhoo** after his ship, the *Corbin*, was wrecked. More recently, a German traveller was banished here for the murder of his girlfriend (see the boxed text 'Brought to Justice' in the Facts for the Visitor chapter).

### Diving

**Milaidhoo Reef** Strong currents flowing through the Kamadhoo Kandu provide an environment for soft corals, which thrive on the reef on the north side of an uninhabited island, Milaidhoo. The reef top, at 2m, is great for snorkelling, and it drops straight down to about 35m. This cliff has numerous caves and overhangs with seafans and sponges.

**Kakani Thilla** The north side of this thilla, at 25m to 30m, retains coral formations in excellent condition, and colourful soft corals fill the overhangs. It's also a home to lots of fish, including napoleons, jackfish, and oriental sweetlips.

**Dhigali Haa** This small thilla, though well inside the atoll, commonly attracts pelagic species (barracuda) and grey reef sharks. Other fish include jacks, batfish and trevally. It's also a good place to see nudibranchs, yellow and orange soft corals and anemones (with clown fish).

**Nelivaru Thilla** From April to November this area is a manta cleaning station, and in good conditions it's OK for quite inexperienced divers. Turtles and schools of tuna are also seen here.

**Miriandoo Thilla** Dropping steep and deep off the outer edge of the atoll, this site is for experienced dive rs only. It's another manta spot from April to November, and also has eagle rays, turtles and sharks.

**Madi Finolhu** This sandy reef has large coral blocks on which black coral grow. Stingrays can be seen on the sand, and mantas also pass through. Good beginners dive (20m).

NORTHERN ATOLLS

## Mapping the Maldives

**Hundreds of thousands of depth soundings were needed to chart the atolls.**

If you've flown to other atolls, you will have seen something of the maze of reefs, channels, sandbars and islands that make up the Maldives. If you've taken a boat trip from your resort, you'll realise that very little of this complexity is visible from sea level. The local boatmen know their way around the atolls from long experience and the tiniest of clues, like a greenish tinge on the underside of a cloud which can indicate a reef in the water below. Other mariners are dependent on accurate navigational charts, the best of which are published by the British Admiralty.

These charts have their origins in a remarkable marine survey done in the 1830s by three British vessels under the command of Robert Moresby. As British trade with India and the Far East flourished, it became important to chart the shipping routes in the Indian Ocean. In particular it was critical to plot safe passages through the Lacadive-Chagos ridge – a chain of reefs, atolls and islands that extends some 2000km south of India. The Maldives, in the centre of this ridge, forms a barrier across the most direct routes between the Middle East and southern India, Ceylon (as it was then) and the Malay Peninsula. More than a few ships had foundered on the Maldives because the reefs and passages were not charted with any accuracy.

Moresby started with the Lacadive (now Lakshadweep) Islands in 1828, but was diverted to the Red Sea where he spent five years surveying and charting. By the time his crews started on the Maldives, in 1834, they must have been a very experienced and highly efficient operation. With only a couple of officers, they worked from north to south, taking hundreds of thousands of depth soundings using a lead-weighted line, painstakingly recording the exact position of each one. This data was plotted precisely on paper, and lines interpolated to show the extent of every reef, the depth of every channel and the location of every island, shoal and sandbar.

It must have been demanding and exacting work – moving around by sail and oar, calculating position with a sextant and ship's clock, recording pages of data by hand and plotting the charts with pen and ink by the light of an oil lamp. They lived on their tiny ships, worked in oppressive heat and were stricken by dysentery and 'fever' (probably malaria which was rife at the time). Some had to return to India and at least one died. The survey of the Maldives took two years and two months, and it was another two and a half years before the final charts were drawn and published in England in December 1839.

The accuracy and thoroughness of the charts was immediately recognised, and they were exhibited to Queen Victoria, then in the second year of her long reign. The charts resulted in an immediate improvement in marine safety and contributed greatly to the scientific understanding of coral reefs. In 1869 the Suez Canal opened, and the amount of shipping in the area increased enormously, with mariners relying on Moresby's surveys of both the Red Sea and the Indian Ocean. Today, the Maldives sits on one of the busiest sea lanes in the world, with cargo ships and supertankers plying from Europe and the Middle East to East Asia. The Admiralty charts are regularly updated with the latest satellite-imaging techniques, but still bear the notation that most depth data is based on lead-line surveys from the original Marine Survey of India.

There are not many memorials to Moresby, but if you sit on any resort island in the Maldives, snorkel around any reef, or go diving on any thilla, there is every chance that it was once visited by a small British boat under his command. The crew would have surveyed every side of your island, charted your reef and plumbed the depths of your dive site over 160 years ago. They were not on holiday.

**Muthafushi Thilla** Overhangs here are home to soft coral and anemones. Many hard corals are in good condition and very colourful, black coral can also be seen. There are large schools of bluestripe snapper.

## Resorts

Though Sonevafushi has been here for quite a few years, several other resorts were developed in the late 1990s as part of an expansion program, which may have increased the supply of resort rooms faster than the growth in demand.

*Reethi Beach Resort* (☎ 232626, **e** info@reethibeach.com.mv), Fonimagoodhoo Island, new sibling to the venerable Reethi Rah Resort, is on a good-sized island with plenty of natural vegetation, soft white beaches, an accessible house reef and expansive lagoon. The buildings, all with thatched roofs, are designed to blend with the environment, and also incorporate some Maldivian design elements – like the deep horizontal mouldings used on Male's old Friday Mosque. It still provides all the mod-cons though – swimming pool, gym, squash and Internet access, while the rooms have air-con, TV, minibar, IDD phone and quality bathrooms.

The dive operation is very professional and reasonably priced. A single dive is US$35, or US$41 with all equipment; there's also discounts for multidive packages. Boat trips are US$12, and a PADI open-water course costs US$462. Nitrox diving is 17% extra, and a nitrox course costs US$148. Windsurfing, sailing and other water sports are popular here, partly because of the wide lagoon, and partly because of the enthusiasm of the staff. With few resorts in the area, you'll probably have good dive sites to yourself.

Guests are mostly German, Swiss and British, on half-board packages that let them make use of the two specialty restaurants and the weekly barbecue, as well as the excellent selection in the main buffet. There's some formal entertainment, but most guests seem happy with a few drinks in the well-patronised and sociable bar. It would be a good resort for kids too, though there are no special facilities nor programs.

The standard rooms with half board are US$91/152 in low season, US$120/197 in high season and a lot more over Christmas. Deluxe villas are US$20 extra per person, and the water villas are US$20 per person more than that. Full board (ie, lunch) is US$19 extra per person. And there's a 10% service charge on top of all that! It's 106km from the airport and transfers are by seaplane (35 minutes, US$220). The resort's Male' office (☎ 323758, fax 328842) is at Ma Sheerazeege, Sheeraazee Goalhi.

*Le Meridien* (☎ 230346), Kihaadhuffaru Island, may not be the Meridien when you get there. This new resort, with 100 rooms, ran into difficulties a few weeks after opening, and promptly closed. One rumour suggested that it would be taken up by the Italian operator Valtur, and operated as a club-style resort. Try contacting the Male' office of Athama Marine (☎ 320157, fax 327748, **e** athamar@dhivehinet.net.mv) to find out what's happening.

*Royal Island* (☎ 230088), Horubadhoo Island, is a new 150-room resort of the Villa group. It's expected to be much more of a natural-style resort than some of their other big, new resorts. Contact Villa Group (☎ 316161, fax 314565, **e** vilahtls@dhivehinet.net.mv), STO Trade Centre, Male', or have a look at its Web site (www.villahotels-maldives.com) for details.

*Sonevafushi* (☎ 230304, **e** soneva@dhivehinet.net.mv), Kunfunadhoo Island, has the biggest resort island in the country (more than 1½km long), with just 51 luxurious villas. Each one is like a small house, comprising natural materials, designer furnishings and rusticated style, but with deluxe features including hairdryer, private safe, CD player and air-con. Anything 'modern' is carefully concealed – no plastic is visible. Villas are well-spaced around the edges of the island, affording complete privacy – they're reached by sandy tracks that wind through the lush vegetation, which is kept as natural as possible. The reception, bar and restaurant areas all have sand floors and cane furniture, and the chickens are free to wander anywhere.

The cuisine is arguably the best in the Maldives – nothing too fancy, but with the

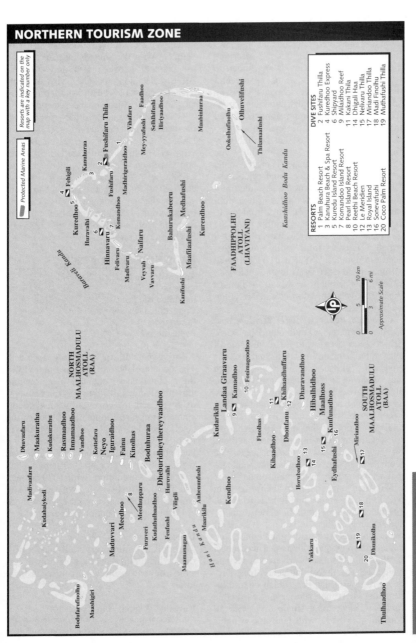

# NORTHERN TOURISM ZONE

Resorts are indicated on the map with a key number only

Protected Marine Areas

**RESORTS**
1 Palm Beach Resort
3 Kanuhura Beach & Spa Resort
5 Kuredu Island Resort
7 Komandoo Island Resort
8 Pearl Island Resort
10 Reethi Beach Resort
12 Le Meridien
13 Royal Island
16 Sonevafushi
20 Coco Palm Resort

**DIVE SITES**
2 Fushifaru Thilla
4 Kuredhoo Express
6 Shipyard
9 Milaidhoo Reef
11 Kakani Thila
14 Dhigali Haa
15 Nelivaru Thilla
17 Mirandoo Thilla
18 Madi Finolhu
19 Muthafushi Thilla

NORTH MAALHOSMADULU ATOLL (RAA)

SOUTH MAALHOSMADULU ATOLL (BAA)

FAADHIPPOLHU ATOLL (LHAVIYANI)

Kaashidhoo Bodu Kandu

Faadhu Kanda

Hani Kandu

Approximate Scale

0      5      10 km
0    3    6 ml

NORTHERN ATOLLS

freshest, finest ingredients, beautifully prepared and presented. Lunch and sometimes dinner are buffet-style, but the offerings change daily, and the wine list is wonderful.

There is the usual range of resort recreations, including a dive school. Picnics on isolated islands are popular, as are the dozens of different massages and treatments offered at the new Raison d'Etre spa. The atmosphere is completely relaxed and delightfully unpretentious – leave your jewellery and your dinner jacket at home. There's a range of villas at various prices, and prices also vary with the season, but the absolute minimum is around US$350/440 for a single/double with full board. As you move from low to high season, and from the comfortable to the sublime, the prices move well over US$1000 a night. Transfers from reality are by seaplane (25 minutes, US$235). The local agent is Bunny Holdings (BVI) Ltd (☎ 326685, fax 3224660), Faamudheyri Magu, Male', or check its Web site (www.soneva-pavilion .com) for details.

*Coco Palm Resort* (☎ 230011, @ cocopalm@ dhivehinet.net.mv), Dhunikolhu Island, is a new top-end resort with 86 rooms and 14 over-water bungalows. The island itself is quite large with beaches all round (though they're narrow in places) and a very accessible house reef. The vegetation has a very natural look but is a little sparse and scrubby – they're working to thicken it up. Architecturally, it's one of the most interesting resorts, with large tent-like thatched pavilions for reception, restaurant and bar areas. The rooms are circular with high, thatched, conical roofs and open-air bathrooms – the deluxe rooms have an individual, free-form plunge pool. Another highlight is the food. All meals are buffet, but the variety, quality and freshness is hard to believe. It's one of the few resorts with really good coffee, and perhaps the only one with perfect avocados.

With no other resorts around, divers here have access to almost untouched sites. Diving is run by Ocean-Pro, which offers professional, personal service at reasonable rates – US$52 for a single dive with all equipment; US$37 with tank and weights only. A PADI open-water course will cost

about US$520 with everything. Whale watching is an option in October and November, when the animals migrate through the channel between Baa and Goidhoo Atolls. Excursions include a visit to Thulhaadhoo, an island well known for producing lacquer work, which you can see and buy.

Coco Palm is quite a pricey resort, with the beach villas ranging from US$200 to US$350, depending on the season. Deluxe villas (with plunge pool!) are US$50 more, and a 'lagoon villa' is twice as much. Add US$25 per person per day for half board, and US$60 for full board (or find an agent with a cheaper package deal). Seaplane transfers cost US$200. The Male' office is Sunland Hotels (☎ 324658, fax 325543), STO Trade Centre.

## FAADHIPPOLHU ATOLL

**Administrative District:** Lhaviyani
**Code Letter:** G
**Inhabited Islands:** 5
**Uninhabited Islands:** 53
**Resorts:** 1
**Population:** 7725

All five islands are relatively crowded. The people of **Naifaru** (population 3132), the capital, have a reputation for making attractive handicrafts from coral and mother-of-pearl, and for concocting local medicines. **Hinnavaru** (population 2700) is the next busiest island. The island of **Maafilaafushi** was inhabited in the 17th century, later abandoned, and is now being resettled with government support. Other populated islands are **Kurendhoo**, with 1020 people, and **Olhuvelifushi** with 340 people. The atoll is a strong fishing centre with a modern tuna canning plant on **Felivaru**.

### Diving

The atoll has some very well-known dive sites, which until recently were only accessible from one resort, and by the occasional safari boat.

**Kuredhoo Express** Subject to strong currents, this demanding dive is a long drift through the channel next to the Kuredu resort. Napoleon

Over-water bungalows, palm trees, sun and shade – a hectic life.

You don't need a small fortune for the good life. Prices at resorts vary, the levels of luxury fluctuate but sand, water, good food and relaxation are found everywhere.

wrasse, grey reef sharks and trevally frequent the channel entrance, while inside are overhangs dripping with soft coral. Look for morays, turtles and stingrays. It's a Protected Marine Area.

**Shipyard** This is another demanding dive, with two wrecks within 50m of each other. Strong currents around these ships have promoted rapid growth of soft and hard corals, which now form a habitat for many types of reef fish. Moray eels and sweepers live inside the wrecks, while nurse sharks cruise around the bottom.

**Fushifaru Thila** This dive is subject to strong currents and is not for beginners. The thila, with lovely soft corals, sits in the centre of a broad channel and attracts mantas, eagle rays, sharks, groper, sweetlips and turtles around it. Cleaner wrasse abound on the thila, which is a Protected Marine Area.

## Resorts

Though Kuredu has been open for over 25 years, the other resorts are more recent (late 1990s), and reflect the upmarket trend in Maldives tourism.

*Kuredu Island Resort (☎ 230337, ✆ info@ kuredu.com),* Kuredhoo Island, is one of the most isolated and most remote resorts in the country and, with 300 rooms, it is also one of the largest. It was established in 1976 as a diving camp and, though it has been upgraded since then, it is still an inexpensive resort in the budget to mid-range bracket. Because of its size, it can offer three a-la-carte restaurants, a couple of bars and a coffee shop – there's even a tea shop where you can get typical Maldivian short eats at typical tourist prices (it's more popular with staff than guests). Recreation facilities include a gym, tennis court, football field and well-used beach volleyball court. It's a well-run resort and, with a young, predominantly European clientele – casual and very sociable. The food is OK, but some people find the rooms a little too basic, and are troubled by mosquitoes, bats and the occasional rodent – the wildlife is hard to control on a large and well-vegetated island, so if this is a problem for you, find another (more expensive) resort.

Swimming and snorkelling are very good and there are the usual excursion trips to nearby fishing villages and deserted islands,

as well as the option of spending 24 hours on an island all to yourself. Diving is a particular attraction, with excellent dive sites not accessible from other resorts.

The ProDivers centre is a five-star PADI facility offering a full range of courses – a beginners resort course with all equipment costs US$198, while a PADI open-water course is US$495 (this might seem a little pricey, but it includes nine dives, boat trips, equipment, books and fees, which are charged as extras on many resorts). A single dive costs US$35 including all equipment, or US$29 with only tank and weights supplied. A 10-dive package is US$314 (US$254 with tanks and weights only). Nitrox diving is available – the US$195 course includes two dives. Boat charge is US$10 per trip (but you can do some good dives directly from the shore). Despite the number of divers here, ProDivers gives personalised attention, and matches divers with others of similar experience and interest. It also runs a complete snorkelling program, with dive instructors taking groups for fish spotting, photography and night snorkelling trips.

Standard room rates with half board start at about US$70/90 in low season, US$85/100 in high season. Superior rooms have air-con, hot water and are on the nicer side of the island – they cost US$20 more. Full board is an extra US$10 per day. All-inclusive rates (including all meals, plus non-premium drinks) are about US$30 more than the half-board rates. Beer is US$3.75 a can, house wine is US$4.75 a glass, and spirits are US$6, so you can figure if it's worth the extra money for an all-inclusive package.

The resort is 129km from the airport and transfer is by a fast boat (4½ to 5 hours, US$90 return) or by seaplane (40 minutes, US$240 return). The resort's agent in Male' is Champa Trade & Travel (☎ 326545, fax 326544, ✆ ctnt@dhivehinet.net.mv), Champa Building.

*Komandoo Island Resort (☎ 230377, ✆ komandoo@dhivehinet.net.mv),* Komandhoo Island, is a new and more upmarket sibling of Kuredu. It has 45 quite pleasant hexagonal rooms, prefabricated in pine from

Finland, complete with air-con, phone, fridge, safe and CD player. The food is good, and the sand-floor bar and restaurant look out to the sand and sea. The diving costs are the same as for Kuredu, though the operation is much smaller. It's fairly quiet, friendly and informal, but doesn't have much character as yet. Full-board rates are around US$175/220 in high season. Transfers are as for Kuredu, and they share the same Male' agent.

***Kanuhura Beach & Spa Resort*** (☎ *230084,* ✉ *reservations@kanuhura.com.mv)*, Kanahuraa Island, another brand new resort, is obviously pitching for the people who want to be pampered. Though the island has beautiful beaches and a prime location, the emphasis is all on the luxury rooms, comfortable lounges and superb spa facilities.

It has 100 'villas' and 'suites', some of them over the water, with introductory prices from US$210 to US$600. It's 125km from the airport, with seaplane transfer (35 minutes, US$295). The Male' operator is SIMDI (☎ 324819, fax 310549, ✉ jens@simdi.com), Neelofaru Magu, or check its Web site (www.kanuhura.com) for details.

The ***Palm Beach Resort*** (☎ *230084,* ✉ *palmbeach@dhivehinet.net.mv)*, Madhiriguraidhoo Island, has a gorgeous site. It is a large, lush island with brilliant beaches, and its 100 rooms are almost invisible from a distance. It is destined to be an upmarket Italian resort operated by Sporting Vacanze (☎ 0039 068411607 in Rome). The Male' office (☎ 314478, fax 314578) is at M Velidhooge, Dhambu Goalhi.

# Southern Atolls

## Highlights

MALE'

- Staying on a former British air force base
- Crossing the equator to Fuamulaku Atoll, but only in good weather
- Visiting the goldsmiths on Ribudhoo and silversmiths on Hulhudheli
- Seeing the mysterious giant black dome on Isdhoo
- Getting there first – new dive sites are being developed
- Travelling the Maldives' longest road, 16 km, by causeway from Gan to Koattey

Most of the atolls south of Male' are outside the tourist zone and there is no regular transport here. Even a chartered safari boat can't go cruising down here without a permit. The only southern atolls with resorts are Felidhoo, which is just south of South Male' Atoll, and Addu, which includes the island of Gan, in the far south of the country. The most spectacular way to see the southern atolls is from the air, flying over most of the atolls and giving a brilliant perspective.

Atolls are listed below, from north to south, under their common, locally used geographical names, with names and details also given for the corresponding administrative atoll or district.

## FELIDHOO ATOLL

**Administrative District:** Vaavu
**Code Letter:** J
**Inhabited Islands:** 5
**Uninhabited Islands:** 19
**Resorts:** 2
**Population:** 1697

Vaavu comprises Felidhoo Atoll and the small Vattaru Falhu Atoll, which is uninhabited. It is the least populated of the administrative districts. The main industry is fishing. There is some boat-building and tourism, but very little agriculture. New resorts may open in the future, though there are no immediate plans. The capital island is **Felidhoo**, which has only about 380 people. **Keyodhoo**, the neighbouring island, is the most populous in the atoll with 530 people and souvenir shops for visitors on excursions from the resort islands. Nearby **Thinadhoo** has just 136 people. **Rakeedhoo**, at the southern tip, with 270 people, is often used as an anchorage by safari boats, especially if they are taking divers to the nearby channel. At the northern edge, **Fulidhoo** has a population of 260 and is an attractive island that is visited on day trips from the resorts and by safari boats. You may see some impressively large boats under construction here.

## Diving

There are at least 24 recognised dive sites in the atoll and, with only two resorts in the area, they are unlikely to become crowded. Some of them are not readily accessible, even from the resorts, and are mostly visited by safari boats. A few of the best-known sites are:

**Devana Kandu** This is a not too demanding drift dive in a channel divided by reefs. There are several entrances to the channel which has overhangs, caves, reef sharks and eagle rays. The southern side has soft corals and lots of reef fish. Farther in, the passages join up and there is a broad area of hard corals, the deeper parts being less affected by bleaching. The whole channel is a Protected Marine Area.

**Fotteyo** An excellent, more challenging dive site in and around a channel entrance – it's worth making several dives here. There are numerous small caves, several large caves and various arches and holes, all decorated with colourful soft coral. Rays, reef sharks, groper, tuna, jackfish, barracuda, turtles and even hammerhead sharks can be seen. Inside the channel are schools of sweetlips and titan triggerfish.

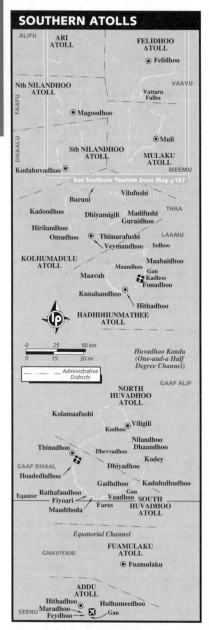

**SOUTHERN ATOLLS**

ALIFU
ARI ATOLL
FELIDHOO ATOLL
⊙ Felidhoo
VAAVU
Nth NILANDHOO ATOLL
FAAFU
Vattaru Falhu
⊙ Magoodhoo
DHAALU
⊙ Muli
Sth NILANDHOO ATOLL
MULAKU ATOLL
Kudahuvadhoo ⊙
MEEMU
See Southern Tourism Zone Map p167
Vilufushi
Buruni
Kadoodhoo
Dhiyamigili   Madifushi
THAA
Hirilandhoo
Guraidhoo
Omadhoo   ⊙ Thimarafushi
LAAMU
Veymandhoo   Isdhoo
KOLHUMADULU ATOLL
Maabaidhoo
Maandhoo   Gan
Maavah   Kadhoo
Fonadhoo
Kunahandhoo ⊙
Hithadhoo
HADHDHUNMATHEE ATOLL

0   25   50 km
0   15   30 mi

Administrative Districts

Huvadhoo Kandu (One-and-a Half Degree Channel)

NORTH HUVADHOO ATOLL
GAAF ALIF
Kolamaafushi
Viligili
Kudhoo ⊙
Nilandhoo
Thinadhoo   Dhevvadhoo   Dhaandhoo
Kodey
GAAF DHAAL
Dhiyadhoo
Hoadedhdhoo
Gadhdhoo   Kaduhulhudhoo
Equator   Rathafandhoo   Gan
Fiyoari   Vaadhoo   SOUTH
Maadthoda   Fares   HUVADHOO ATOLL

Equatorial Channel

FUAMULAKU ATOLL
GNAVIYANI
⊙ Fuamulaku

ADDU ATOLL
Hithadhoo ⊙   Hulhumeedhoo
SEENU   Maradhoo   ✈
Feydhoo   Gan

---

**Rakeedhoo Kandu** This is a challenging dive in a deep channel – the east and west sides are usually done as separate drift dives. Broad coral shelves cover overhangs and caves, which have seafans and black coral. Turtles, napoleon wrasse, sharks and schools of trevally are often seen. The upper reef offers excellent snorkelling in calm conditions.

**Vattaru Kandu** This is a remote channel dive on the southern edge of Vattaru Falhu. It is not too demanding unless the currents are running at full speed. Around the entrance are many caves and overhangs with soft corals, sea fans and abundant fish life – barracuda, fusilier, and white-tip reef sharks. Turtles are sometimes seen here, and manta rays from December to April.

## Resorts

*Dhiggiri (☎ 450593)*, Dhiggiri Island, was completely renovated in the late 1990s and is now a mid-range resort with 45 rooms. It's a small island, splendidly isolated, with good dive sites nearby. It's a club-style Italian resort operated by Bravo Club, with all the guests booked through Alpitur in Italy. Transfers are by speedboat (52km, 1½ hours). The local operator is Safari Tours (☎ 323524, fax 322516), Chandanee Magu, Male'.

*Alimatha (☎ 450575)*, Alimathaa Island, like Dhiggiri, was completely renovated in the late 1990s. It is a bigger resort, with 102 comfortable rooms, and it also has 100% Italian clientele who book through Alpitur and come for the Bravo Club style. Alimatha is about 60km from the airport and transfers are by speedboat (1¾ hours, US$105). The Male' operator for both resorts is also Safari Tours.

## MULAKU ATOLL

**Administrative District:** Meemu
**Code Letter:** K
**Inhabited Islands:** 9
**Uninhabited Islands:** 25
**Resorts:** 2
**Population:** 4186

This atoll is also called Mulakatholhu. **Muli** is the capital island, but **Dhiggaru**, in the north of the atoll, is the most populated. **Kolhuvaariyaafushi** and **Boli Mulah** islands grow lots of yams.

The atoll was included in the tourism zone in the late 1990s, and apart from a few safari boats it has been little explored by divers.

## Resorts

*Medhufushi (☎ 460026)*, Medhufushi Island, due to open in mid-2000, is to be a medium-sized resort. It will have a natural style and 120 rooms of various types, including 46 over-water bungalows with every convenience and comfort. The introductory prices are very reasonable, starting at US$130/190 for a single/double room with full board in low season. The resort is 129km from the airport and transfers will be by seaplane (40 minutes, US$220 return). The resort's Male' office (☎ 324933, fax 324943, ✉ sale@aaa.com.mv) is AAA Hotels & Resorts on the 3rd floor of the STO Trade Centre.

*Hakuraa Club (☎ 460014, ✉ hakuraa@dhivehinet.net.mv)*, Hahuraahuraa Island, is a newly opened club-style resort catering mainly to British and German guests on all-inclusive packages. All the rooms are over-water bungalows shaped like boats pointing out to sea, with pleasant interiors and curious, tent-like roofs. The island has a fair beach, on the far side of the island from the bungalows, and a very wide lagoon, which is not good for snorkelling. Another disadvantage is the very long walk between the rooms and boat jetty – in fact the whole layout of the island seems inconvenient. Introductory rates are very moderate for a fancy new resort – from around US$160/190 including full board, drinks, snacks, snorkelling and windsurfing equipment. The resort is about 133km from the airport, with transfers by seaplane (40 minutes, US$240). The resort's Male' office (☎ 318077, fax 318073) is on Roashanee Hingun.

## NORTH NILANDHOO ATOLL

**Administrative District:** Faafu
**Code Letter:** L
**Inhabited Islands:** 5
**Uninhabited Islands:** 10
**Resorts:** 1
**Population:** 2614

The capital island, **Magoodhoo**, is a fishing village with a very traditional Islamic community. On the nearby island of **Nilandhoo**, the Aasaari Miskiiy is the second oldest mosque in the country, built during the reign of Sultan Mohammed Ibn Abdullah (1153–1166). It is made of dressed stone and the interior is decorated with carved woodwork. It's possible that the stones were recycled from the ruins of earlier, pre-Islamic temples.

Thor Heyerdahl's book *The Maldive Mystery* devotes an entire chapter to this island. His expedition unearthed a number of phallic stone carvings, similar to the lingam associated with the Hindu god Shiva in his manifestation as the creator. Examples of these images can be seen in the National Museum in Male'. Heyerdahl's expedition also found ruins believed to have been part of an ancient gate, one of seven surrounding a great pagan temple complex. Of Nilandhoo, Heyerdahl wrote:

Five teams of archaeologists could dig here for five years and still make new discoveries ... the magnitude of this prehistoric cult centre seemed quite out of proportion to the size of the island.

The island of **Dharaboodhoo** is known as a place where turtles come to lay their eggs, struggling up the beaches during the southwest monsoon. As in many other places, the turtle numbers have declined in recent years, but there is now a total ban on the capture of turtles and the sale of turtle products, so there is hope that the species may once again thrive here.

## Diving

The atoll has only recently been included in the tourism zone and has been little explored by divers – even safari boats visited infrequently. The opportunity to dive the pristine sites will be the big attraction of new resorts in the area.

## Resort

*Filitheyo (☎ 460025, ✉ fili@aaa.com.mv)*, Filitheyo Island, a beautifully designed and finished resort is on a large, well-vegetated, triangular island. The house reef is easily accessible on two sides of the island, and beaches are good on most of the shoreline. The public buildings are spacious, open-sided Balinese-style pavilions with palm thatch roofs and natural finishes. The 109 guest rooms have a natural look, with air-con, satellite TV, minibar, hairdryer and partly open-air bathroom as standard features. The 16 overwater villas have a private sun deck. Other facilities include a beautiful pool, gym, clinic, water sports and a 1st-class diving operation.

This is a top-quality resort, and the introductory prices look like a bargain – from US$86/116 to US$118/160 for the standard rooms with full board, depending on the season. It's 120km from the airport and transfers are by seaplane (35 minutes, US$210). The resort's Male' office (☎ 324933, fax 324943, @ sale@aaa.com.mv) is AAA Hotels & Resorts, STO Trade Centre.

## SOUTH NILANDHOO ATOLL

**Administrative District:** Dhaalu
**Code Letter:** M
**Inhabited Islands:** 8
**Uninhabited Islands:** 50
**Resorts:** 2
**Population:** 4199

The capital island, **Kudahuvadhoo**, has a mysterious archaeological mound and an old mosque, which Heyerdahl said had some of the finest masonry he had ever seen, surpassing, in his opinion, that of the famous Inca wall in Cuzco, Peru. He was amazed to find such a masterpiece of stone-shaping art on such an isolated island, although it had a reputation in the Islamic world for finely carved tombstones. The waters around Kudahuvadhoo have seen several shipwrecks, including the 1340-ton *Liffey*, which went down in 1879, and the *Utheem*, which hit the same reef in 1960.

Uninhabited **Maadheli**, also known as Salazar or Temple Island, has ruins which have not yet been investigated, including an ancient mosque and the foundations of what appear to be dwellings.

In the north of the atoll are the so-called 'jewellers islands'. **Ribudhoo** has been long known for its goldsmiths, who are believed to have learnt the craft from a royal jeweller banished here by a sultan centuries ago. Another version is that they developed their skills on gold taken from a shipwreck in the 1700s. The nearby island of **Hulhudheli** is a community of traditional silversmiths. Most of the gold and silver work on sale in Male' now seems to be imported, though the gold chains and medallions worn by many children may be made in these islands. Many of the craftspeople here are now making jewellery, beads and carvings from black coral and mother-of-pearl.

## Resorts

Like Meemu and Faafu, Dhaalu Atoll has only recently been included in the tourism zone, and the two resorts here were both opened in the late 1990s. A big attraction of these resorts is their access to infrequently explored dive sites.

*Vilu Reef* (☎ 460015, @ info@vilureef .com.mv), Meedhufushi Island, was the first resort to open in this atoll. A mid-range resort, it has an unusual spiral design for its main restaurant and its 68 air-con beach villas. The rooms are well equipped and have a natural style, and the resort provides a full range of recreational facilities including tennis, gym and snooker. Divers are well catered for by Dive Explorer, which offers a variety of dive trips and courses, including a nitrox course. Guests are mostly young German speakers, and the resort is lively at night with a disco, crab races and other light entertainment. Prices are around US$180/220 with full board in high season. The resort is 129km from the airport, and transfers are by seaplane (35 minutes, US$230). The resort's Male' office is Sun Travel (☎ 325977, fax 320419, @ suntrvl@dhivehinet.net.mv), 8 Boduthakurufaanu Magu, or check its Web site (www.vilureef.com) for details.

*Velavaru Island Resort* (☎ 460028, @ info@velavaru.com.mv), Velavaru Island, is on a sparsely vegetated island with great beaches, but not much else going for it. The public areas are under large domed roofs, but they look somehow inelegant. The 66 rooms are in pairs in small

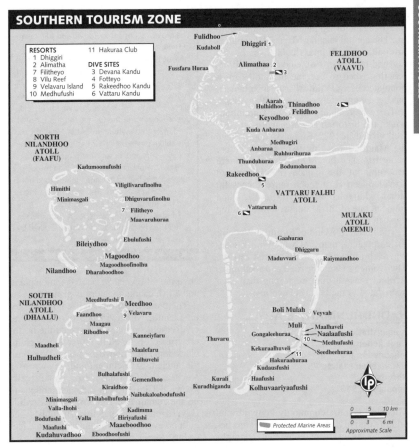

## SOUTHERN TOURISM ZONE

| RESORTS | 11 Hakuraa Club |
|---|---|
| 1 Dhiggiri | |
| 2 Alimatha | **DIVE SITES** |
| 7 Filitheyo | 3 Devana Kandu |
| 8 Vilu Reef | 4 Fotteyo |
| 9 Velavaru Island | 5 Rakeedhoo Kandu |
| 10 Medhufushi | 6 Vattaru Kandu |

*Protected Marine Areas*

0   5   10 km
0   3   6 mi
Approximate Scale

semicircular buildings around the beach-front, so each room has an awkward wedge shape. Architecturally, this resort is not quite right. The meals are buffet-style and OK, but the selection is limited. The main attraction here would be the diving, and the rates are reasonable – US$44 for a single dive with full equipment, US$31 with tank and weights only. An open-water course will cost about US$520 with everything included. It's not a bad resort, but at the quoted full-board rates of US$100/145 in low season, US$210/240 in high season, it doesn't seem like very good value. It's

about 132km from the airport, and transfers are by seaplane (35 minutes, US$230). The resort's Male' office (☎ 324658, fax 325543) is in the STO Trade Centre, Orchid Magu, or check its Web site (www.velavaru.com) for details.

## KOLHUMADULU ATOLL

**Administrative District:** Thaa
**Code Letter:** N
**Inhabited Islands:** 13
**Uninhabited Islands:** 54
**Resorts:** 0
**Population:** 8189

Kolhumadulu is a great circular atoll and one of the major fishing regions of the country. The capital island of Thaa is **Veymandhoo** although **Thimarafushi**, which was ravaged by fire in 1902 and again in 1905, has flourished to become the atoll's most populated island. **Vilufushi**, the next largest, has been completely covered by the village.

There is a sultan's grave on **Guraidhoo**, which the historian and archaeologist HCP Bell visited in 1922. Sultan Usman I ruled the Maldives for only two months before being banished here. On **Dhiyamigili** there are ruins of the palace of Mohammed Imaaduddeen II, a much more successful sultan who ruled from 1704 to 1721 and founded one of the Maldives longest-ruling dynasties.

The northern island of **Buruni** is a centre for carpenters, many of whom work elsewhere, building boats and tourist resorts. The women make coir rope and reed mats. Around the mosque are tombs that have been dated to the late 18th century.

## HADHDHUNMATHEE ATOLL

**Administrative District:** Laamu
**Code Letter:** O
**Inhabited Islands:** 12
**Uninhabited Islands:** 75
**Resorts:** 0
**Population:** 9101

This atoll is more commonly known by its administrative name of Laamu, perhaps because it's easier to spell than the geographical name – Hadunmati, Hadhunmathee, Hadhunmathi etc.

Laamu is one of the major fishing centres in the country and freezer ships anchor near the former capital, **Hithadhoo**, collecting fresh fish direct from the dhonis. There's an airfield on the island of **Kadhoo**, which has flights from Male', but you need to check their frequency. Kadhoo is linked by causeways to the large island of **Fonadhoo** to the south, which is now the atoll capital. The causeway also goes north to the islands of **Maandhoo** and **Gan** to the north, forming one of the longest stretches of road in the country – all of 12km. Maandhoo has a

### The Toddy Tapper's Daughter

The Maldives' answer to *Romeo and Juliet* is an old folk tale of star-crossed lovers from the island of Buruni. Dhon Hiyala was the beautiful daughter of a poor but pious toddy tapper, and she fell in love with a local silversmith named Ali Fulhu, who made her gifts of exquisite jewellery. Hiyala's father was known for his eloquence in reading the Quran and this brought the family to the attention of the Male' sultan. The sultan's men noticed the lovely girl with the fine jewellery and, despite her protests, she was taken to the palace in Male'. Ali Fulhu followed, succeeded in finding her, and they escaped from the capital in Ali's boat. The sultan was furious and his guards gave chase. Soon overtaken by the faster boat, the lovers leapt into the sea rather than be captured, and were devoured by a sea monster and never seen again.

government-owned STO refrigeration plant, and a fish canning factory is planned.

There are numerous archaeological sites on Laamu, with evidence of pre-Muslim civilisations on many islands. At the northeastern tip of the atoll, on **Isdhoo**, a giant, black dome rises above the palms. Who built the ancient artificial mound, known as a *hawitta*, and for what reason, is not really known. HCP Bell believed such mounds to be the remains of Buddhist stupas, while Heyerdahl speculated that Buddhists had built on even earlier mounds left by the legendary Redin people. For many years the mound was a landmark for boats navigating between the atolls, but it didn't save the British cargo ship *Lagan Bank*, which was wrecked here on 13 January 1938. The Friday Mosque on Isdhoo is around 300 years old. It was probably built on the site of an earlier temple because it faces directly west, rather than towards Mecca, which is to the north-west.

Bell also found quite a few mounds on Gan (or Gamu) Island, which he also believed to be Buddhist stupas, and he found a fragment of a stone Buddha face, which he estimated was from a statue over 4m high. Almost nothing remains of these structures

**Top Right & Left:** You only need to snorkel down to a few metres to see some of the best marine life. **Bottom:** Village volleyball, near Male', is a good way to spend much of a day, or a week – or a whole holiday.

**Top Left:** Windsurfing in the Maldives is good for beginners, but try not to fall off in shallow water over a coral reef! **Top Right & Bottom:** Heavy holiday traffic, under sail across the lagoon.

because the stones have been removed to use in more modern buildings. There are mounds on several other islands in Laamu, including Kadhoo, Maandhoo and Hithadhoo – one is over 5m high.

## NORTH HUVADHOO ATOLL

**Administrative District:** Gaaf Alif
**Code Letter:** P
**Inhabited Islands:** 10
**Uninhabited Islands:** 83
**Resorts:** 0
**Population:** 7300

This is the northern half of the giant Huvadhoo Atoll, which is separated from Laamu by the 90km-wide Huvadhoo Kandu, also called the One-and-a-Half-Degree Channel, because of its latitude. It's the safest place for ships to pass between the atolls that make up the Maldives. Because it's such a big atoll, and perhaps as a response to the 'southern rebellion' (see South Huvadhoo Atoll), Huvadhoo is divided into two parts for administrative purposes. Huvadhoo is one of the largest true coral atolls in the world.

**Viligili**, the capital island, is also the most populated with about 5000 people. A little farther south, the island of **Kudhoo** has a new ice plant and fish-packing works. The atoll also has some productive agriculture, with 644 acres of arable land. Some 214 cultivated acres are on **Kodey** (population 200), which has four hawittas. Heyerdahl discovered a limestone carving of the Hindu god Makara here.

**Dhevvadhoo**, in the centre of the atoll, is not well placed for fishing or farming, but the islanders are famous for their textile weaving and coir rope making. There are also hawittas on Dhevvadhoo, and mosques from the 16th and 17th centuries.

## SOUTH HUVADHOO ATOLL

**Administrative District:** Gaaf Dhaal
**Code Letter:** Q
**Inhabited Islands:** 10
**Uninhabited Islands:** 154
**Resorts:** 0
**Population:** 10,400

Geographically isolated from Male', but strategically located on the Indian Ocean trade routes, Huvadhoo had independent tendencies dating back many years. It had its own direct trade links with Sri Lanka, and the people spoke a distinct dialect almost incomprehensible to other Maldivians. **Thinadhoo**, the capital of Gaaf Dhaal, was a focal point in the 'southern rebellion' against the central rule of Male' during the early 1960s. So much so, that troops from Male' invaded in February 1962 and destroyed all the homes. The people fled to neighbouring islands and Thinadhoo was not resettled until four years later.

Meanwhile, **Gadhdhoo**, which now has more than 2000 people, became the main island in the atoll. Women on Gadhdhoo make superb examples of the mats known as *tundu kunaa*, which are woven from special reeds found on the island of **Fiyoari**.

Nearby is the island of **Gan**, which is much larger, but now uninhabited, although people from Gadhdhoo gather coconuts and bury their dead here. Gan has an ancient Muslim cemetery, and a profusion of ancient mounds.

### The Island of Cats

The island of Gan, in South Huvadhoo Atoll, is also called the 'Island of Cats', though it has not been inhabited for many years and there is no evidence of any cats ever living here. It's quite a big, well-vegetated island, and it has extensive ruins as well as a big Muslim cemetery. It is thought that there was once a large and impressive limestone pyramid here, and many finely carved stone artefacts have been found. According to local legend, the island was once invaded by giant cats, which killed many of the people and caused the rest to flee in terror. The survivors settled on smaller islands nearby and Gan was abandoned. This story may have its origins in an attack by roving Sinhalese bandits, who made many forays to attack unprotected settlements. These marauders were called 'lion people', and there is evidence that they wore savage looking feline masks and lion-like costumes to terrorise their victims.

In the south of the atoll, only about 20km from the equator, the island of **Vaadhoo** has several hawittas, and a mosque that dates from the 17th century. The mosque is elaborately decorated inside and has a stone bath and some ancient carved tombstones outside.

There is a small airport on the island of **Kaadedhoo**, near Thinadhoo, which has regular flights to/from Male' five times per week.

## FUAMULAKU ATOLL

**Administrative District:** Gnaviyani
**Code Letter:** R
**Inhabited Islands:** 1
**Uninhabited Islands:** 0
**Resorts:** 0
**Population:** 10,000

Across the equator, in the southern hemisphere, Fuamulaku (also called Foammulah) is not really an atoll, but rather a solitary island stuck in the middle of the Equatorial Channel. It is about 5km long, densely vegetated and surrounded by a steep, rough coral beach. With two freshwater lakes, it's very fertile and about the lushest island in the Maldives, producing fruits and vegetables that won't grow elsewhere, including mangoes and oranges. Yams grow so well here that they're now the local dietary staple.

Fuamulaku is divided into eight districts. The main landing point is at **Rasgenfanu**, which is the biggest village and the administrative capital, but sometimes boats must land at other points. Sandy roads crisscross the island, and there are lots of motorcycles and small pick-up trucks.

The island has no lagoon and lacks a protective coral barrier reef. The coral-shingle beach drops straight down to deep water and there are vicious currents and no safe anchorage – boats must always be moored on the leeward side of the island. Landing a boat is only possible in calm weather, limiting fishing activity. Often, very small fishing boats must be used to ferry passengers and goods ashore. The national government intends to provide a permanent jetty some-

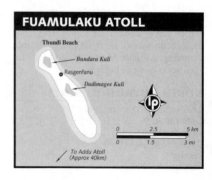

where on the island, but to date it has not found a suitable site.

The island's people are noticeably different from those in the rest of the country. They look bigger and healthier than other islanders and, apparently, live longer. Thor Heyerdahl wrote in *The Maldive Mystery*:

The people were also exceptionally beautiful and displayed far more variety in physical type than we had seen in Male'.

Despite Fuamulaku's apparent isolation, it's actually on a sort of marine freeway – the Equatorial Channel has long been used by navigators passing between the Middle East, India and South-East Asia. Currents rip through the channel at speeds of up to five knots, going eastwards in July and westward in January.

Many travellers have stopped here. Ibn Battuta visited in 1344, stayed for two months and married two women. Two Frenchmen visited in 1529 and admired the mosque, which they described as very ancient and made of massive stones. In 1922 HCP Bell explored the island, investigating the hawittas, the carved tombstones and the stone bath outside the mosque.

It's not an easy destination for modern travellers. You'll need a permit, then a plane from Male' to Addu Atoll, which is 50km away. There's now a semi-regular speed launch between Addu and Fuamulaku, which carries about 20 people and takes just over an hour if the weather is OK. There's an office in Addu where you can book tickets.

## ADDU ATOLL

**Administrative District:** Seenu
**Code Letter:** S
**Inhabited Islands:** 7
**Uninhabited Islands:** 20
**Resorts:** 1
**Population:** 21,000

This is the main economic and administrative centre in the south of the country, and the only area to rival Male' in size and importance. It has an airport capable of handling large aircraft and, with four substantial islands linked by causeways, it has a 16km stretch of drivable road.

There is an independent streak in the Addu folk – they even speak differently from the people of Male'. Tensions last came to a head in the 1960s under the leadership of Abdulla Afif Didi, the elected president of the 'United Suvadiva Islands'. The short-lived southern rebellion was quashed by an armed fleet sent south by Prime Minister Ibrahim Nasir. Afif fled the country, but is still talked about on his home island of Hithadhoo. He has since resided in the Seychelles, where he ultimately rose to the position of foreign minister.

The biggest influence on Addu's modern history has been the British bases, first established on Gan during WWII as part of the Indian Ocean defences. In 1956, when the British could no longer use Sri Lanka, they developed a Royal Air Force base on Addu as a strategic Cold War outpost. The base had around 600 personnel permanently stationed here, with up to 3000 during periods of peak activity. The British built a series of causeways connecting Feydhoo, Maradhoo and Hithadhoo Islands and employed most of the population on or around the base. In 1976 the British pulled out, leaving an airport, some large industrial buildings, barracks and a lot of unemployed people who spoke good English and had experience working for Westerners. When the tourism industry took off in

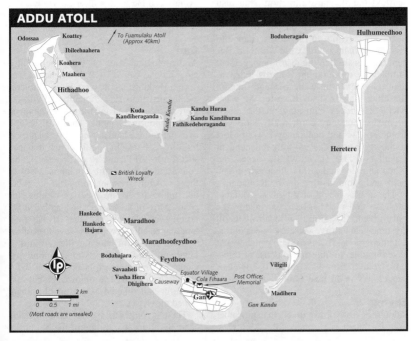

ADDU ATOLL

the late 1970s, many of the men of Addu went to Male' to seek work in resorts and tourist shops. They have never lost their head start in the tourism business and to this day, in resorts all over the country, there's a better than even chance that the Maldivian staff will be from Addu.

Tourism development in Addu itself has been slow to start. The first resort, established in the old RAF buildings on Gan, suffered from irregular flight connections in small planes – luggage sometimes did not arrive until the guests were due to depart! Also, with most Maldivian resorts being marketed in the tropical paradise mould, an old military base didn't hold much appeal.

Now there is a 40-seat jet providing a link to Male' with capacity for tourists *and* their luggage. The Gan resort has changed ownership a couple of times, but the current operators have a good reputation for efficiency. The resort offers not just sun, sea and the standard attractions, but also unparalleled access to some of the most interesting, attractive and unspoiled villages in the country, not to mention a chance to see the remnants of this Cold War relic. Recent reports are that the resort management is not very encouraging towards independent travellers who want to spend time on the other islands. They'd prefer the usual package tourists who stay on the resort premises, but they can't really stop you from leaving, and occupancy is pretty low so they give good deals to fully independent travellers (FITs). If you want to access the other islands, make this clear when you book and avoid visiting during Ramadan.

The nearby island of **Viligili** is available for lease, and a bid has been accepted by the government, though a new resort may still be some years away. There are hopes of direct international flights to Gan, which would save the time, trouble and expense of transfers from Male'. This doesn't, however, seem likely in the near future.

## Diving

Addu sees vastly fewer divers than any other area in the tourist zone of the Maldives.

New dive sites are still being discovered here. The diving highlights are the turtles, sharks, manta rays and other large fish that can be seen at various times of the year. September to December is the best time for whale sharks and January to April is best for mantas. Perhaps because it is close to the equator, Addu has suffered especially badly from coral bleaching, and nearly all the coral in the lagoon was killed as a result of the sea temperature increases associated with the 1998 El Niño event. The best-known dive is an old wreck:

**Wreck of the *British Loyalty*** This oil tanker was torpedoed in 1944 by a Japanese submarine, which fired through an opening in the antisubmarine nets at the entrance to Gan Kandu. The *British Loyalty* was disabled and stayed in the atoll until 1946 when it was towed to its present location and used for target practice by another British ship. The wreck lies in 33m of water with its port side about 16m below the surface. It now has a good covering of hard and soft corals, and big holes a diver can easily swim through into the hull. Turtles, trevally and many reef fish inhabit the encrusted decks.

## Gan

Archaeological sites on Gan, including a large mound which HCP Bell believed was once a Buddhist stupa, were levelled to create the airstrip in 1956. A number of villages were also destroyed and the residents moved to neighbouring islands. The British took over the entire island and constructed airport buildings, barracks, jetties, maintenance sheds, a NAAFI canteen, golf course, tennis courts and all the comforts of home. Many of these structures remain, some run-down but not ruined, others are used for various purposes. Most of the island's lush native vegetation was cleared, but the British then landscaped with new plants – avenues of casuarina, clumps of bougainvillea, swaths of lawn and even roses. It's much more spacious than most resort islands and it has a slightly weird and eerie atmosphere, but very peaceful and relaxed – like an old, abandoned movie set.

There is some activity, but most times it's scarcely noticeable. Some of the old buildings have been taken over by foreign-owned garment factories, which employ mostly Sri Lankans. They come on contract, work long hours and live in the former barracks. Why do these businesses set up here instead of Sri Lanka or Bangladesh? Because those countries already produce more garments than their US import quota allows, while the Maldives does not.

Some other things to see include a memorial to those who served on the base, including Indian regiments such as the 13th Frontier Force Rifles and the Royal Bombay Sappers & Miners. Dozens died here 'in the service of their country', though the atoll saw no action at all apart from the 1944 attack on the *British Loyalty*. Big guns, which were part of the WWII defences, now guard the memorial. Across the road is the post office, some telephones and a branch of the Bank of Maldives. The cinema seems to have closed and the golf course is overgrown. Nearby is a densely vegetated compound, which was once a plant nursery. A small mosque, built by Pakistanis working for the RAF, is still standing. It's a little more elaborate than a Maldivian mosque, but no longer in use.

You might also notice the satellite dish near the resort's reception area – it points straight up. Gan is less than half a degree south of the equator, and a geostationary satellite sits directly overhead. There's also a few radio masts around. Unlike other resorts, with their calculated cut-off-from-the-world atmosphere, it's not hard to imagine this place as a Cold War listening post in constant communication with everywhere, though it's probably one of the most isolated places on earth.

**Post & Communications** The post office is east of the resort entrance, on the road to the airport, and there are phones outside where international calls can be made with a Dhiraagu card. The resort may offer Internet access to its guests. There's a cybercafe in Hithadhoo.

**Places to Stay & Eat** *Equator Village* (☎ 588019), Gan Island, is a budget resort,

quite different from any other in the Maldives. The 60 comfortable, air-con rooms are in long straight lines, built as they are on the foundations of old barracks, but they're spacious and well furnished. The reception, bar and dining areas have been created from the old sergeant's but thoroughly redecorated in very unmilitary pink, white and grey. These open-sided spaces with their cane furniture and ceiling fans look out onto a sizable freeform swimming pool and through palm trees to the blue sea beyond. The full-size billiard table is a handsome inheritance from the Brits, as are the first-class tennis courts. At one time, the meals were cooked and served in true English style, roast beef and all, but they now offer a wider selection. Nevertheless, both the food and the service can be somewhat starchy. The Maldivian barbecue buffets are better and much more relaxed.

The only decent beach is a few hundred metres east of the resort. The dive school has standard prices – US$45 for a single dive with all equipment; a PADI open-water course costs about US$460.

Guests are from various countries, including a few British ex-servicemen. Single/double rooms will cost from around US$72/124 in the low season to US$101/140 in the high season. This is an 'all-inclusive' rate – that means three meals, some snacks and standard house wine, beer, spirits and water, plus bicycle use, a fishing trip and an island hopping trip are included. The local operator is Gan Invest (☎ 322212, fax 318057, ✆ kaimoo@dhivehinet.net.mv), H Kandige, Dheefuram Goalhi, Male'.

A nonresort eating option is *Cola Fihaara*, the old NAAFI shop, on a corner between the resort and the airport. It's a really pleasant spot with picnic tables under a big shady tree and a very 1960s outdoor sculpture. A light meal, such as fish and chips or fish curry, will cost under Rf 55. Ice cream and soft drinks are also available. The neighbouring islands have local tea shops, which are very inexpensive and serve real Maldivian food, but they won't save you any money because lunches and snacks will be included in your Equator Village rate anyway.

**Getting There & Away** Air Maldives flies from Male' to Gan and back, usually in the afternoon, but check because the schedule is changeable. The standard fare for foreigners is US$119 one way, US$238 return, but packages to the island charge US$180 for return transfers. The views are great from either side of the plane.

Private yachts should report to the NSS here by radio to arrange security and customs clearance, but will probably be told to continue to Male' for health and immigration checks to complete the 'clear-in' process.

**Getting Around** The best way to get around Gan and across the causeway to the neighbouring villages is by bicycle, and they're included in the Equator Village rates. If you're only going as far as Feydhoo, you could easily walk. There are also taxis and minibuses going between the islands. A taxi all the way to Koattey is around Rf 100.

## Feydhoo, Maradhoo & Hithadhoo

A new causeway between Gan and Feydhoo connects with the British-built causeways to Maradhoo and Hithadhoo, so you can travel over 16km, via several villages, to **Koattey** at the north-western tip of the atoll – this is the longest stretch of road in the country. There are no spectacular attractions along the way, but the villages are an absolute delight.

Like most Maldivian villages they are laid out on a rectangular grid with wide, straight, sandy streets and white coral-stone houses. A few motorcycles, taxis, trucks and minibuses will be seen, but for most of the day the streets are empty. In the early morning, and especially in the evening, locals will be out walking or cycling, sitting outside their houses or leaning against the low front walls. Shady trees overhang the streets and you can usually catch a glimpse of the sea at one end of the street or the other.

Most of the houses have corrugated iron roofs, but are otherwise traditional. Older buildings are made of coral stone, while newer ones are of concrete blocks. There's

usually a courtyard or an open space with a shady tree and a *joli* or *undholi* providing a cool place to sit in the heat of the day. Notice the big, square chimney blocks – there are wooden racks inside where fish are hung to be smoked. Another distinctive feature can be seen at street junctions, where walls and buildings all have rounded corners.

There are several mosques – a large, new, white one in Feydhoo; a smaller blue one, also in Feydhoo; and several older ones, on the sandy back roads, that look a little like tiny churches. A big telecommunications station has been built with Japanese aid and there's a new high school, one of the few outside Male'. Other facilities include a power station, hospital and several shiny new phone boxes.

In between the villages are coconut plantations, swampy lakes and a surprising amount of woodland. The coast is mostly too rocky or shallow for bathing, but there's a break in the reef up at Koattey where it's OK. This place is also called Demon Point – it once had a sultan's fort, and later a British gun emplacement, but there is nothing left to see now.

**Post & Communications** As well as some postal agencies and a sprinkling of public phones, Hithadhoo has a 'cyberstation' Internet cafe on the main street. It opens from 7.30 am to 3 pm Sunday to Thursday, 4 pm to 6 pm Friday, Saturday and holidays. It charges Rf 15 for the initial connection, plus Rf 20 for the first 15 minutes, and Rf 1 per-minute after that. It's a good place to meet local students.

**Places to Eat** There are several local tea shops in these villages, serving tea, cakes and 'short eats', and some will have a more substantial fish curry. In Hithadhoo, the *Scoop* restaurant has been recommended. It's no problem getting something for lunch or dinner, but visitors are supposed to be back at Gan before dark. Though you don't need a permit to visit these islands, they do have the same legal status as inhabited islands in other parts of the tourism zone: visitors are not allowed to stay the night.

**Responsible Tourism** The relatively free access to these unspoilt villages is the great attraction of Addu. Please remember that they are conservative Muslim communities, and behave with appropriate decorum and respect. Dress modestly, don't enter mosques uninvited, don't give presents or sweets to kids and don't even think about alcohol. If visitors behave inappropriately, then access will surely be restricted in the future. As yet, there are none of the souvenir shops that are such an eyesore on other islands frequented by tourists – it would be a shame if local people thought that there was a demand here for tourist schlock.

## Hulhumeedhoo

At the north-east corner of the lagoon, this island has two adjoining villages, Hulhudoo and Meedhoo, jointly known as Hulhumeedhoo, with a combined population of 2300. Local legend has it that an Arab was shipwrecked here in about AD872, and converted the islanders to Islam 280 years before the people of Male'. The cemetery is known for its ancient headstones, many of which are beautifully carved with the archaic Dhives Akuru script. This island is not connected to Gan by a causeway, so you'll need to charter a dhoni to get here. Equator Village may do a day excursion here.

# Language

Divehi has its own script, Thaana, which was introduced by the great Maldivian hero Thakurufaanu after he tossed out the Portuguese in the 16th century. Thaana looks like shorthand, has 24 letters in its alphabet and is read from right to left (their front page is our back page).

The Romanised transliteration of the language is a potpourri of phonetic approximations, and words can be spelt in a variety of ways. This is most obvious in Maldivian place names. For example: Majeedi Magu is also spelt Majidi, Majeedhee and Majeedee; Hithadhoo also becomes Hithadhu and Hitadhu; and Fuamulak can be Fua Mulaku, Foahmmulah or, thanks to one 19th century mariner, Phoowa Moloku.

To add to the confusion, several islands have the same name (there are six called Viligili), and there are names for the 19 administrative atolls, which do not coincide with the 26 natural atolls which have completely different names.

There is no officially correct, or even consistent, spelling of Divehi words in official English language publications.

Maldivians are pleased to help you learn a few phrases of Divehi, and, even if you only learn a few words, the Maldivians you meet will be very appreciative of your interest.

The best phrasebook available is *Practical Divehi* by M Zuhair (Novelty Press, Male', 1991). It's available from the Novelty Bookshop in Male' and in a number of the resort shops. Here are a few words and phrases to whet your appetite.

## Greetings & Civilities

| | |
|---|---|
| Hello. | *a-salam alekum* |
| Farewell. | *vale kumu salam* |
| Peace. | *salam* |
| Hi. | *kihine* |
| See you later. | *fahung badaluvang* |
| How are you? | *haalu kihine?* |
| Very well. (reply) | *vara gada* |
| Fine/Good/Great. | *barabah* |
| OK. | *enge* |
| Thank you. | *shukuria* |

## Useful Words & Phrases

| | |
|---|---|
| Yes. | *aa* |
| No. | *noo* |
| How much is this? | *mi kihavaraka?* |
| What is that? | *mi korche?* |
| What did you say? | *kike tha buni?* |
| I'm leaving. | *aharen dani* |
| Where are you going? | *kong taka dani?* |
| How much is the fare? | *fi kihavare?* |

| | |
|---|---|
| I/me | *aharen/ma* |
| you | *kale* |
| she/he | *mina/ena* |
| name | *nang, nama* |
| expensive | *agu bodu* |
| very expensive | *vara agu bodu* |
| cheap | *agu heyo* |
| enough | *heo* |
| now | *mihaaru* |
| little (for people, places) | *kuda* |
| mosquito | *madiri* |
| mosquito net | *madiri ge* |
| bathroom | *gifili* |
| toilet | *fahana* |
| inside | *etere* |
| outside | *berufarai* |
| water (rain, well) | *vaare feng, valu feng* |

## Some Useful Verbs

| | |
|---|---|
| swim | *fatani* |
| eat | *kani* |
| walk | *hingani* |
| sleep | *nidani* |
| sail | *duvani* |
| go | *dani* |
| stay | *hunani* |
| dance | *nashani* |
| wash | *donani* |

## People

| | |
|---|---|
| friend | *ratehi* |
| mother | *mama* |
| father | *bapa* |
| atoll chief | *atolu verin* |

| island chief | kateeb |
| VIP, upper-class person | befalu |
| white person (tourist or expat) | don miha |
| community religious leader | gazi |
| prayer caller | mudeem |
| fisherman | mas veri |
| toddy man | ra veri |
| evil spirit | jinni |

## Places

| atoll | atolu |
| island | fushi or rah |
| sandbank | finolhu |
| reef or lagoon | faru |
| street | magu |
| lane or small street | golhi or higun |
| mosque | miski |
| house | ge |

## Time & Days

| today | miadu |
| tomorrow | madamma |
| yesterday | iye |
| tonight | mire |
| day | duvas |
| night | reggadu |
| week | hafta |
| month | mas |
| year | aharu |

| Monday | horma |
| Tuesday | angaara |
| Wednesday | buda |
| Thursday | brassfati |
| Friday | hukuru |
| Saturday | honihira |
| Sunday | aadita |

## Numbers

| 1 | eke |
| 2 | de |
| 3 | tine |
| 4 | hatare |
| 5 | fahe |
| 6 | haie |
| 7 | hate |
| 8 | ashe |
| 9 | nue |
| 10 | diha |
| 11 | egaara |
| 12 | baara |
| 13 | tera |
| 14 | saada |
| 15 | fanara |
| 16 | sorla |
| 17 | satara |
| 18 | ashara |
| 19 | onavihi |
| 20 | vihi |
| 30 | tiris |
| 40 | saalis |
| 50 | fansaas |
| 60 | fasdolaas |
| 70 | hai-diha |
| 80 | a-diha |
| 90 | nua-diha |
| 100 | sateka |

## FOOD & DRINK

Fish and rice are the staple foods. Any substantial meal, with rice and roshi, is called 'long eats', and might include the following:

*mas* – fried fish; usually refers to skipjack tuna or bonito

*valo mas* – smoked fish

*mas huni & hana kuri mas* – dried, tinned, fried or cold fish mixed with coconut, onion, chilli and spices

*mas riha* – fish curry

*kandukukulhu* – a special tuna curry

*garudia* – the staple diet of fish soup, often taken with rice, lime and chilli

*rihakuru* – garudia boiled down to a salty sauce or paste

*bai* – rice

*roshi* – flat, unleavened bread

*modunu* – a simple salad

*aluvi* – potato

*paan* – bread

*bis* – egg

'Short eats' or *hedhikaa* is the selection of little sweet and savoury items that is displayed on the counter of a local tea shop.

*gulas* – fish ball; deep-fried in flour and rice batter

*kuli boakiba* – spicy fish cake

*bondi bai* – rice pudding; sometimes with currants

*kastad* – sweet custard

*foni boakiba* – gelatin cakes and puddings

The range of drinks is very limited. Tea shops will always serve *bor feng* (drinking water), and of course *sai* (tea). Unless you ask otherwise, tea comes black, with *hakuru* (sugar). Kiru (milk) isn't a common drink, and is usually made up from powder. In local villages you might get raa (palm toddy).

Most fruit is imported, but the following are grown locally:

*kurumba* – coconut, especially a young or new coconut

*donkeo* – little bananas

*bambukeyo* – breadfruit

*bambukeyo hiti* – breadfruit used in curries

*bambukeyo bondibai* – breadfruit used in desserts

After dinner, many Maldivians chew betel, a combination of *foah* (areca nut), some cloves and lime paste wrapped in *bileiy.*

# Glossary

Here, with definitions, are some unfamiliar words and abbreviations you might meet in this book or while you are in the Maldives.

**animator** – extroverted person employed in some resorts to promote group activities and good times, and ensure that no-one is left out of the fun; the Club Med equivalent is a 'GO'
**atoll** – a ring of coral reefs and/or coral islands surrounding a lagoon; the English word 'atoll' is derived from the Divehi *atollon*

**bashi** – popular girls' team game with tennis ball and net
**BCD** – Buoyancy Control Device; a vest that holds air tanks on the back and can be inflated or deflated to control a diver's buoyancy and act as a life preserver (also called a BCV – Buoyancy Control Vest)
**bodu beru** – literally: 'big drum'; bodu meaning big; made from a hollow coconut log and covered with stingray skin; bodu beru is Maldivian drum music, often used to accompany dancers
**BSAC** – British Sub Aqua Club; organisation that sets diving standards, training requirements and accredits instructors, like PADI

**cadjan** – mat made of coconut palm leaves
**carrom** – a popular board game, like a miniature snooker; players use their fingers to flick flat, round counters from the edges of a square wooden board, trying to knock other players' counters into the four corner holes
**chew** – wad of areca nut wrapped in a betel leaf, often with lime, cloves and other spices; commonly chewed after a meal, or at any time by those with the habit
**CMAS** – Confederation Mondiale des Activities Subaquatiques; a French organisation that sets diving standards, training requirements and accredits instructors, like PADI
**coir** – fibre made from coconut husks, traditionally used for ropes, mats etc

**Dhiraagu** – the Maldives telecommunications provider, it is jointly owned by the government and the British company Cable & Wireless
**dhoni** – a Maldivian boat, probably derived from an Arab dhow. Formerly sail powered, many dhonis are now equipped with a diesel engine
**Divehi** – the language and people of the Maldives, also spelt 'Dhivehi'
**Divehi Raajje** – 'Island Kingdom'; what Maldivians call the Maldives

**fandhita** – magic, wizardry
**faru** (or faro) – ring-shaped reef within an atoll, often with an island in the middle
**feylis** – traditional sarong, usually dark with light-coloured horizontal bands near the hem
**finolhu** – a sparsely vegetated sand bank
**FIT** – Fully Independent Traveller; in the Maldives, every effort is made to book these people into a resort as soon as possible!
**fushi** – island

**giri** – a coral formation that rises steeply from the atoll floor and almost reaches the surface; *see also* thilla

**hawitta** – ancient mound found in the southern atolls; archaeologists believe these mounds were the foundations of Buddhist temples
**hiki mas** – dried tuna fillet; a traditional export, especially to Sri Lanka where it is called 'Maldive fish'
**hotel** – a small cafe or tea shop is often called a 'hotel' in Male', but definitely will not provide accommodation
**house reef** – coral reef adjacent to a resort island, used by guests for snorkelling and diving; guests from other resorts can't dive on a house reef without permission

**inner-reef slope** – where a reef slopes down inside an atoll; *see also* outer-reef slope

**jinni** – a witch or wizard, sometimes coming from the sea

**joli** (or jorli) – a net seat suspended from a rectangular frame; typically there are four or five seats together outside a house

**kandiki** – sarong worn by women under the *libaas*
**kandu** – a sea channel; connecting the waters of an atoll to the open sea; feeding grounds for sharks, rays and turtles – good dive sites, but subject to strong currents
**kateeb** – elected chief of an island
**kunaa** – traditional woven mat

**lagoon** – the shallow body of water enclosed by a reef, particularly between an island and its fringing reef
**libaas** – traditional dress with collar and cuffs, and embroidered with gold thread

**madrasa** – government school
**magu** – street
**maktab** – Islamic religious school
**mas** – fish
**MATI** – Maldives Association of Tourism; a private tourist industry organisation
**miskiiy** – mosque
**mudhim** – muezzin; the person who calls Muslims to prayer
**mundu** – man's sarong, usually made with a chequered cotton fabric with a darker panel at the back
**munnaaru** – a minaret, a mosque's tower

**nakaiy** – two-week period associated with a specific weather pattern; the year is divided into 27 nakaiy
**NAUI** – National Association of Underwater Instructors; another dive-training body, that gives accreditation, like PADI
**NSS** – National Security Service; the Maldivian army, navy, coast guard and police force

**outer-reef slope** – the outer edge of an atoll facing open sea, where reefs slope down towards the ocean floor; *see also* inner-reef slope

**PADI** – Professional Association of Diving Instructors; the best known of several organisations that set diving standards, training requirements and accredit instructors (also said to stand for 'Put Another Dollar In')

**pelagic** – relating to the open sea, as opposed to the sheltered atoll waters; pelagics are open-sea fish such as tuna and barracuda

**Quran** – also spelt Koran; Islam's holy book

**raa** – toddy; the sap of a palm tree, consumed as a fresh or slightly fermented drink
**Ramazan** – Maldivian spelling of Ramadan, the Muslim month of fasting
**Redin** – legendary race of people believed by modern Maldivians to have been the first settlers in the archipelago and the builders of the pre-Islamic *hawittas*
**reef** – ridge or plateau close to the sea surface; Maldivian atolls and islands are surrounded by coral reefs
**reef flat** – the shallow area of reef-top between a lagoon and where the reef slopes down into the deeper surrounding water
**roshi** – unleavened bread

**SAARC** – South Asia Association for Regional Cooperation; a regional trade and development organisation which comprises Bangladesh, Bhutan, India, Maldives, Nepal, Pakistan and Sri Lanka
**sai** – tea
**SSI** – Scuba Schools International, accreditation organisation, like PADI
**STO** – State Trading Organisation

**Thaana** – Divehi script; the written language unique to the Maldives
**thilla** – a coral formation that rises steeply from the atoll floor and reaches to within five to 15m of the surface; *see also* giri
**toddy** – *see* raa
**toddy tapper** – a person who extracts the sap of a palm tree to make toddy
**tundu kunaa** – finely woven reed mats, particularly those from Gaaf Dhaal

**undholi** – a wooden seat, typically suspended under a shady tree so the swinging motion provides a cooling breeze

**vedi** – a large *dhoni* used for trading between Male' and the outer atolls
**VSO** – Voluntary Service Overseas; British overseas aid organisation

# Acknowledgments

## THANKS

Many thanks to the following travellers who used previous editions of the Maldives and wrote to us with helpful hints, useful advice and interesting anecdotes about travelling in the Maldives.

Adrian Hoskins, Alex Suslin, Aminath Nazla, Annie Salvitti, Ben Renehan, Bernie Tynas, Brian Goodman, CL Pout, Chen Min, D Atherton, Dee McMath, Edward Dawson-Damer, Elena Masiero, Emanuela Mencaglia Martignoni, Geoff Kershler, Gerard Newcombe, Gunther Meyer, Hans-Lothar Kruger, John Deacon, Katja Meyer, Lawrence Lemoine, Louise Hoskins, Marzia Beltrami, Michel Kostovic, Mike Gaffney, Namita Pendharker Lulla, Paul Garcia, Philip Kenny, Richard Pennington, V Tacito, Vanita Hulme.

# LONELY PLANET

You already know that Lonely Planet produces more than this one guidebook, but you might not be aware of the other products we have on this region. Here is a selection of titles which you may want to check out as well:

**Goa**
ISBN 1 86442 681 X
US$16.99 • UK£10.99

**Sri Lanka**
ISBN 1 86442 720 4
US$16.95 • UK£10.99

**Kerala**
ISBN 1 86442 696 8
US$15.95 • UK£9.99

**South India**
ISBN 1 86442 594 5
US$24.95 • UK£14.99

**India**
ISBN 1 86442 687 9
US$25.95 • UK£15.99

**Healthy Travel Asia & India**
ISBN 1 86450 051 4
US$5.95 • UK£3.99

**Available wherever books are sold.**

# Lonely Planet Guides by Region

L onely Planet is known worldwide for publishing practical, reliable and no-nonsense travel information in our guides and on our Web site. The Lonely Planet list covers just about every accessible part of the world. Currently there are 16 series: Travel guides, Shoestring guides, Condensed guides, Phrasebooks, Read This First, Healthy Travel, Walking guides, Cycling guides, Watching Wildlife guides, Pisces Diving & Snorkeling guides, City Maps, Road Atlases, Out to Eat, World Food, Journeys travel literature and Pictorials.

**AFRICA** Africa on a shoestring • Botswana • Cairo • Cairo City Map • Cape Town • Cape Town City Map • East Africa • Egypt • Egyptian Arabic phrasebook • Ethiopia, Eritrea & Djibouti • Ethiopian Amharic phrasebook • The Gambia & Senegal • Healthy Travel Africa • Kenya • Malawi • Morocco • Moroccan Arabic phrasebook • Mozambique • Namibia • Read This First: Africa • South Africa, Lesotho & Swaziland • Southern Africa • Southern Africa Road Atlas • Swahili phrasebook • Tanzania, Zanzibar & Pemba • Trekking in East Africa • Tunisia • Watching Wildlife East Africa • Watching Wildlife Southern Africa • West Africa • World Food Morocco • Zambia • Zimbabwe, Botswana & Namibia
**Travel Literature:** Mali Blues: Traveling to an African Beat • The Rainbird: A Central African Journey • Songs to an African Sunset: A Zimbabwean Story

**AUSTRALIA & THE PACIFIC** Aboriginal Australia & the Torres Strait Islands •Auckland • Australia • Australian phrasebook • Australia Road Atlas • Cycling Australia • Cycling New Zealand • Fiji • Fijian phrasebook • Healthy Travel Australia, NZ & the Pacific • Islands of Australia's Great Barrier Reef • Melbourne • Melbourne City Map • Micronesia • New Caledonia • New South Wales • New Zealand • Northern Territory • Outback Australia • Out to Eat – Melbourne • Out to Eat – Sydney • Papua New Guinea • Pidgin phrasebook • Queensland • Rarotonga & the Cook Islands • Samoa • Solomon Islands • South Australia • South Pacific • South Pacific phrasebook • Sydney • Sydney City Map • Sydney Condensed • Tahiti & French Polynesia • Tasmania • Tonga • Tramping in New Zealand • Vanuatu • Victoria • Walking in Australia • Watching Wildlife Australia • Western Australia
**Travel Literature:** Islands in the Clouds: Travels in the Highlands of New Guinea • Kiwi Tracks: A New Zealand Journey • Sean & David's Long Drive

**CENTRAL AMERICA & THE CARIBBEAN** Bahamas, Turks & Caicos • Baja California • Belize, Guatemala & Yucatán • Bermuda • Central America on a shoestring • Costa Rica • Costa Rica Spanish phrasebook • Cuba • Cycling Cuba • Dominican Republic & Haiti • Eastern Caribbean • Guatemala • Havana • Healthy Travel Central & South America • Jamaica • Mexico • Mexico City • Panama • Puerto Rico • Read This First: Central & South America • Virgin Islands • World Food Caribbean • World Food Mexico • Yucatán
**Travel Literature:** Green Dreams: Travels in Central America

**EUROPE** Amsterdam • Amsterdam City Map • Amsterdam Condensed • Andalucía • Athens • Austria • Baltic States phrasebook • Barcelona • Barcelona City Map • Belgium & Luxembourg • Berlin • Berlin City Map • Britain • British phrasebook • Brussels, Bruges & Antwerp • Brussels City Map • Budapest • Budapest City Map • Canary Islands • Catalunya & the Costa Brava • Central Europe • Central Europe phrasebook • Copenhagen • Corfu & the Ionians • Corsica • Crete • Crete Condensed • Croatia • Cycling Britain • Cycling France • Cyprus • Czech & Slovak Republics • Czech phrasebook • Denmark • Dublin • Dublin City Map • Dublin Condensed • Eastern Europe • Eastern Europe phrasebook • Edinburgh • Edinburgh City Map • England • Estonia, Latvia & Lithuania • Europe on a shoestring • Europe phrasebook • Finland • Florence • Florence City Map • France • Frankfurt City Map • Frankfurt Condensed • French phrasebook • Georgia, Armenia & Azerbaijan • Germany • German phrasebook • Greece • Greek Islands • Greek phrasebook • Hungary • Iceland, Greenland & the Faroe Islands • Ireland • Italian phrasebook • Italy • Kraków • Lisbon • The Loire • London • London City Map •·London Condensed • Madrid • Madrid City Map • Malta • Mediterranean Europe • Milan, Turin & Genoa • Moscow • Munich • Netherlands • Normandy • Norway • Out to Eat – London • Out to Eat – Paris • Paris • Paris City Map • Paris Condensed • Poland • Polish phrasebook • Portugal • Portuguese phrasebook • Prague • Prague City Map • Provence & the Côte d'Azur • Read This First: Europe • Rhodes & the Dodecanese • Romania & Moldova • Rome • Rome City Map • Rome Condensed • Russia, Ukraine & Belarus • Russian phrasebook • Scandinavian & Baltic Europe • Scandinavian phrasebook • Scotland • Sicily • Slovenia • South-West France • Spain • Spanish phrasebook • Stockholm • St Petersburg • St Petersburg City Map • Sweden • Switzerland • Tuscany • Ukrainian phrasebook • Venice • Vienna • Wales • Walking in Britain • Walking in France • Walking in Ireland • Walking in Italy • Walking in Scotland • Walking in Spain • Walking in Switzerland • Western Europe • World Food France • World Food Greece • World Food Ireland • World Food Italy • World Food Spain **Travel Literature:** After Yugoslavia • Love and War in the Apennines • The Olive Grove: Travels in Greece • On the Shores of the Mediterranean • Round Ireland in Low Gear • A Small Place in Italy

# Lonely Planet Mail Order

**L**onely Planet products are distributed worldwide. They are also available by mail order from Lonely Planet, so if you have difficulty finding a title please write to us. North and South American residents should write to 150 Linden St, Oakland, CA 94607, USA; European and African residents should write to 10a Spring Place, London NW5 3BH, UK; and residents of other countries to Locked Bag 1, Footscray, Victoria 3011, Australia.

**INDIAN SUBCONTINENT & THE INDIAN OCEAN** Bangladesh • Bengali phrasebook • Bhutan • Delhi • Goa • Healthy Travel Asia & India • Hindi & Urdu phrasebook • India • India & Bangladesh City Map • Indian Himalaya • Karakoram Highway • Kathmandu City Map • Kerala • Madagascar • Maldives • Mauritius, Réunion & Seychelles • Mumbai (Bombay) • Nepal • Nepali phrasebook • North India • Pakistan • Rajasthan • Read This First: Asia & India • South India • Sri Lanka • Sri Lanka phrasebook • Tibet • Tibetan phrasebook • Trekking in the Indian Himalaya • Trekking in the Karakoram & Hindukush • Trekking in the Nepal Himalaya • World Food India  **Travel Literature:** The Age of Kali: Indian Travels and Encounters • Hello Goodnight: A Life of Goa • In Rajasthan • Maverick in Madagascar • A Season in Heaven: True Tales from the Road to Kathmandu • Shopping for Buddhas • A Short Walk in the Hindu Kush • Slowly Down the Ganges

**MIDDLE EAST & CENTRAL ASIA** Bahrain, Kuwait & Qatar • Central Asia • Central Asia phrasebook • Dubai • Farsi (Persian) phrasebook • Hebrew phrasebook • Iran • Israel & the Palestinian Territories • Istanbul • Istanbul City Map • Istanbul to Cairo • Istanbul to Kathmandu • Jerusalem • Jerusalem City Map • Jordan • Lebanon • Middle East • Oman and the United Arab Emirates • Syria • Turkey • Turkish phrasebook • World Food Turkey • Yemen  **Travel Literature:** Black on Black: Iran Revisited • Breaking Ranks: Turbulent Travels in the Promised Land • The Gates of Damascus • Kingdom of the Film Stars: Journey into Jordan

**NORTH AMERICA** Alaska • Boston • Boston City Map • Boston Condensed • British Columbia • California & Nevada • California Condensed • Canada • Chicago • Chicago City Map • Chicago Condensed • Florida • Georgia & the Carolinas • Great Lakes • Hawaii • Hiking in Alaska • Hiking in the USA • Honolulu & Oahu City Map • Las Vegas • Los Angeles • Los Angeles City Map • Louisiana & the Deep South • Miami • Miami City Map • Montreal • New England • New Orleans • New Orleans City Map • New York City • New York City Map • New York City Condensed • New York, New Jersey & Pennsylvania • Oahu • Out to Eat – San Francisco • Pacific Northwest • Rocky Mountains • San Diego & Tijuana • San Francisco • San Francisco City Map • Seattle • Seattle City Map • Southwest • Texas • Toronto • USA • USA phrasebook • Vancouver • Vancouver City Map • Virginia & the Capital Region • Washington, DC • Washington, DC City Map • World Food New Orleans  **Travel Literature:** Caught Inside: A Surfer's Year on the California Coast • Drive Thru America

**NORTH-EAST ASIA** Beijing • Beijing City Map • Cantonese phrasebook • China • Hiking in Japan • Hong Kong & Macau • Hong Kong City Map • Hong Kong Condensed • Japan • Japanese phrasebook • Korea • Korean phrasebook • Kyoto • Mandarin phrasebook • Mongolia • Mongolian phrasebook • Seoul • Shanghai • South-West China • Taiwan • Tokyo • Tokyo Condensed • World Food Hong Kong • World Food Japan  **Travel Literature:** In Xanadu: A Quest • Lost Japan

**SOUTH AMERICA** Argentina, Uruguay & Paraguay • Bolivia • Brazil • Brazilian phrasebook • Buenos Aires • Buenos Aires City Map • Chile & Easter Island • Colombia • Ecuador & the Galapagos Islands • Healthy Travel Central & South America • Latin American Spanish phrasebook • Peru • Quechua phrasebook • Read This First: Central & South America • Rio de Janeiro • Rio de Janeiro City Map • Santiago de Chile • South America on a shoestring • Trekking in the Patagonian Andes • Venezuela  **Travel Literature:** Full Circle: A South American Journey

**SOUTH-EAST ASIA** Bali & Lombok • Bangkok • Bangkok City Map • Burmese phrasebook • Cambodia • Cycling Vietnam, Laos & Cambodia • East Timor phrasebook • Hanoi • Healthy Travel Asia & India • Hill Tribes phrasebook • Ho Chi Minh City (Saigon) • Indonesia • Indonesian phrasebook • Indonesia's Eastern Islands • Java • Lao phrasebook • Laos • Malay phrasebook • Malaysia, Singapore & Brunei • Myanmar (Burma) • Philippines • Pilipino (Tagalog) phrasebook • Read This First: Asia & India • Singapore • Singapore City Map • South-East Asia on a shoestring • South-East Asia phrasebook • Thailand • Thailand's Islands & Beaches • Thailand, Vietnam, Laos & Cambodia Road Atlas • Thai phrasebook • Vietnam • Vietnamese phrasebook • World Food Indonesia • World Food Thailand • World Food Vietnam

**ALSO AVAILABLE:** Antarctica • The Arctic • The Blue Man: Tales of Travel, Love and Coffee • Brief Encounters: Stories of Love, Sex & Travel • Buddhist Stupas in Asia: The Shape of Perfection • Chasing Rickshaws • The Last Grain Race • Lonely Planet … On the Edge: Adventurous Escapades from Around the World • Lonely Planet Unpacked • Lonely Planet Unpacked Again • Not the Only Planet: Science Fiction Travel Stories • Ports of Call: A Journey by Sea • Sacred India • Travel Photography: A Guide to Taking Better Pictures • Travel with Children • Tuvalu: Portrait of an Island Nation

# Index

## Text